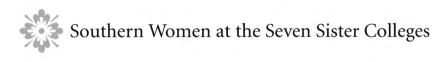 Southern Women at the Seven Sister Colleges

Southern Women *at the* Seven Sister Colleges

Feminist Values

and Social Activism,

1875–1915

JOAN MARIE JOHNSON

The University of Georgia Press • Athens and London

© 2008 by the University of Georgia Press

Athens, Georgia 30602

All rights reserved

Set in Minion by Bookcomp, Inc.

Printed and bound by Thomson-Shore

The paper in this book meets the guidelines for
permanence and durability of the Committee on
Production Guidelines for Book Longevity of the
Council on Library Resources.

Printed in the United States of America

12 11 10 09 08 C 5 4 3 2 1

Library of Congress Cataloging-in-Publication Data

Johnson, Joan Marie.

Southern women at the seven sister colleges : feminist
values and social activism, 1875–1915 / Joan Marie Johnson.

     p. cm.

Includes bibliographical references and index.

ISBN-13: 978-0-8203-3095-2 (hardcover : alk. paper)

ISBN-10: 0-8203-3095-7 (hardcover : alk. paper)

1. Women—Southern States—History. 2. Women social
reformers—Southern States—History. 3. Sex role—
Southern States—History. 4. Social problems—Southern
States—History. 5. Southern States—Social conditions—
1865–1945. I. Title.

HQ1438.S63J64 2008

305.48'9621097509034—dc22   2007039031

British Library Cataloging-in-Publication Data available

For my parents, Joseph and Dorothy Infosino
With love and gratitude

CONTENTS

ix   Acknowledgments

1   Introduction

13   ONE. "In the Wonderland of the Mind": The Benefits of a Liberal Arts Education

40   TWO. "We Do Want More Southern Girls to Come": Entrance Requirements, Preparatory Departments and Schools, and Alumnae Networks

62   THREE. From Homesick Southerners to Independent Yankees: The Campus Experience

78   FOUR. A Southerner in Yankeeland: Southern Clubs, Yankee Ways, and African American Classmates

109   FIVE. After College: The Marriage and Career Dilemma

143   SIX. After College: The Activist

175   Notes

207   Bibliography

223   Index

ACKNOWLEDGMENTS

It has been a pleasure to complete this book with the generous assistance of so many over the years. I am grateful to the staffs at archives, especially at the women's colleges studied herein, who maintain such full records of their institutions and alumnae. I would like especially to thank Patricia Albright at the Archives and Special Collections, Mount Holyoke College; Nanci Young at College Archives, Smith College; Wilma R. Slaight at Wellesley College Archives, Margaret Clapp Library; and Dean Rogers and others at the Vassar College archives for their assistance in tracing information on alumnae and obtaining photographs for the book. I also thank the archivists at the following special-collection libraries, where I read the letters of alumnae and their parents and other relatives: the University of Kentucky; Special Collections, Robert W. Woodruff Library, Emory University; the South Caroliniana Library at the University of South Carolina; Special Collections, Perkins Library, Duke University; the North Carolina State Archives; and the Southern Historical Collection, Wilson Library, the University of North Carolina. Interlibrary loan librarians fulfilled hundreds of requests for me while at Northeastern Illinois University, and the librarians at the Newberry Library in Chicago also provided valued service while I was a scholar-in-residence there.

Thanks are also due to the Spencer Foundation for the Small Research Grant that I received in 2001–2, which enabled me to complete a great deal of the research for and writing of this book, including funding for a research trip to Wellesley, Smith, and Mount Holyoke colleges. I would especially like to thank Jim Grossman and the staff at the Newberry Library in Chicago for administering the grant and providing a wonderful place to study and superb research facilities to me as a scholar-in-residence. I also received a grant as an Archie K. Davis Fellow to travel to archives in North Carolina from the North Caroliniana Society and a Women's Studies Research Grant, from Special Collections, Perkins Library at Duke University.

I would like to thank many colleagues for their support and encouragement, including Regina Morantz for pointing out to me, while I was in graduate school, that one of the most interesting things about the Poppenheims was their northern education, and Carol Bleser for her support of my earlier project editing the Poppenheim letters for publication. I thank Amy McCandless, Melissa Walker, June Sochen, Linda Eisenmann, Patricia Palmieri, Francesca Morgan, Anne Knupfer, Kathleen Clark, Marjorie Spruill, Valinda Littlefield, Karen Cox, Anne Firor Scott, Rebecca Montgomery, Joan Cashin, Belinda Gergel, Carolyn

Bashaw, Patrick Miller, and Jane Turner Censer for their support. I would also like to thank the anonymous readers at the *History of Education Quarterly* and the University of Georgia Press for invaluable advice. Nancy Grayson at the University of Georgia Press and her staff have been wonderful as they have helped make this a better book.

Finally I would like to thank my family and friends for their support of my work. My book club, friends from TCC who share coffee at Peet's and days at the beach, and friends and neighbors from St. A's, Seward Street, and Hastings Avenue are a constant source of fun and support (and occasionally, much-needed childcare). Thank you also to Janel Miller for her loving presence in our lives. I appreciate the encouragement my family has always shown me, including my sisters, Anne Marie Infosino and Monica Infosino; and my brother and sister-in-law, Andrew Infosino and Silvia Cecchini. I wish that my mother-in-law, Anne M. Johnson, had lived to see the publication of this book, for she and my former father-in-law, Dr. Charles J. Johnson, were both lifelong educators. Their children all imbibed the importance of education from them.

I also thank my parents, Joseph and Dorothy Infosino, to whom this book is dedicated, for encouraging my education for as long as I can remember. Their insistence that education came first was something I lived and breathed my entire youth. I cannot thank them enough for the sacrifices they made to prioritize the education of their children. My own education pushed me to excel, provided me with confidence in my abilities, and imbued me with feminist values and progressive ideals; it undergirds this book. Finally I thank my daughters, Darci, Sophie, and Elise, who make each of my days special, and my husband, Don, whose unwavering love and support make it all possible.

Southern Women at the Seven Sister Colleges

INTRODUCTION

Margaret Preston, a member of a prominent family from Lexington, Kentucky, attended Bryn Mawr College from 1904 to 1906, initially against her will. Letters between Margaret and her parents while she was away at school reveal a homesick young woman, at first uninterested in scholarship. Unused to being on her own, spoiled, and needy, Margaret appealed to her mother for support and whined constantly about Bryn Mawr. She complained that the other girls were "ugly and look disagreeable" and that she had bags under her eyes because "Bryn Mawr is a warranted Beauty destroyer."[1] Overwrought with stress, she had a nervous breakdown and almost did not return for her second year. However, once back at school, as Margaret matured she began to develop academically. She focused less on returning home, beauty, and boys and more on her classes. She ignored her mother's requests for her to leave Bryn Mawr early for Christmas vacation in order to attend a dance because she would lose credit if she missed class. Although she had earlier told her mother that she would have preferred that her aunt fund a trip to Europe rather than her education at Bryn Mawr, she now suggested that if she stayed four years to complete her degree, she might have a chance to graduate with honors. Apparently, her aunt did not choose to extend her financial support because Margaret stayed only two years.[2] However, she returned home to Lexington a more bold and self-confident woman.

When Margaret eventually married at the age of thirty-two, she was far different from the young, homesick freshman who entered Bryn Mawr. Her husband, Philip Johnston, respected her intellectual abilities and interest in literature, presenting her with works by Ibsen, Shelley, Scott, and Keats.[3] Before their marriage Margaret wanted to eliminate the word "obey" from a wife's marriage vow. Although her Episcopalian priest denied her request, Margaret made it clear to Philip that her vows to him were not about obedience but about mutual respect.[4] Her ability to enter the marriage as an equal partner came from her own sense of self developed while at Bryn Mawr as well as from the strength of her relationships with other women, especially her mother. Once married, Margaret did not work for wages but dedicated herself instead to woman suffrage and the League of Women Voters and held local and statewide offices of the women's auxiliary of her church and women's clubs. She returned to college in 1938, eventually earning a bachelor of arts degree from the University of Kentucky.

Margaret's letters reveal a woman changed by the college experience. Challenged to think for herself in an academic setting, she grew into an independent, able woman. She also became a woman suffragist and infused her marriage with modern ideas concerning gender equity. Margaret was part of a small but influential group of over one thousand white southern women who went north to the best women's colleges—Vassar, Wellesley, Smith, Mount Holyoke, Bryn Mawr, Radcliffe, and Barnard, called the Seven Sister colleges—at the turn of the century due to the relative dearth of academically rigorous women's colleges in the South. A collective biography of these students is important because they disproportionately formed an elite female leadership in the South and forged new roles for women, especially in social reform and education. Their educational background is crucial to understanding the influences and motives of the women who were central to the social reform movement in the Progressive Era South. They melded together new possibilities for independence and leadership learned in the North with traditional southern gender roles. The southern lady ideal encompassed domesticity, purity, submissiveness, and piety as well as charm, dependence, grace, and manners. The life choices of students who left the South for college significantly elucidate both the meaning of higher education for southern women and changing gender roles for women at the turn of the century. The experiences of the women in this book—both at college and after—in great measure explain how women of the New South emerged in the early twentieth century. A northern college education enabled them to challenge southern patriarchal society, to take public roles heretofore closed to women, and to assert their independence, intelligence, and equality. While some would not have called themselves feminists because they were not actively working to assert women's full equality with men, they defended women's capabilities and advanced women's rights through their activism and achievements.

In studying the movement of women educators, writers, editors, and reformers into public life in the early republic, historian Mary Kelley explored "the role schooling at female academies and seminaries played in mediating this process." According to Kelley, "the large majority of the women who claimed these careers and who led the movement of women into the world beyond their households were schooled at these institutions." One hundred years later the influence of formal education is unmistakable. Although relatively few women attended college at the turn of the twentieth century, historian Lynn Gordon asserts that "women who did not go to college also made their mark on the world, but increasingly college women led others in achievement."[5] Colleges fostered self-confidence and intellectual curiosity and encouraged their graduates to go beyond the traditional domestic role expected of women at the time. However, with many professions still closed to women, alumnae had to negotiate new roles, found new organizations, and pioneer new career fields. Historian Sarah Wilkerson-Freeman contends that "the efforts of these graduates set the agenda of social reform for the first decades of the twentieth century."[6] In the South many of these college women had studied in the North.

The accomplishments of college women are particularly striking given the small numbers of college women at the time: in 1870 the rate of American women who had attended college was just under 1 percent; in 1880 it was 1.9 percent; in 1890 it was 2.2 percent; in 1900 it was 2.8 percent; and by 1920 it had reached only 7.6 percent.[7] Yet despite the unlikelihood that women would have bachelor's degrees, college graduates were present wherever a reform movement or a women's club or a school was founded. The *Woman's Who's Who in America,* published in 1914, recognized thousands of prominent women in the professions and volunteer work. A study of a sampling of the entries shows that an astonishing 43.8 percent had bachelor's degrees, with an even higher number, 63.4 percent, attaining some level of higher education.[8]

Moreover, in the South a diploma from a college in the North was an even more significant indicator of achievement than a local degree. The relative importance of northern colleges is evident from the fact that in 1917 818 college graduates living in southern states joined the Southern Association of College Women (SACW). Although some were undoubtedly transplants rather than native southerners, almost half (384) had graduated from a college outside of the South, and 141 of those had graduated from one of the Seven Sister colleges. Historians focusing on northern students (or southern students at southern colleges) have not yet studied these women, although it is impossible to understand the impact of college education on southern women without attention to those who left the South for their degrees.[9]

Southerners who went north had little choice: in the 1870s and 1880s women's colleges in the South generally did not offer the bachelor's degree. Even by 1915, when there were half a dozen or so legitimate southern women's colleges, the Seven Sister colleges retained their reputation as the best women's colleges in the country, equivalent to the best men's colleges such as Harvard and Amherst. Southern colleges were bound by student populations that were "more Protestant, more rural, more conservative, and less affluent than their Northern and Western counterparts." Not surprisingly, "southern institutions have been slower to raise matriculation and graduation standards, to revise the classical curriculum, and to eliminate in loco parentis than schools in other regions of the country." To ensure that students learned to be southern ladies, colleges in the region also retained strict social codes for years after northern colleges had loosened their restrictions.[10] Those seeking the best education had to leave the South. Ironically, as historian Rebecca Montgomery has pointed out, the lack of colleges for women in the South, which was a result of the desire to keep women in traditional gender roles, had the reverse effect: it "pushed southern daughters out of their region and into the seedbed of the women's rights and Progressive movements."[11]

Why did these southern women seek a prestigious and rigorous classical education? While some students desired a professional career, most students' lack of practical aims suggests that they sought the intangibles of a liberal education: a general bettering of themselves, sharpening of their minds, and building of their characters. Most believed that a college education would, in short, make them better women. Thus, they did not anticipate the revolution: many did not realize how much the experience threatened traditional understandings of what it meant to be a southern lady.

Despite most colleges' professed determination to produce "a womanly woman," self-realization and intellectual development pushed students to reconsider their ideas of gender equality. Exposure to feminist professors (who explicitly advocated women's equality with men) and progressive reform opportunities caused southern women to broaden their ideas of what was proper and appropriate behavior for women.[12] Students took courses with feminists and reformers, listened to speeches by Jane Addams and Florence Kelley, investigated factory conditions, volunteered at settlement houses, and otherwise were introduced to the world of social reform and broadened opportunities for women. They voted in mock presidential elections and in college elections for class and student government presidents, contests that many southern women won. They organized meetings, gave speeches, and learned parliamentary procedure. In the classroom and the library, colleges taught women to think for themselves and to "value their own thinking and themselves."[13]

Higher education was so powerful an influence because the experience pushed southern women to create new possibilities for themselves while working within the boundaries of traditional gender roles. Southern women in the late nineteenth century were raised to be pure, pious, domestic, dependent, and protected women. The burgeoning woman's rights movement in the North was slower to catch on in the South due to the general conservatism of the region and the entwined racial and gendered social hierarchy. Those who ventured north for an education were well positioned to combine femininity with feminism and create a New Southern Woman for the twentieth century. They brought home to the South the feminist values they learned at college—that women were intellectually capable, that women were equal to men (if still different from them), that women had much to offer in professional and public life, that women had a duty to serve the larger community beyond the confines of the home, that women deserved full political citizenship, including the vote, that women could seek and find satisfaction in professional life and single life rather than depending on marriage. Thus, these alumnae provide important clues as to how feminist values spread.

This book follows historian Anne Firor Scott's pioneering research on Troy Female Seminary in which she suggested that the graduates of this prestigious nineteenth-century woman's seminary disseminated the feminist values they learned there. Founder Emma Willard believed in the intellectual capacity of women: that they could "learn any academic subject" and that they could become professionals—that is, teachers—well before women took over the field.[14] Her students fanned out across the country, creating their own schools modeled after hers as well as taking on paid and volunteer work, motivated by the seriousness of purpose and sense of self-worth as women they had developed at Troy. Furthermore, preliminary research shows that, like the group of southern women studied in this book, Troy graduates were more likely than the general population to remain single and, if married, to have fewer children. Scott admits that while the women who attended Troy were a "self-selected" (or parent-selected) group, they nevertheless suggest "the beginning of a new personality type."[15] Southern women who went to the North to attend prestigious women's colleges echo her findings. They, too, believed in women's capabilities and worked to spread their new ideas of what a woman could be and do. Significantly, many returned home to found schools of their own and teach the values they had imbibed in the North. The influence of this small group of educated women was felt in communities throughout the South.

According to historians Elna Green, Sarah Wilkerson-Freeman, and Rebecca Montgomery, a northern education or other northern exposure characterized many reformers and suffragists in the South. They strongly believed in the power of education and wanted to transform the educational opportunities available to southern girls, opening schools, reforming school systems, and promoting coeducation at southern universities. Having experienced the influence of education in their own lives, they hoped to expose other women to its life-changing effects, which included both a reordering of gender roles in families and greater economic opportunities for women. Orie Latham Hatcher, a Vassar graduate from Virginia who also taught at Bryn Mawr, was determined to improve educational standards for women and to help them find more professional opportunities utilizing their education in Virginia and the region. Hatcher's biographer called her "an importer to the South of educational and employment ideas for women that were developing in other parts of the nation," an apt description of many of the women in this study.[16]

These women were also very likely to support woman suffrage, establish women's clubs, and become leaders in social activism; they also disproportionately directed women into the social welfare branch of Progressive Era reform in the region.[17] Some women such as Virginia Foster Durr, who attended Wellesley from Alabama, later became involved in the movement for interracial cooperation and civil rights. Like suffragists and other social reformers, these women cited their educational experiences in the North as influencing their decision to become activists. Access to higher education in the North did not make most of these women radical reformers; it did, however, inspire many to create new and acceptable ways for women to work for change within their society. Although not all women who went north returned as suffragists or otherwise activist or professional women, a large number did. Likewise, although not all suffragists and activists in the South were northern educated, many still had some connection to the North or an unusually strong education. Several important reformers born in the antebellum South and active in the 1880s such as Caroline Merrick of New Orleans, Elizabeth Johnson and Lide Meriwether of Tennessee, and Belle Kearney of Mississippi had exposure to northern teachers, including Emma Willard and her protégées.[18]

The majority of southern students who attended Wellesley, Vassar, Mount Holyoke, and Bryn Mawr at the turn of the twentieth century returned to the South to live after graduation.[19] Once they were home, they found that a northern education affected their life choices. College graduates married at about half the rate of the general female population. Many struggled with the choice between career and marriage after college. This dilemma was even more salient for southern students, many of whom were expected not to work for wages but to remain southern ladies. In their postgraduate choices southern students resembled their northern counterparts more than they did their southern sisters who had remained at home for college. They married at rates comparable to those of their fellow students at elite northern colleges (50–65 percent); these marriage rates were considerably lower than the national average and lower than those of graduates of southern women's colleges. These low marriage rates are not surprising considering the level of community service work performed and the feminist values imbibed by many alumnae. Yet northern-educated southern women also worked for slightly lower wages than their northern contemporaries, and they chose to attend schools that produced fewer working graduates, suggesting that many did not believe paid employment was proper or ladylike. Most came from middle-class and upper-class families and were not obligated to work out of financial necessity. Their choices suggest that in creating a new southern woman they compromised: while many did not desire wage work, they still experienced a "social claim" and therefore became activist volunteer women.[20] Student letters reveal that the independence these women gained at northern schools was not a natural phase in their growth but a Yankee characteristic learned in the North. They had to reconcile their newly found autonomy with the tradition of dependence and need for protection assumed of southern women; their choices concerning marriage, career, and social activism were thus fraught with tension.

Southern women who attended college in the North were profoundly changed by the experience. While they were at school southern students nurtured their regional identity. They represented the South and its racial mores to their classmates, and they sought each other's fellowship in campus southern clubs. Fred Hobson argued in *Tell about the South* that southerners had a "rage to explain" that compelled them to justify and defend southern identity, given the southern history of slavery and racism.[21] Southern students shared that need to defend the South and promote their southern identity. Their defense of the South and desire for respect offer insight into how the Lost Cause, the movement to honor the Confederacy and find meaning in defeat, operated in the daily lives of southerners. Furthermore, in an example of northerners choosing reconciliation over racial justice, schools like Vassar deferred to white southern students when they refused to admit African American students, while other schools like Wellesley admitted black students and forced white southern students to reconsider their prejudices. These students' experiences demonstrate the ways in which northerners and southerners interacted in the decades following the Civil War.

In *Southern Women at the Seven Sister Colleges* I examine the effect that education had on the lives of women. Rather than focusing on the relative lack of higher educational opportunities for women in the South, I concentrate on the many southerners who were passionate about women's education. I explore why students sought a classical liberal arts education, how they prepared for college entrance examinations, what it was like to be a southerner on a northern campus, and what influence these women's education had on their subsequent lives and communities.

In this book I examine the approximately one thousand southern white students who attended Vassar, Smith, Wellesley, Mount Holyoke, Bryn Mawr, and, to a lesser extent, the coordinate colleges, Radcliffe and Barnard, primarily from 1875 to 1915.[22] Although these women represented such a large percentage of college-educated women in the South, fellow southerners made up a very small portion of their classes. Wealthy southern families commonly sent daughters north for an education early in the antebellum period, but this practice slowed as the Civil War approached.[23] Historian John Hope Franklin found that a campaign by southerners to encourage both men and women southern students to attend colleges and universities in their own section worked better in the immediate postbellum years than before the war; numbers of southern students at institutions like West Point and Princeton remained fairly low in the early 1870s.[24]

By the 1880s, when Vassar, Smith, and Wellesley opened their doors, southern girls once again began traveling north. The first southerners graduated from Smith and Wellesley in 1880 and from Mount Holyoke in 1883. While only twenty southerners attended Smith from 1875 (when the school opened) to 1900, in the next fifteen years the number climbed to almost 150. Southern students increased in number and percentage of their class, especially after 1900. At Smith southern students represented less than 1 percent of their class in the 1880s but 12.8 percent between 1910 and 1915. Vassar and Wellesley showed similar increases, with southern students at Vassar making up 14 percent of their class by 1915. Southerners attended Bryn Mawr and Mount Holyoke in much smaller numbers. Southern women made up only between 5 and 8 percent of their class through 1910 at Bryn Mawr. At Mount Holyoke the numbers were even smaller. Only sixty-seven brave southern students attended Mount Holyoke between 1875 and 1915, compared with over three hundred at Wellesley and Vassar. At Mount Holyoke a southerner generally found herself one of only a handful of southern students at the school. Most of her classmates came from Massachusetts, New York, Pennsylvania, and other New England states.[25]

In order to gain a richer understanding of southern students' experiences at school I located collections of letters between students and home written during their college years.[26] A dozen extensive collections are available, along with several smaller collections. Family correspondence provides a unique opportunity to observe the socialization of women through the advice and questions between southern mothers and fathers and their daughters in the North. I also compiled a database of the approximately one thousand southern students who attended Vassar, Wellesley, Bryn Mawr, Smith, and Mount Holyoke between 1875 and 1915.[27] For the vast majority of these students basic biographical information can be gleaned from alumnae directories, such as whether or not they returned to the South after graduation, married, had children, pursued graduate studies, or worked for wages. Although this material is primarily based on information provided to the school by alumnae, schools and alumnae kept in close contact at the turn of the century, ensuring the relative accuracy of data. Wellesley College, for example, even noted in its directory when an alumna lost contact with the college, although such notations were rare. More extensive information is available for approximately three hundred of these students, especially women who became social activists, suffragists, clubwomen, educators, or professionals. Alumnae biographical files are a treasure trove of information. While school officials gathered published accounts of alumnae achievements, alumnae themselves listed their leadership (offices held, years involved) in various volunteer organizations in alumnae surveys and wrote letters to their classes detailing their postgraduate lives and providing their own assessment of their lives and their impact on their communities. They sometimes addressed issues such as whether or not they would attend the college again and what their education meant to them. Their files also contain obituaries and other public records such as published articles about more prominent women. Taken together, biographical information and college letters as well as the larger trends discernible from data available for southern women educated at northern colleges provide evidence of the profound influence of these women's years in the North. This approach places the students, rather than the institution, at the center of this study.

I have focused on the years from 1875 to 1915, after the opening of Smith and Wellesley in 1875 and before World War I, because students in the 1920s had somewhat different social lives and experiences due to the fact that they were no longer the "pioneers" of women's colleges and to the changing mores of the decade. This allowed me to determine if there were changes between the 1880s, when southerners were few and far between, through the early 1910s, when they made up from 11 to 14 percent of their classes at Smith, Vassar, and Wellesley. Furthermore, this period coincided with the Progressive social reform era, when students would have been likely to be influenced by professors caught up in the reform fervor of the time. I limited this study to these elite northern women's colleges because they were considered to offer the best education for women at the time in a single-sex setting, which was preferred by many southern families. These colleges consistently turned out high-achieving women— women whose career and volunteer work propelled them into collections such as *Who's Who of American Women* and *Who's Who in America* at higher rates than women who attended other women's colleges or coeducational institutions.[28] The atmosphere engendered leadership in women and provided a safe space for women to pursue intellectual interests rather than domestic ideals. Furthermore, the women's colleges maintained excellent records of their students. The Seven Sisters, with their rigorous academic requirements, attracted many of the brightest southern students. I chose to focus on the five independent women's colleges in the Seven Sisters, with only cursory attention to the two coordinate colleges, Radcliffe and Barnard, because the women's colleges generally provided a fuller campus experience.

Where applicable, I have made comparisons using secondary literature on southern women at southern colleges and on women at coeducational universities such as Cornell and the University of Michigan, although the number of southern women at these institutions was extremely low.[29] Several women in the study attended both a women's college and a university, often for a graduate degree, notably Sophonisba Breckinridge, the reformer who received her bachelor of arts degree from Wellesley and her doctorate and doctor of law degrees from the University of Chicago; Gertrude Weil, who received her bachelor of arts from Smith and then took several courses at Cornell; and Lilian Wyckoff Johnson, who attended Wellesley and then received her doctorate from the University of Chicago. Weil complained that at Cornell "there are too many men . . . and every once in a while you hear the word Co-ed uttered in such a way as to make you ashamed to be one." Interestingly, one of the first students at the University of Chicago was a southerner, Elizabeth Messick Houk of Memphis. She arrived by carriage to a brand new university and was given a cot to sleep on in the room of Marion Talbot, dean of women.

Southern students at northern colleges were fairly typical of women college students at the turn of the century. College women were the daughters of the upwardly mobile middle class, of professionals and businessmen. In a survey of college women conducted in 1902, over half had fathers who were either professionals or classed as commercial. Mount Holyoke drew the most farmers' daughters.[30] Not surprisingly, out of fifty-six southern Smith College students whose fathers' occupations were listed in the college registers, twenty-two were "businessmen," including bankers, merchants, and manufacturers, and seventeen were professionals, including ministers, educators, doctors, and lawyers or judges. Only one father specified his occupation as farmer, and one described himself as a planter.[31] Well-known southern students such as Sophonisba Breckinridge, Gertrude Weil, and others had lawyers, merchants, and teachers for fathers. The small number of southern students at Mount Holyoke, where in contrast there was a preponderance of farmers' daughters, underscores the professional and commercial status of most southern college students' families. Historian Barbara Sicherman argues that college students were less identifiable by their wealth than by their parents' educational level or, at least, aspirations.[32]

While these were not the wealthiest families in America, they were certainly comfortable. One survey of female college graduates from 1869 to 1898 found that their parents' salaries were approximately three times the national average and that parents paid out 20–25 percent of their annual income on tuition and room and board, which together often cost four hundred dollars annually.[33] Many southern students seemed to be able to afford college without much sacrifice.

Southern students who went north were primarily from Kentucky, Tennessee, and Maryland. Fewer students came from Deep South states; they would have had to travel farther both literally and figuratively.[34] Out of approximately one thousand students between 1875 and 1915, 25 percent hailed from Kentucky. Tennessee, Maryland, and Texas followed, with 15, 13, and 11 percent, respectively. Of the Deep South states, only Georgia had more than 5 percent, with 8 percent, while Mississippi and Louisiana provided only a tiny fraction of the students, together sending only thirty students out of over one thousand. Women in border states may have had more familiarity or interactions with northerners, although, as will be evident, that did not diminish their regional affinity; they still wore their southern identity on their sleeves. Although some Louisiana students may have chosen to attend Sophie Newcomb in New Orleans, other states with good women's colleges such as Georgia (Agnes Scott) and Maryland (Goucher) sent many students north anyway. Certain towns such as Lexington, Louisville, and Chattanooga were well represented because they had strong preparatory schools nearby.[35] Furthermore, students predominantly came from small towns or small cities. Only one-third of southern students at northern colleges were from the fourteen southern cities large enough to be included in the top one hundred most populous cities in the nation in 1900.[36] College life, with its independence and progressive atmosphere, was profoundly different from their hometowns for women who came from small communities.

The SACW also probably influenced some students from the states where it was most active, including Tennessee, where it was founded, and Alabama. Of the eighteen meetings this organization of college women held between 1903 and 1921, six were in Tennessee, three were in Georgia, and two each were in Kentucky and Alabama. Alabama's relatively high number of students for a Deep South state (fifty-two, or 5 percent of the total) may have been due to the Montgomery branch of the SACW, which was quite active. It secured tuition scholarships for Alabama students to attend Mount Holyoke, Smith, and Wellesley as well as southern schools.[37]

Margaret Preston was forced to confront her ideas about southern womanhood while she was away at school. She and other students sought greater opportunity for themselves and other women yet still remained southern ladies in their manners, their duty to family, and their sense of place. Many northern female college students in these pioneer generations and southern girls who remained in the South also encountered the homesickness and growth characterized here. Yet because of the intensity of expectation that southern women conform to proper gender roles, especially because of the intersection of race and sex, and the shock of traveling so far from home, the experience of southern girls at northern schools appears different. Southern schools were considered less academically demanding than northern colleges and less likely to foster independence. Southern parents and educators sometimes focused more on marriage preparation than on intellectual stimulation.[38] Northern-educated southern women's ability to find some balance between the prescriptions of proper ladylike behavior and expectations of dependence with their experiences of independence, intellectual growth, and increased opportunity for women seems to have been all the more precarious. They had to finesse a new southern womanhood, a southern lady who was somewhere in between, who was active but proper, who had expanded possibilities for education and reform work but was still protected and did not entirely denounce chivalry. Examining how other women in Margaret's position wrestled with the new ideas they had learned up north and the traditional prescriptions of the South will help us better understand who the social reformers and woman suffragists of the Progressive Era South were. Furthermore, the experiences of these women "in the land of Yankees" illustrate the power of education to change an individual—and her community.

CHAPTER ONE

"In the Wonderland of the Mind"

The Benefits of a Liberal Arts Education

May Belle Stephens Mitchell was a Catholic Atlantan who studied at Bellevue Convent in Quebec before completing her education at the Atlanta Female Institute with honors. May Belle's aunts
Mary and Sarah Fitzgerald, who went to Charleston for their education and
"returned to bring learning and literature to the back country," also played a
role in her education. Immersed in a love for literature, May Belle became a
leader of the Atlanta Woman's Study Club and an active suffragist. The mother
of *Gone with the Wind*'s author, Margaret Mitchell, May Belle wanted Margaret
to be educated also, not necessarily for career preparation but so that she would
be able to survive whatever life threw at her. Margaret recalled that as a child
she had not wanted to learn math. May Belle explained that just as the world
had changed dramatically during the Civil War, it could change again during
Margaret's lifetime, and she had to be able to land on her feet. Education was
the key to survival, "so for God's sake," May Belle told Margaret, "go to school
and learn something that will stay with you. The strength of women's hands
isn't worth anything[,] but what they've got in their heads will carry them as far
as they need go."[1] Although May Belle might not have envisioned the successful
career that Margaret eventually had, she knew that she did not want Margaret
to play the helpless, dependent female role so typical in the South. Rather, she
wanted Margaret to be able to think for herself and to use her intellect—and
training available at a liberal arts school like Smith College was central to that
goal. Margaret's mother thought Smith the best women's college in the country,
and after graduating from Atlanta Seminary Margaret would attend there.[2]

Why did southern women like Margaret Mitchell travel hundreds of miles
to join the select few at women's colleges in the North? What did they hope to
gain from higher education? Why did they go north rather than attend one of
the women's colleges closer to home? Understanding why such young women
wanted to go north as well as what their experiences were once they arrived on
northern campuses is key to explaining their leadership in women's activism
during the Progressive Era. Armed with diplomas, these northern-educated

southern women would help create new roles for women in the early-twentieth-century South.

The desire of such women to improve their minds is the first clue as to what drove them to such activism. As was the case with Margaret Mitchell, most southern families wanted their daughters to have the best classical education available so that they would learn to think and to better themselves. While a few had professional training in mind, most sought the intangibles of a liberal arts education. Those women strong-minded enough to go went north because they were interested in a rigorous liberal education that they could not find at southern women's colleges. For the best classical education available, such women sought out schools modeled after the preeminent men's colleges—Harvard, Yale, Amherst. This meant traveling north to the Seven Sisters: Wellesley, Vassar, Smith, Mount Holyoke, Bryn Mawr, Radcliffe, and Barnard. Southern women's colleges, which had the reputation of being finishing schools and featured a curriculum to match, simply could not compare. (Ironically, southern schools in the early nineteenth century may have provided more opportunities for a classical education than they did after the Civil War.) That such northbound students demanded a more rigorous classical education than could be found locally reveals their sense of self, intelligence, curiosity, and discipline, qualities that would serve them well in their postcollege lives as activist women. Campus life and classes provided additional skills, exposure, and experience to complement the leadership qualities this self-selected group already embodied.

Many of these students at the Seven Sisters were not interested in the teacher training that was becoming more readily available for southern women at this time. They did not seek career placement but rather character development and intellectual training. Because of their elite economic status, many of them were unsure how important the economic independence that a profession could provide was. They sought self-realization instead.

A survey of Harvard alumnae who attended the Harvard Annex or Radcliffe College during its first fifty years reveals how alumnae thought about the "aspects of college life" that made "the most important contribution to a girl's development." Nearly three-quarters of the alumna respondents surveyed chose "scholastic training (through developing the power to use the mind on the problems of life)" as the highest contribution college had made to their lives. They selected "character formation (through promoting habits of 'doing the job,' consideration of others, sportsmanship, mental and moral honesty)" as their education's second-highest value. The third and fourth aspects of college life, "training in citizenship in the broad sense" and "contact making," lagged well behind. These choices closely mirror the sentiments of southern women at northern colleges, who valued their scholastic training and character formation highly.[3]

By the early nineteenth century formal educational opportunities for women across the nation were slowly growing. The Republican Mother ideal, which argued that mothers played a crucial role educating sons to be virtuous citizens of the republic, justified some level of education for women as future mothers. In addition, by the mid-nineteenth century the growth in primary schools and the growing use of women as teachers led to the need for more women to be educated.[4]

Academies and seminaries were the prime means of higher education for women in the early to mid-nineteenth century. The two most well known were located in the North: Emma Willard's Troy Female Seminary in Troy, New York, was founded in 1821, and Mary Lyon's Mount Holyoke Female Seminary, in Mount Holyoke, Massachusetts, started in 1837 (it did not become Mount Holyoke College until 1893). These seminaries provided serious academic training in a boarding school setting but did not offer a full classical curriculum leading to a bachelor of arts degree.

There were also a growing number of seminaries in the South. While historian Barbara Solomon has argued that the number of academies grew slowly in the South due to the lack of public schools, in her study Christie Farnham found vitality in the growth of the seminaries and academies for the wealthy. There was no fear or expectation in the South that educated women would work, Farnham notes, because only the daughters of the wealthy were educated. Southerners therefore did not hesitate to open female colleges during the antebellum period, though quality often lagged. Georgia Female College, for example, was chartered in 1837 and opened in 1838, although many historians have dismissed it because the school admitted twelve-year-old girls and did not offer the same classical course as men's colleges. Similarly, Mary Sharp College in Winchester, Tennessee, which opened in 1853, offered a bachelor's degree, although its academic quality, too, was suspect.[5]

Many of these academies, seminaries, and "colleges" did not last, but southerners saw college education as "emblematic of class, a means to a type of refinement that labeled one a lady worthy of protection, admiration, and chivalrous attention."[6] Formal education marked class, refinement, and—surprisingly—marriageability. The South Carolina Female Collegiate Institute in Barhamville, for example, attracted the daughters of planters. One father wrote that "a girl will be more respected with an education than with wealth," implying that a main purpose of a woman's education at the institution was improved marriage prospects.[7] Students took courses in math, history, languages (especially French), geography, religion, grammar, composition, literature, science (especially astronomy), and sometimes Latin. Yet despite the fact that students took more than art, music, or sewing, they still focused on becoming southern belles. They wanted to become ladies—healthy, refined, pure, and religious—but not intellectuals. Teachers, many of whom were from the North, found the students to be lacking in purpose. One teacher complained, "It is not in them to be smart."[8] Historian Catherine Clinton argues that students took their education, married, and then lived on isolated plantations in the same domestic situation as their mothers and grandmothers who were not educated, thus putting their education to little effect. Furthermore, Clinton contends there was a profound difference between North and South: northerners defined virtue to mean industriousness, whereas to southerners it meant chastity.[9] Therefore, it is no surprise that although Farnham found support for a classical curriculum, parents and teachers remained reluctant to teach southern girls certain subjects. One southern educator "warned against having students exposed to the 'squabblings of heathen gods and goddesses,'" expressing his distaste for learning foreign languages.[10] Implicit in this history of southern antebellum academies is the assumption that southern parents and educators did not question their daughters' intelligence but rather the propriety of developing women's intellect in the same manner as men's.

Growing out of the antebellum tradition of academies and seminaries, a number of lasting and rigorous women's colleges began to appear immediately after the Civil War due to changing opportunities for women and to a general trend of growth in higher education. In the North, Vassar opened in 1865, then both Smith and Wellesley in 1875, and Bryn Mawr in 1885. Vassar had strict rules regulating students' days, including both academics and social activities, and students there earned the reputation of being serious about both their work and social and women's issues.[11] Smith College was established by Sophia Smith upon her death. The board of trustees desired to open a women's college equivalent to the best for men. There was no preparatory department, and strict entrance requirements meant that only fourteen young women were admitted into the first class. Called the College Beautiful, Wellesley was established by Henry and Pauline Durant with the intention of offering the best instruction, a beautiful setting, a religious atmosphere, and an all-female faculty. Durant's missionary zeal was later minimized by trustees and the administration, which stressed academic excellence. Dr. Joseph Wright Taylor, a Quaker, founded Bryn Mawr just outside Philadelphia, with an academic system modeled on Johns Hopkins University. Bryn Mawr's first president, M. Carey Thomas, pushed her students to achieve academic excellence.[12] Although opened in 1837 by founder

Mary Lyon, Mount Holyoke began as a seminary and did not begin offering the college course until fifty-one years later. In 1893 Mount Holyoke received a new charter as a college only. The college was known for its religious emphasis and training of missionaries and teachers. The Harvard Annex began when Arthur Gilman and a committee of women convinced a group of Harvard professors to offer courses to women, who were to take the same entrance exam as Harvard male students. Twenty-five students began the program in the fall of 1879. In 1893 Harvard Annex became Radcliffe College, officially related to Harvard.[13]

Despite the classical curriculum of southern antebellum seminaries, long-lasting and "real" southern colleges for the most part did not appear until the late 1880s and 1890s. Those that offered a liberal arts education (as opposed to the seminaries or secondary schools, normal schools for teachers, and finishing schools) were still considered less rigorous than northern schools.[14] The most notable included Mary Baldwin in Virginia, Agnes Scott College in Georgia, Woman's College of Baltimore (also known as Goucher, after its president), Randolph-Macon College in Virginia, and Sophie Newcomb College in Louisiana. Yet these colleges were too little, too late. In her address to the Conference on Southern Education held in 1907 in Memphis, Lilian Wyckoff Johnson asked why southerners thought they had to send their daughters north for the best education available.[15] Students at southern colleges "had fewer ties to faculty, less enthusiasm for careers, and little interest in suffrage" in comparison to students at northern schools. They also retained strict social codes governing dress, smoking, dancing, fraternization with men, and drinking for decades longer than their northern counterparts.[16]

The major problem at southern schools was that southern educators and families were comparatively more concerned with whether higher education "unsexed" women and made them "manly."[17] According to John Franklin Goucher, president of Woman's College of Baltimore, a woman's potential for motherhood was why she "is of a more intense nature, has keener insight and stronger passions, is more conscientious in details and less skillful in generalization than man."[18] Women's education, accordingly, should not only cultivate their womanliness but recognize their different virtues and ultimately be centered upon creating better mothers.[19] Dr. D. B. Johnson of Rock Hill, South Carolina, argued that schools for women should be separate, be equivalent but not identical, and fit women for their lives and sphere.[20] These ideas were not limited to educators but extended to family members as well. Historian Lynn Gordon found that in the South "most Southern families clung to their daughters and to conservative notions of Southern womanhood."[21]

Southern educators believed that the southern lady ideal—women should be pious, pure, domestic, submissive, charming, and dependent—could be taught primarily by the example of women teachers but also through classes such as Bible study. Although Wellesley and Smith Colleges also claimed that they created true women (Smith College catalogs stated that as a women's college it aimed "to preserve and perfect every characteristic of a complete woman-hood"), southern schools proclaimed themselves the guardians of womanli-ness. John M. McBryde, Jr., of Sweet Briar argued that while northern colleges focused solely on providing an equal education to that of men, the Woman's College of Baltimore "was the first college for women to announce a distinctive policy for women. 'The ideal entertained by the founders of the College is the formation of womanly character for womanly ends.'" Randolph-Macon College in Virginia was known not only for its academic strength but also for its often-quoted statement: "We wish to establish in Virginia a College where our young women may obtain an education equal to that given in our best colleges for men, and under environments in harmony with the highest ideals of womanhood, where the dignity and strength of fully developed faculties and the charm of the highest literary culture may be acquired without loss to woman's crowning glory: her gentleness and grace." McBryde believed that although women were capable of academic work, schools could not neglect to train the finer qualities of women, for which he stressed literature, music and art, and domestic science.[22] Through these subjects women would be taught to cultivate good taste, manners, and character; in short, they would be all the more womanly. Thus, by 1911 75 percent of students at North Carolina's Greensboro Female College were studying music, while only 10 percent of Vassar students were.[23]

Significantly, the interest in creating ladies first and scholars second invariably meant that the level of scholarship available at the southern schools was less rigorous because southern schools feared fostering "grinds." While M. Carey Thomas built an atmosphere of scholarship at Bryn Mawr, President Goucher of Baltimore Woman's College believed it was more important to have students with grace and social skills than intellectual prowess. He ensured that at Goucher the dormitories (called college homes) were far enough from the classrooms to enforce a separation between home life and academics. Social life was more important to many students and their parents. Sophie Newcomb's president, Brandt Van Blarcom Dixon, had to ask parents' assistance in cutting back on students' social activities, which he believed were interfering with their academic achievements.[24] A short story written by a Bryn Mawr alumna from Baltimore suggests that students were well aware of the need to defend themselves against being called grinds or bluestockings. In "A Diplomatic Crusade," by Edith Campbell Crane, Marjorie has just encountered a man named Mr. Ballantyne who was against modern women. She tells her roommate that the question of whether or not women should go to college has been answered in the affirmative. But, she complained, Mr. Ballantyne still thought that women had to prove that they should be in college. This put pressure on college women "to be so broad-spirited and alert and interested in everything, that we shall simply convince these people that college training is the best thing that ever happened to women—especially Bryn Mawr training." Marjorie ultimately not only convinced Ballantyne to send his own daughter to Bryn Mawr but started a crusade among students to push for well-rounded achievement, for them to play basketball and join the glee club in addition to their studies. Given the emphasis on scholarship at Bryn Mawr, Crane's need to explain that students were not too driven by academics alone is striking. Perhaps she encountered similar sentiments at home in Baltimore.[25]

Furthermore, Amy McCandless argued that in the early twentieth century parents saw schools as places to shelter young women before marriage rather than as institutions designed to challenge them intellectually. Well into the twentieth century southern parents inordinately desired to continue to regulate the details of their daughters' lives. Southern schools like Agnes Scott College retained their social restrictions much longer than their northern counterparts— Agnes Scott still had 10:00 p.m. lights out in 1913, while Vassar abandoned a set time in 1899.[26] Many southern colleges viewed the northern colleges as their model and had northern teachers, yet they remained more closely tied to rules and to Christian evangelicalism longer.[27]

Southern women venturing to northern colleges had to be either not too concerned with remaining womanly or convinced that northern colleges would not endanger their femininity. Vassar and Wellesley offered some reassurance that girls would be protected, but they did not go as far as Agnes Scott College outside Atlanta, which assured parents that "every effort is made to give . . . the character of a Christian home. . . . Care is taken to render the home life of the student . . . conducive to the cultivation of those graces which mark refined women. . . . Instruction in manners and etiquette is given by the Lady Principal." Southern women also had to want the intellectual challenge that northern colleges offered. Historian Louise Boas said that southerners sent their daughters to local schools to learn manners, but if they really wanted an education, they sent them north.[28]

Such a strong focus on remaining southern ladies was related to the web of sex and race in the South, where any threat to the gender hierarchy implied a danger to the greater southern social order and therefore to segregation and the racial oppression of African Americans. In the most common version of southern sex and race mores, southern white men protected southern white women from the brutality of black men through segregation and disfranchisement. Recognizing that while women gained protection they also lost many rights, Smith graduate and North Carolina journalist Nell Battle Lewis quipped in 1925 that the educated woman was "inconsistent with the chivalric ideal." This, she argued, is why it took longer for higher education to catch on in the South. "In southern chivalry, the queen and the concubine were inseparably connected. The same system produced them both." Thus, slavery held down both black and white women.[29] Southern schools paid homage to these ideals when they clung to Lost Cause images of the happy plantation and the antebellum belle. The 1932 catalog for Limestone College in Gaffney, South Carolina, explained that "Limestone College strives to preserve as a precious elixir of life all that was finest in the civilization of the Old South—its exalted ideals of manhood and womanhood, its liberal culture at its best, its peerless standards of unsullied honor, the delicate charm of its manners, and the ineffable beauty of its social life."[30]

These ideas concerning gender roles influenced how southern educators viewed their students. Sophie Newcomb president Dixon said about his students: "The southern girl . . . is inclined to be self-willed and exacting, but not self-reliant; alert and quick-witted but not persistent and steady, eager for novelty and possessing a fine initiative but changeable and dependent on others for results. She lacks the discipline which comes from interest in that which requires hard work. . . . She has not been required to fend for herself, is guarded and supervised continually."[31] Southern women complained that such low standards for southern girls only served to reinforce women's inferiority. They wanted women's intellectual abilities to be nurtured and recognized.

There were few choices for students who did not want to leave the South. Southern states led the nation in opening state-supported normal and industrial schools for women that offered career preparation but not a classical education. Endorsed in part by Populist politicians, Winthrop Normal and Industrial School in Rock Hill, South Carolina, and North Carolina Normal and Industrial School were both chartered in 1891. Mississippi Industrial Institute and College opened in 1884, and similar schools for women opened in Georgia in 1889, Alabama in 1893, Texas in 1901, and Florida in 1905. The Florida Female College was founded when the legislature essentially abolished all existing public higher education and chartered a university for men and a college for women. The college stressed domestic science and had a normal school, although it did not have professional schools like its male counterpart.[32] These schools were inexpensive and drew farmers' daughters and young women who could not afford to go north in addition to those who wanted to teach.[33]

Because of these limitations, only seven southern women's colleges were accredited by the Association of Colleges in 1917: Agnes Scott, Goucher, Converse,

Florida State, Randolph-Macon, Sophie Newcomb, and Westhampton.[34] When Sophie Newcomb was founded in 1886 as a coordinate college with Tulane in New Orleans, President Dixon wanted the school to compare academically to northern colleges. Unfortunately, the school could not attract enough qualified students to allow it to abandon its preparatory department. In 1907 only 135 of 433 students were enrolled in the bachelor's degree program, yet its commencement speaker claimed that it was the pride of the South as the only southern school to rank with Vassar and Wellesley. Students saw marriage as inevitable, and school officials bemoaned the tendency of parents to encourage students (many of whom lived at home) to prioritize social events over studies. Founded to educate Christian mothers in 1889, Agnes Scott College in Decatur, Georgia, just outside Atlanta, did not confer the bachelor's degree until 1906.[35]

When Mary Caroline Crawford wrote a book in 1905 describing various women's colleges, detailing the stereotypes of the students who attended each, she played up the lack of seriousness of students at southern colleges. While she discussed the bookishness and hard work of Vassar and Bryn Mawr students, Crawford referred to the southern schools in terms of their focus on creating ladies. According to her, Randolph-Macon produced "the purest type of southern college girl" based on the "ladylike conduct" expected of her. Despite this characterization, Randolph-Macon, Sophie Newcomb, and Goucher were at least recognized for having some academic standards. Other southern colleges did not fare as well, with Hollins summarized as a college where students were treated with the "respect and attention which their sex ever receives at the hands of good society in Virginia"; Mary Baldwin Seminary described as a school that emphasized purity and refinement; Agnes Scott portrayed as a place that focused on developing Christian women, using the Bible as a textbook; and the Woman's College in Richmond, Virginia, dismissed as a school with such paternalistic rules that students were even told when they needed an umbrella.[36]

With the opening of Vassar and other women's colleges during the last decades of the nineteenth century, popular magazines as well as academic journals debated higher education for women. Opposing sides weighed in on whether women should go to college, whether higher education for women should be the same as that for men, and whether women should attend all-female or coeducational institutions. The most notable educators, including Charles Eliot, president of Harvard University, Charles F. Thwing, president of Western Reserve University and Adelbert College, Alice Freeman Palmer, president of Wellesley, and M. Carey Thomas, president of Bryn Mawr, contributed to the debate. Southern women and their families undoubtedly read some of these articles as they decided whether and where to attend college.

By the 1880s the answer to whether women were intellectually capable of higher education seemed settled. Vassar had already been producing college graduates for twenty years, both Wellesley and Smith were open, some prominent universities in the Midwest and West admitted women, and female scholars such as M. Carey Thomas had returned from Europe with doctoral degrees, all seemingly proving that women were capable of the most rigorous academic work. Although much of the debate now turned to how best to educate women, southern students at northern colleges recognized that some Americans had lingering doubts as to women's capabilities. In 1906 William L. Felter from Girls' High School in Brooklyn, New York, argued that women should learn the history of physics rather than quantitative physics because they were more suited for the historical than the quantitative approach. Daisy Lee Worthington, a Kentucky Vassar alumna, dashed off a heated reply. Worthington claimed that women were just as intellectual as men but had not always been given the same opportunities.[37]

Southern students probably encountered family members, friends, or neighbors who persisted in their belief that women were not as intellectual as men or that women were less talented at some subjects such as Greek and math, stereotypes that persist into the twenty-first century. In 1891 Vassar student Josie Simrall recounted to her father a story told by her physics teacher, Miss Whiting, who had described to her students the visit of Sir Richard Temple, a British politician, to Vassar College. Temple expressed his disbelief that Whiting actually taught physics to young women. According to Temple, women did not possess enough imagination to understand physics. Whiting "sedately" replied that she had just heard from an authority at Harvard that women could not learn mathematics because they had too much imagination. While male authorities debated, she implied, women were learning.[38]

While many of the southern students studied here complained about the difficulty of the work, they did not usually attribute their struggles to an inherent lack of talent on the part of their sex. Perhaps the all-female setting strengthened many students' views of women's capabilities. Kentuckian Margaret Preston came closest to blaming her troubles on her sex. Constantly complaining about her work during her first year at Bryn Mawr, she seemed to think that even if she and other women were intellectually capable, they were not emotionally or physically strong enough to bear the pressures of college. She found college work extremely difficult and, at first, suffering from homesickness, was overwhelmed. Unable to make friends, she mocked the teas and other social activities at the college and struggled with the intensity of the work and competition. She confessed to her mother, "I feel all the time as if I ought to like it here and be interested in the work and yet I am not." The stress of exams upset her "fearfully," which she blamed in part on the fact that "girls take everything so hard" and partly on her approaching menstrual period. She told her mother, "I don't think I was ever made for college or competitive things, they worry me so." Describing examinations as "a tremendous strain," she proclaimed, "I am sure boys don't sob as Elizabeth and Helen did to-night."[39]

Margaret's allusion to her menstrual period reflected the concerns of Edward Clarke, who published *Sex in Education* in 1874.[40] In it he argued that women should not attend college even though they were capable of doing so; if they did attend, their education should be different so as to protect their fertility. Clarke thought that women were not capable of expending energy to the reproductive physical functions and the muscles at the same time as to the brain; therefore, if they overstudied in the crucial years of adolescence, they would be underdeveloped physically, miss their periods, and become infertile. Men's reproductive organs, on the other hand, developed with less effort, leaving them more energy for their brains. One of his examples was a Vassar student who exercised while having her period, causing her to faint and eventually develop hysteria and dysmenorrhea. He blamed her small breasts on arrested physical development.

As a doctor, Clarke presented a scientific argument linking women's destiny to their biology, a premise his opponents were hard pressed to challenge. College-educated women and their supporters found it difficult to refute Clarke's essential point, that women's most important function was motherhood, so, rather than argue with his basic principle, they disagreed with his findings. They tried to show that college did not make women weaker but improved their health because schools required exercise. In 1885 the Association of Collegiate Alumnae surveyed its members, and the results of 705 replies (almost half coming from Vassar alumnae) showed that 78 percent of alumnae claimed to be in excellent or good health.[41] Furthermore, a smaller number classified themselves as below fair health than the number who did so upon entering college, demonstrating improvement, and a higher number saw themselves as in good or excellent health in comparison to average women or working girls. The ACA thus proved that college did not physically harm women, although it would still have to answer to whether college women married less often, had fewer children, or otherwise disavowed the maternal impulse while leaving their maternal organs intact.

Letters between southern students and their families show they were almost consumed with worry over health. Several students had late periods while at college. Margaret Preston blamed her emotional depression on her late period. When she told her mother she was crying because of her exams, Margaret added that her upcoming period might be exacerbating the problem.[42] Fellow Kentuckian Sophonisba Breckinridge also experienced infrequent periods and was concerned enough to consult the Wellesley campus doctor, a woman named Dr. Speakman. At home, her mother, Issa, consulted a male doctor, who reassured her that it was entirely normal, despite Dr. Speakman's alarm. He suggested that the female campus doctor erred because she did not really know Sophonisba.[43] South Carolinian Julia Hammond wrote to her mother and speculated that because she did not get her period until two months after she arrived at Radcliffe, "though I had no physical ill effect from this suppression, I think emotionally it was depressing."[44] While these students experienced temporary fluctuations in their cycles, probably due to stress, they did not suffer long-term physical consequences from their education. Comparatively lower fertility rates for married college graduates were due more to age (many married later) or choice rather than debilitation.

Southern parents were concerned enough over their daughters' health to remind them over and over again that health came before academics. Isabella Simrall put her daughter's health first, admonishing Kentuckian Josie to guard her health "even if you have to sacrifice your collegiate course for it."[45] She was specifically concerned with Josie's nervous system and the danger that examinations posed to it if Josie taxed herself through the amount of study and her dread of it.[46] Parents explained to their daughters that they would achieve even more academically if they prioritized rest and health. Issa Breckinridge followed this logic the farthest, telling Sophonisba that if she stayed healthy she might even become president of Wellesley one day. Issa again stressed Sophonisba's limitless possibilities when she wrote her: "You have birth—you have breeding—you have character and intellect—if you have health what may you not hope to be in this world—and in the next."[47] While many college parents were concerned for their daughters' health, southern parents were particularly concerned with their children's unfamiliarity with cold winters and frequently offered advice on how to avoid catching a cold.

A few students ignored their parents' warnings and succumbed to exhaustion. Goldsboro, North Carolina, native Eva Stanley wrote a year after her graduation from Mount Holyoke: "After all the 'ologies, 'osophies, and 'onomies of my Senior year, I was very much worn out and had grown so thin that my friends and relatives thought it would be best for me to take a rest, so I have given myself up to good times."[48] Margaret Preston's health was the most jeopardized by her stress. She apparently had a nervous breakdown at the beginning of her sophomore year. Her doctor advised her mother to dissuade Margaret from returning to Bryn Mawr because she was in an "overwrought, nervous condition, suffering in fact from neurasthenia." When Margaret returned anyway her attitude improved, probably due to her achievement in the classroom, which reduced her level of stress, although it was possibly due to the "tonic" she was taking.[49]

The concerns over health shared by parents and students were so strong that school catalogs emphasized at great length the college's calisthenics, outdoor life, gymnasiums, and other health programs and the ventilation and heating of the buildings. Smith College even bragged that there were no deaths on campus until the fall of 1885, ten years after the school opened, noting that even in this case the student lived with her parents in town, not on campus![50]

Beyond the question of whether women were capable of higher education and whether it harmed them physically, late-nineteenth-century Americans still asked why women needed a college degree. What was the purpose of higher education? Should it be a liberal education—training to think, to stretch the mind, to become the best, most thoughtful, most cultured, most appreciative, most disciplined person one can be? Or should it be of a more practical sort, more directly connected to one's vocation in life? If the latter, for women should it be for motherhood? For housekeeping? For better companionship as a wife? Would a general liberal education suffice? Or was a more specific domestic science or home economics course required? Furthermore, what of those women who did not marry? Should women receive training for teaching, farming, or professional careers? The best northern women's colleges believed in training the mind as preparation for any facet of life, regardless of gender. Southern students who chose these schools wanted a liberal education, despite those in the South who disapproved.

A classical curriculum generally included courses in Greek, Latin, modern languages, science, mathematics, political economy, and literature. In the antebellum academies and seminaries, Latin and Greek were generally offered as electives, and women students read less difficult texts than their male counterparts. However, historian Christie Farnham points out that despite these differences in course difficulty, many southerners believed that being conversant in the classics was evidence of a young woman's education and status, and they did not bar female students from these subjects. Furthermore, knowledge of the classics helped students appreciate Western civilization, read the Bible in Latin or Greek versions, and learn grammar in modern languages. Mathematics and sciences trained the mind to think logically and enabled women to investigate the world around them. Rhetoric and composition helped students learn to express themselves. Still, in those seminaries and academies the informal curriculum also included inculcating young women in the art of becoming southern ladies, that is, socializing them into the separation of spheres, stressing domestic duties, benevolence, and manners. Parents also insisted that their daughters receive training in the "ornamentals," or music, art, and embroidery.[51]

Most late-nineteenth-century Americans and certainly many southerners believed that "the highest function of womanhood is motherhood" and that God designed women to be physically, mentally, and emotionally adapted to this purpose. Those against women receiving the same education as men argued that because most women would be wives and mothers, their education should be tailored to fit them for this role. They contended that, like the antebellum academies and seminaries, colleges for women should encourage health, purity, grace, good temper, culture, and taste. Classes in art, music, and literature should teach taste and the art of conversation.[52] Even Radcliffe and Smith students encountered this perspective from S. Weir Mitchell, who stressed womanliness and the importance of women not trying to be like men. If colleges tended to make women choose careers over marriage, he argued in a speech at Radcliffe, then colleges should be shut down. He patronizingly told his audience to make sure they were properly trained in domestic skills and to remember to dress well and retain their charm, something professional women sometimes neglected. He encouraged students to learn English literature "for its charm" and science in order to be better able to boil rice, among other things.[53] When North Carolinian Gertrude Weil heard him speak at Smith several years later, she called him an "old fogy."[54]

Initially, Vassar, Wellesley, Smith, Holyoke, Radcliffe, and Bryn Mawr did not offer courses in home economics. They stood firmly by their intention to offer women the same kind of classical education that was offered in the best men's colleges. But by the early twentieth century the clamor for domestic science, brought about in part in response to low marriage rates for college graduates, grew loud enough that even Vassar introduced some courses. Some female educators, including Marion Talbot, hoped to make homemaking more professional and thus more worthy and valued. Yet despite her efforts, Vassar's domestic science courses attracted limited enrollment, and Wellesley offered a domestic science course for only two years.[55] Annie Allen's survey of one hundred college women, the majority of whom were at Holyoke, Smith, Wellesley, and Vassar, found only thirteen who wanted household economics in the curriculum, underscoring its lack of popularity. Despite the lack of such classes, most women grew to appreciate their role as homemakers. Only three in Allen's survey said that they grew to value domestic duties less while in college, while forty-four saw a greater value in domestic work.[56]

Defenders of liberal education argued that neither men nor women needed to take courses in psychology to prepare for parenthood, and women did not go to college to learn how to cook. Students who made the effort to go to Wellesley or Bryn Mawr wanted to take languages, sciences, math, or history. M. Carey Thomas conceded that infant psychology, the chemistry of cooking, and physiology with regard to motherhood and wifehood could be offered as electives, although she dismissed each as unnecessary or not appropriate in a college. Rather, contended Charles Thwing, if women used a liberal education to learn how to think, to appreciate, and to be righteous, they would use those broad principles as mothers, wives, and housekeepers or perhaps even wage earners, just as men use those principles as lawyers and businessmen.[57] On the one hundredth anniversary of Vassar's founding, Dean C. Mildred Thompson, a Vassar graduate from Atlanta, reiterated Vassar's commitment to liberal arts education, which should, according to the college's founder, Matthew Vassar, contribute to "intellectual culture" rather than be practical or useful. Thompson argued that schools needed to remember their duty to "liberate the mind to learn, to want to learn" rather than to take on the responsibilities of the home or church and teach domestic skills or religious dogma. Thompson also told Georgians gathered at a celebration for Georgia State Woman's College that Georgia needed more educated women, quipping, "As man does not live by bread alone, so woman does not live by the baking of bread alone."[58]

Despite these broad views, educators had to be wary of causing women to be discontented with their primary role as wife and mother. Cornelia Phillips had been tutored and attended classes at the University of North Carolina in the 1840s. Twenty years later she expressed her impatience with her life and her desire to "take wings and fly and leave these sordid occupations. . . . I think sometimes it is cruel to cultivate tastes that are never to be gratified in this world."[59] If colleges in the post–Civil War period were not careful, a larger than expected percentage of their graduates might seek fulfillment beyond domestic roles.

Some southern educators preferred domestic science to a classical curriculum. A Randolph-Macon professor criticized Bryn Mawr for its emphasis on liberal arts and academic rigor, arguing that its students were deficient in "knowledge of the housewife."[60] Although she wanted to encourage independence rather than good taste and manners in southern women, southern educator Celeste Parrish also argued that higher education should also teach women the practical skills of child rearing and housewifery through home economics or domestic science and child psychology courses.[61] She and others even recognized that some women would not marry, would be widowed, or would be otherwise impoverished and therefore would need to be able to teach or take up other wage work.[62] Vassar graduate Orie Latham Hatcher, who headed the Southern Women's Educational Alliance (later known as the Alliance for Guidance of Rural Youth), also considered education the key to aiding women find better employment opportunities, as did Wellesley alumna Lilian Wyckoff Johnson. Johnson's vision for a southern women's college was broad: in 1901 she suggested that college should prepare women for motherhood and homemaking, train them for livelihoods, and provide an "all-around" education through courses in the humanities and arts. By the time she became president of Western College for Women in 1904, Johnson, who was partially influenced by Charles Dabney, president of the University of Tennessee, and Philander Claxton of the Southern Education Board, was convinced that women needed to be trained in home economics in order to fit them for their duties as mothers and social reformers.[63] Although Parrish, Hatcher, and Johnson were attuned to the need for increasing the economic independence of working women through improving their educational and wage opportunities, other southern alumnae focused more on the personal growth that a liberal arts education provided those who could afford it.

This debate between the merits of a liberal education and a practical education that stressed home economics was evident at the opening of Smith College in 1875. In an address at the inauguration of the Reverend L. Clark Seelye as college president, Professor W. S. Tyler, president of the Smith board of trustees, emphasized the importance of a liberal education without regard to gender. He argued that a college education "is that education of the whole man [*sic*] which makes the most of the best there is in us, and thus prepares us for the fullest accomplishment of the highest and best work in life of which we are severally capable. This highest education, which is the proper sphere of the college, is quite irrespective of occupations, professions and pursuits." He therefore concluded that such a liberal education should also be irrespective of gender or class. Yet in his address President Seelye backed away from Tyler's gender-neutral beliefs and focused more on the education of intelligent mothers for the benefit of the race. Furthermore, Seelye admitted that some women in the past had had to ostracize themselves or become "coarse and repulsive" in order to get an education. But, he argued, knowledge was attractive, and he asked, "May we not preserve the social graces and add to them those which come from intelligence?" Finally, to assuage any doubts of parents or critics, he claimed, "It is not the aim nor the tendency of the higher education to make woman less feminine, or less attractive in those graces peculiar to her sex. It is to preserve her womanliness that this College has been founded."[64] The differences between these two men were especially interesting because Sophia Smith, the founder of Smith College, argued quite forcefully for women's higher education as a means of fighting against the oppression of women. She founded Smith "with the design to furnish for my own sex means and facilities for education equal to those which are afforded now in our Colleges to young men." Smith believed that increasing educational opportunities for women would result in higher wages for women and more opportunities for them to influence the morals of their families and society. Yet despite her strong challenge to sex discrimination, Smith also backed away from gender-neutral ideas, claiming, "I would have the education suited to the mental and physical wants of woman. It is not my design to render my sex any the less feminine, but to develop as fully as may be the powers of womanhood, and furnish women with the means of usefulness, happiness, and honor, now withheld from them."[65] Sophia Smith wanted an education for women equal to that of men because she believed that women were capable, though they had been held back by society, and that education would end that oppression. She recognized that some women would marry, but others could contribute to society as workers and citizens. Yet Smith wanted her college to acknowledge the differences between the sexes and to adjust women's education to those differences, thus preserving their womanliness rather than threatening it.

This debate over the value and purpose of higher education for women was meaningful to southern students who chose a northern college. Letters written by southern students and their families consistently emphasize the value of a rigorous classical education. They believed the sacrifice it took to go north for an education was worth it, and they were not there for domestic training. After Josie Simrall had difficulty with exams, her mother reassured her that it was worth it, that "you were taking more freely from these days of great opportunities, than you could or would do if you were at home." Josie apparently agreed, declaring that the benefits of college outweighed her exhaustion. She considered it one of her greatest blessings.[66] Despite the high cost of Vassar (most of the colleges charged three to four hundred dollars per year in tuition and room and board), the Poppenheim family, who sent four daughters to Vassar from Charleston, South Carolina, believed the educational experience merited the financial sacrifice. Mary Elinor Poppenheim told her daughter Mary that friends probably did not send their daughter to Vassar because of the expense. But, she added, "I am reconciled to your being away when I see the advantages and know how many want to go who can't. When you come home we will realize the benefit to all."[67] Sometimes perceptions of the benefits of education varied from family member to family member. Alabamian Virginia Foster Durr said she was different because although she wanted "to be popular and marry well," she also "was just dying to go to college. Anyway Daddy finally agreed to send me to Wellesley, because he was convinced I had brain enough to go to college." Her mother, however, agreed to the plan for Virginia to attend Wellesley because she hoped that Virginia would meet a potential husband there.[68]

Students like Virginia were at school because they had the support of their families. Very few young women went to school against the will of their parents.[69] In the 1850s the parents of Mary Fuller, originally from Mississippi, demonstrated their support for higher education by moving to New Jersey to be closer to their children, with Mary at Mount Holyoke and her brothers at

Princeton. Students understood that their education was not just for themselves but would benefit the entire family, especially mothers who had not had
enough access to formal education. Daughters therefore dutifully went to college to please their parents. Lilian Wyckoff Johnson went to Wellesley because
her father wanted her to. He had sent her older sisters to Vassar, and they were
the first female students from Memphis to go to the Northeast for college. She
recalled that "he literally made me go to Wellesley in 1879."[70] Mary Elinor Poppenheim also supported her daughters' tenure at Vassar College. Educated at
Edgefield Academy in South Carolina, Mary Elinor decided that her daughters
should attend Vassar. Louisa remembered that her mother wanted them to go
despite Charleston society's resistance to the idea. She described her older sister
Mary as having been "taken to Vassar by mother who decided to enter her."
Louisa also recalled that she found exams stressful because she so desperately
wanted to please her parents.[71]

Like the Poppenheims, many students had the support of their mothers, especially if the mother was educated herself. Few mothers would have had the
opportunity to obtain college degrees, although many went to academies and
seminaries. Hope Summerall's mother, Ellen Mitchell, had been educated in the
1840s by her father, a University of North Carolina faculty member who brought
his daughters to classes and tutored them. Hope believed that her mother had
been frustrated by the fact that neither her intellect nor her ambitions could be
fulfilled in domestic life. Undaunted, Hope also believed in the value of education, and when her husband did not want to send their daughter to college, she
sold property held in her own name and sent her to Bryn Mawr. While Mary
was at college Hope extended her own world by becoming involved in women's
clubs and other organizations. She found reading Ibsen and Shaw with her book
club to be "intoxicat[ing]"; feminist literature and the study of woman suffrage
soon followed. Mary M. Chamberlain graduated in the class of 1915.[72]

These daughters felt the responsibility of educating not only themselves but
also their mothers, sisters, and other relations as well.[73] Isabella Simrall, who
had attended Daughters College in Harrodsburg, Kentucky, in the 1850s clearly
valued education, often writing Josie of the many intellectual opportunities the
family sought at home: Josie's younger sisters attended a lecture on Norway,
and Isabella went to a series of lectures on history. However, she wished that
Josie's sister Bart (Mary Barton) was "putting her time to as good use as you
are yours. I hope often after this first winter of gay dissipation." She wrote Josie
that she read that Gladstone was to publish a paper on Alypian religion: "I look
forward to great pleasure when you come home our reading together—I expect
you to stimulate me to self-cultivate. I do so little of it now."[74] Like Mary Elinor
Poppenheim, Isabella hoped that Josie would bring home fashion and culture

as well as the intellectual curiosity she had learned while in the North and at college, telling her that maybe she would have some ideas about landscaping their home influenced by the grounds at Wellesley.[75] Like many southerners, these mothers saw the North—especially New York—as offering the latest in fashion, and they hoped to benefit from their daughters' exposure to the newest trends.

Gertrude Weil's mother, Mina, was also an intellectual whose husband, Sol, once wrote to her that he was "jealous of your books," implying that she was more interested in science and math than in him. Educated at Wilson Collegiate Seminary for Young Ladies in North Carolina, Mina did her best to study on her own while her daughters were at Smith so that she would remain up-to-date. She supported the decision for Gertrude to undertake a college education and told her to focus on her studies rather than fashion, a warning hardly necessary for Gertrude. However, Mina was unable to sway Gertrude on her choice of school. Gertrude's Aunt Sarah, originally from Boston, wanted her to attend Smith, which she did over her mother's objections that Smith was too pretentious.[76]

The support of fathers was even more important than that of mothers. A survey of Vassar alumnae from the classes of 1865–90 showed that students were five times more likely to credit their father's influence in their choice of college than their mother's. This was true for Sophonisba Breckinridge. Her mother supported Sophonisba, reminding her that she had "intellect and culture beyond most girls of [her] age," but the driving force behind her choice was her father.[77] Sophonisba was his favorite, and he pushed her to obtain a good education (her older sister Ella was considered more the belle of the family). Her mother claimed that Sophonisba was "Papa's sole only hope for an educated daughter" and the object of his love. Sophonisba later claimed that William's desire for her to be educated came in part from his experiences attending Centre College in Kentucky. While the college was coeducational, women, including several of William's cousins, who completed the same courses as men were not awarded a diploma. She wrote later that his experience of studying side by side with intellectually talented women "undoubtedly influenced his attitude toward women and their intellectual capacity." Sophonisba also claimed in her autobiography that she was a dull child, motivated to study only by her love for her father. "I cared a great deal about grades because it pleased my Father to have me make good grades, and justified his position with reference to the treatment of women." Perhaps the desire to please her father pushed her to become an intense student who constantly strove for perfection. Her father had high expectations for her, telling her "to uphold the family reputation 'for good thinking and courageous utterance,'" noting that "the name has been connected with good intellectual work for some generations—for over a century—you must preserve this connection for the next generation." Her brilliant performance at Wellesley and her long academic career reflected her passion for detail and hard work and earned her a reputation in her own right.[78]

Orie Latham Hatcher's father and a wealthy sponsor urged her to attend Vassar. Called "the second Virginia woman ever to go North to college" by the *New York Times*, feisty Orie was a contemporary of Mary Cooke Branch Munford. Mary was a Virginia suffragist and reformer who wanted a college education so badly that she was "strong-minded to a degree that made Richmond society gasp." So was the Hatcher family. According to legend, a family friend told William Hatcher that he would rather see his daughter "in hell than send her to a Yankee college." William reportedly replied, "Well, you see yours in Hell, mine's going to Vassar."[79] Orie Hatcher's mother was also well educated. She graduated from Fluvanna Institute in Virginia and then continued her education at Albemarle Female Institute. Orie's strong will attracted others to work with her when she later organized an organization to better southern women's education and vocational opportunities. Like many of the other women in this study, she was a dynamo whose organization thrived due to the strength of its leader's personality and dedication.

Mary and Linda Neville both attended Bryn Mawr from Lexington, Kentucky, because their father wanted them to. Linda claimed that he insisted that "his daughters should not grow up ignorant." Furthermore, John Neville believed that education freed his daughters from marrying for support by making them capable of supporting themselves if necessary.[80]

Other relatives also played a role in pushing for academic achievement. Tennessean Maria Daviess had an uncle who told her, "You have shown decided symptoms of intellect, and I want you here by me so I can see it develop. You are all the girl I have got and I want to make you into as great a woman as if you were a boy." He sent her to Nashville College for Young Ladies because it was "the best school for girls in the South" and then Science Hill Academy before Wellesley College.[81] Margaret Preston attended Bryn Mawr due to the generosity of her aunt Jessie Draper, who paid for her tuition for two years.

Overcoming the burdens of travel, expensive tuition and board, and sometimes community or family disapproval required an intense dedication to acquiring such a rigorous classical education. Just getting to college was difficult enough. Students took either a train or a boat. The Poppenheims, for example, sailed from Charleston to New York and then took the train to Poughkeepsie to attend Vassar College. When Mary left for school she had to have her parents accompany her to school in the fall and come to get her when she came home for a vacation and at the end of the year. The boat ride took several days, as did the train trip. When Mary Comer planned to take a train home from Smith College to Savannah, she hoped that if she left New York on Sunday at four o'clock she would be home in time for Tuesday evening's entertainment.[82]

To add to their difficulties, even family members and friends sometimes disapproved. Margaret Mitchell's older brother Stephen, himself Harvard educated, did not want her to go to Smith. According to him, college "was the ruination of girls," and northern schools were even worse.[83] Agnes Raoul captured southern society's reaction to southern college women when she wrote home to Atlanta from New York on her way to school: "Vassar is not such a strange place to the people in this part of the country and they do not open their eyes wide with amazement at the mention of going there."[84]

For each southern student who matriculated, there were others who did not have the money or the support to go. Susan Clay Sawitzky of Lexington, for example, great-granddaughter of Henry Clay, desperately wanted to go to college, but her mother would not allow her to leave Lexington. Belle Kearney, who became a leader of the Woman's Christian Temperance Union, was influenced by a northern teacher and dreamed of attending a northern college, but her father could not afford her tuition at the academy she was attending. She continued to read voraciously but drifted aimlessly until she opened a school for children in her home against her father's wishes, as he did not approve of women working for wages.[85] Some knew of the frustration of older female friends or relatives who had been unable to obtain a formal education. A fifteen year old in 1860 expressed her "wish to go to studying again for I feel more than ever before my great ignorance in all that pertains to knowledge." Left on her own, she read eagerly, including Milton's *Paradise Lost*. A young mother in Georgia in 1857 also felt the limitations of self-study. After reading Macaulay's essays she wrote in her diary, "I look back at the past ten years of my life with much regret, for I feel that I have not devoted this time to intellectual culture as I should have. My mind has I fear shrunk instead of expanding. . . . Oh that I could lend some aid to lift the cloud which obscures our southern intellectual sky."[86]

Those after the war who were able to travel north for education counted themselves among the lucky. They especially appreciated the quality of the education found at the Seven Sister colleges. The Richmonds of Tennessee understood that not all women (or men) had the opportunity to take the kinds of classes offered at Vassar or to pursue a bachelor's degree. Mrs. Richmond reported to her daughter Grace that when a male friend heard what she was studying at Vassar, he claimed it was more than the men learned at the University of Tennessee. Grace herself realized her relative privilege as a female college student at Vassar, telling her mother of a student who had completed her coursework at the University of Wisconsin but did not earn a diploma and so had to go to Vassar to get one.[87] While some students valued the entire experience of college (classes, extracurricular activities, and social life), the intense Sophonisba Breckinridge focused on what she could learn in the classroom. She even told her mother that she did not plan to attend any more costume parties "because things like these take so much time and don't pay."[88]

Alabamian Helen Keller went to Radcliffe because it was the closest she could get to proving herself at the best school in the country—Harvard. In her autobiography she claimed that she entered Cambridge School for Young Ladies in 1896 in order to prepare for Radcliffe because as a child she had visited Wellesley and declared, "Some day I shall go to college—but I shall go to Harvard!" When asked why Harvard and not Wellesley, she replied that there were only girls at Wellesley.[89] Helen went despite the disapproval of many of her friends and advisors who did not believe she was capable of the work—she wanted to prove her intellectual abilities. While southern students often complained about the hard work or that they were homesick, they took their schooling seriously, they appreciated the opportunity to get a college degree, and they believed themselves to be the better for it.

Margaret Preston came to an appreciation of her education at Bryn Mawr more slowly than some other students. She initially did not want to attend Bryn Mawr and, unhappy and homesick, asked her mother if she had to return after Christmas break and then pleaded against returning for her sophomore year. She told her mother that while she appreciated the fact that her aunt was funding her education, she would rather have spent the fifteen hundred dollars traveling to Europe.[90] Despite the nervous breakdown she experienced at the start of her second year, Margaret completed the year and ultimately did quite well in her studies, passing all her courses, some with high marks.[91] Although her aunt had only agreed to pay for two years, Margaret eventually even entertained some thoughts of staying to complete her degree, discussing the possibility of adding extra courses to her schedule in order to be able to graduate with her class. "I don't suppose there is one chance in ten that [I] would come back, and I certainly don't want to except that I should like to have a degree from Bryn Mawr," she wrote, but then she talked about how her friends told her she was doing so well and could be one of the seniors who took honors if she stayed.[92] While she was initially overwhelmed by the work, once she found herself capable she too began to value her education.

Although most parents and students stressed the value of college, the benefits of a classical education were difficult to enumerate. Students were sometimes vague about what exactly they gained at college. While some sometimes mentioned career preparation, most spoke more ambiguously of opportunity and self-improvement and of developing their potential. North Carolinian Sue Hall told her family that she hoped to return home from Wellesley "so much wiser and better in every respect," while Charles Simrall wrote to his wife when she accompanied Josie to Vassar in the fall of 1889, "I have great hopes and ambitions for her, not so much for her mental accomplishments as that she will develop into a good and grand woman."[93] Sophonisba Breckinridge received instructions and assurances from an O. S. Sumner, who told her, "You must remember you are a real Ky. Lady and can do much. I am satisfied you are at one of the best schools in the states—You can acquire those accomplishments that will fit you for the highest and most responsible duties of [your] life." Sue Hall accomplished her aims, later writing on her alumnae survey that she credited Wellesley with "broadening my knowledge of my country and my fellow men and women." Martha Cecil, who became a missionary to China after her graduation from Wellesley, later claimed that Wellesley gave her "love of beauty, a discriminating sense of value, a passion for truth, an appreciation of the patience of real scholarship, [and] enduring friendships."[94] For southerners from small towns, a liberal education and exposure to different people and a different culture was broadening. Fifty years after graduation, Lucy Penniman of Vassar recalled:

> I came to college from a small southern town. I had little interest in the world or its people beyond my own small horizon. Four years far from home, contacts with many people and exposure to the inspiration and joy of education would have shaped my life at any college, but it is specifically Vassar I thank for giving me a broad vision of life, an eagerness to learn more and more, a proud kinship with her Alumnae and, above all, for friends, who would never have been mine, had I not entered Vassar in September 1909.[95]

Her Vassar experience certainly fulfilled the goals of a liberal arts education, as did Eleanor Belknap's. For her fiftieth reunion Eleanor informed her classmates that her education had only begun at Vassar and continued informally through contact with professionals in the fields of medicine, law, and journalism and formally through lectures at the local university.[96] Vassar produced lifelong learners.

The absence of practical aims suggests that the intangibles of a liberal education were precisely what these students sought; they wanted to learn to think more analytically, to appreciate the world around them, and to express themselves more clearly. Such a fully realized potential was appropriate for either motherhood or a career or perhaps even for both. From a lecture on the philosophy of a collegiate education she heard at Vassar, Grace Richmond learned that acquiring knowledge for its own sake was not worthwhile, but "it is the great power the mind acquires that is advantageous."[97]

The one specific area of education that southern students did seem to appreciate was to be well read in literature. Alabamian Julia Strudwick Tutwiler considered herself fortunate to have spent a year at Vassar and was disappointed that she was not able to stay long enough to complete her education. She begged her younger sister to stay in school, explaining her own situation to Ida. Despite a lack of support or encouragement, Julia had studied at home during the Civil War, holding on to her desire to go to college. Suffering from ill health, she asked to go to Vassar, which opened just after the war, to regain her health. However, she was expected to come home at age seventeen and a half simply because it was time, although "I cried my eyes nearly out at the thought of being through life the same ignorant unfinished creature that I then felt myself." Julia did not tell her parents that she wanted to stay longer at Vassar because she did not want them to think her ambitions were due to a lack of love for home, and she worried about the expense. She told her sister that she missed "that systematic and thorough teaching that is given in boy's colleges, and *now* in many girls' schools," and encouraged Ida to remain at school. Julia did not believe that her sister had any intellectual weaknesses. "There is no reason why your education should not be just as thorough and complete as Father's," she wrote. "You have his abilities to obtain such a one." Furthermore, she argued that their father would appreciate being able to discuss literature and other subjects with Ida, particularly because their brothers were "so averse to literature."[98]

Julia Tutwiler, who admitted to having had a difficult year at Vassar, still valued the systematic study and group experience that she found only at college. She recognized her sister's abilities and pushed for her to develop and use her intelligence. She saw education as a means of self-improvement that would also make Ida a better daughter. She did not mention career training, despite her long teaching career; she did not mention studying anything other than literature and classical subjects (e.g., no domestic science); and she expressed no more utilitarian purpose, simply to be well educated and well versed in literature and other subjects.

Julia Tutwiler was not the only student to mention literature specifically. When Mary Poppenheim's younger sister Ida initially failed the Vassar entrance examinations, Mary wanted her to obtain as much education and polish as she could at home through reading good novels. Taking her role as an older sister and advisor seriously, Mary instructed Ida to avoid reading too many "trashy story papers." Mary conceded that if Ida insisted on reading novels, she should "read such ones that are the talk of the day." Familiarity with these novels demonstrated one's culture, and the novels themselves had the power to teach through the morals and characters they illustrated. "The nineteenth century is an analytical age," she explained, "and traits of character are clothed as people and these people are worked into novels."[99] Mary's high ideals once caused her to wonder at a friend's "ignorance" evident in a letter. Although Mary was not specific as to whether the letter was poorly written or showed a lack of knowledge on a particular subject, she clearly believed that her friend had not taken full advantage of her education. "What can she have done with the time she spent at school?" Mary asked her mother. Mary wanted to improve her writing skills, telling her mother that she planned to work harder at her essays. "I think an easy style is almost absolutely necessary to an educated woman," she opined. "What is the use to have the thoughts if you can't express them properly."[100] The comments from these students suggest that they believed that a well-read person made a good companion, one who could converse easily and was familiar with many things, but, more importantly, that reading improved the mind. Students like Mary Poppenheim read at home for pleasure and in preparation for college. Reading for courses made her and other students more able to read critically and to think for themselves.

In the early nineteenth century young women fortunate enough to attend an academy or seminary as well as many without the benefit of a formal education relished reading as "intellectual food." They read everything from history to political theory to novels, discussed their reading with each other, and considered their reading as both improving and pleasurable. Historian Barbara Sicherman found that, several generations later, young women of the late nineteenth century also read "for self-improvement, for sociability, and for emotional sustenance." For M. Carey Thomas and many others, reading provided the opportunity to explore the classics and enjoy the kind of intellectual stimulation formerly thought of as available to men only. Carey and her friends read together, sharing ideas and acting out characters. She turned to books in good times and in bad times, for comfort and for pleasure.[101] Sicherman also argued that reading had the potential to be subversive because it opened up opportunity, imagination, and the articulation of desires and possibilities. *Little Women*, for example, a book read by the Poppenheims, featured Jo, a character whom female readers saw as adventurous, breaking with convention, and wanting to write (even though she ultimately married).[102]

These same opportunities and pleasures are evident in the letters of many southern students who frequently mentioned the books they were reading. Mary Poppenheim described her reaction to various authors, discussing her views on Charlotte Brontë, George Eliot, and Charles Kingsley and her interpretation of the *Aeneid*, which differed from that of her professor. She and her friends even discussed who was most like which character in novels by Charles Kingsley and William Makepeace Thackeray. Mary was thrilled when her friends compared her to Torfrida, the heroine of Kingsley's *Hereward the Wake, "Last of the English,"* who displayed unceasing faithfulness to her flawed husband.

Smith College student Mary Comer also was a voracious reader. She provided her mother with the reading lists from literature class, used her spending money to buy the books, and complained that she was reduced to buying plain volumes while she thought jealously of her mother's beautiful editions. She therefore dipped into her savings account for an extravagant purchase—a fifty-dollar set of Thackeray's works, which she told her mother she preferred to a new suit for spring. Mary's reading list included *The Vicar of Wakefield* by Oliver Goldsmith, *The School for Scandal* by Richard Brinsley Sheridan, *The Life of Samuel Johnson* by James Boswell, *Evelina* by Fannie Burney, *Clarissa, or, The History of a Young Lady* by Samuel Richardson, *The Heart of Midlothian* and *Rob Roy* by Sir Walter Scott, and author Jane Austen. She and her friends read novels and plays aloud, which they believed was the best way to appreciate them.[103]

Helen Keller also lost herself—or found herself—in books. Once she learned to read, her disabilities seemed to disappear. Helen devoted a large portion of her autobiography to her reactions to books and authors. Beginning with the first story she read as a child, she explained how books affected her emotionally and intellectually and how she entered the worlds of the ancient Greeks and Romans, British history, and every other type of literature. "In the wonderland of the Mind," she wrote, "I should be as free as another."[104]

Because students came to college wanting to think and read critically, they complained when teachers did not foster their independent thinking. Some of the most beloved professors, including Vassar's Lucy Salmon, were known for pushing students to think critically. Salmon introduced her students to historical analysis of primary materials rather than memorization of dates, names, and events. Other teachers failed to live up to this standard. Florence Harrison complained that the teachers at Bryn Mawr graded according to how well students agreed with them—the low grade she received on a paper on Robert Louis Stevenson was raised when she changed it to reflect her professor's love for Stevenson rather than her own dislike.[105]

The southern women who attended northern colleges believed that women were as capable of higher education as men, and they wanted to be broadened by a liberal education, which would make them better mothers as well as give them the potential to succeed in any career. They did not attend college to take classes in home economics, although they did want to remain womanly. Most desired to improve their character, many wanted to become more conversant in literature, and a few learned skills for teaching or other employment. In the process they learned to think critically and independently. These skills were crucial to leadership in the progressive reform and woman suffrage movements.

For some students, the supportive atmosphere of a women's college was a continuation of the atmosphere at their preparatory school. The next chapter explores how young southern women prepared to attend college and chose which women's college to attend based on the reputation of each school and on networks of alumnae.

CHAPTER TWO

"We Do Want More
Southern Girls to Come"

Entrance Requirements, Preparatory

Departments and Schools, and

Alumnae Networks

 Both of Connie Guion's parents wanted her to have a college education. Her father had attended the University of North Carolina, and her mother had inherited a set of classics and read aloud to the children every night. More importantly, her sister was also involved in the family decision for Connie to attend Wellesley. Connie's older sister Laura worked at the post office in Charlotte, contributing her salary to the family budget. Laura's friend Alex Haskell had sisters at Wellesley and Radcliffe. When he told Laura that Wellesley was the best school for women, Laura decided to pay for Connie to attend Miss Kate Shipp's school in Lincolnton, North Carolina, to prepare her for Wellesley. From there, Connie contacted Wellesley but learned that she needed more Latin and other requirements before she could enter. Shipp advised her to settle for Converse College for Women in Spartanburg, South Carolina, which Shipp considered "a good Southern college." Never one to back down from a challenge, Connie insisted on Wellesley. Wellesley's dean, Miss Pendleton, suggested that Connie attend Northfield Seminary in Massachusetts, founded by the Reverend Dwight Moody, a friend of the Durants, Wellesley's founders, to complete her preparatory work, noting, "We do want more Southern girls to come to Wellesley." With the support of her family, Connie immediately began preparing to move north, much to the surprise of friends. She recalled that when a neighbor asked her mother how she could let Connie go north, Mrs. Guion retorted, "I'm sending Connie up North to find the family silver those damnyankees stole from us during the War between the States." Because Connie's only goal was to prepare herself as quickly as possible to get to

Wellesley, she never graduated from Northfield, instead leaving as soon as she passed the Wellesley entrance exams. Northfield not only prepared her academically, it also furnished a one-hundred-dollar scholarship toward her tuition at Wellesley.[1]

Connie's experiences capture many of the facets of southern women's struggle to obtain an adequate preparatory education before attending northern colleges. Like Connie, many students decided to attend college through the encouragement of family and friends but found themselves unable to pass difficult entrance examinations. Several studied with a private tutor, while others attended a local public or private school, supplemented with private study. Those like Connie, with inadequate preparation available close to home, had no choice but to leave for the North even earlier and finish their secondary education at a northern preparatory school. Well-established preparatory schools developed a reputation for sending students to the Seven Sister colleges. Prep schools both in the South and in the North often pushed their students to a particular college, and college alumnae developed networks back home to draw students to their alma mater. These networks were crucial to cultivating educational opportunities for southern women. Most significantly, alumnae often opened their own schools, where they prepared students for northern colleges and trained them for leadership. The education of one young woman at Vassar or Wellesley, therefore, could translate into increased educational prospects for hundreds of other women. The dispersal of alumnae of the Seven Sister colleges around the South resulted in increased social activism in many areas of reform by southern women, as is shown later in this book, but the most immediate—and perhaps most important—reform they embraced was educational improvement in their hometowns. The impact of education on an individual was significant enough to make her want to share that experience with as many other young women as possible in her community. Alumnae who served as teachers and education reformers knew firsthand the high standards and rigorous expectations for scholarship at northern colleges. They were best situated to prepare other southern women. Furthermore, even their students who did not go north were still exposed to many of the values and demands of northern colleges through the alumnae teaching in southern schools.

Southern students were often frustrated with their lack of adequate preparation and felt insecure until they established themselves academically at college. Virginian Orie Latham Hatcher believed her educational background was inferior to that of her Vassar classmates, claiming, "in practically every class which I entered students from other sections [of the country] had whole tracts of information about the subject which I did not possess." What made it worse was that "no one was surprised, because I was from the South." She was unsure of her academic status for her first one and a half years because Vassar doubted the quality of the education she had received at Richmond Female Institute.[2] Although Elizabeth Avery Colton had already received a bachelor of arts from Statesboro Female College in North Carolina, she still had to spend a year in the preparatory department at Mount Holyoke.[3] Similarly, Frances Bell Hatcher had a bachelor of arts and a master of arts from the University of Missouri when she entered Radcliffe, and she received a second bachelor of arts the following year. Emma Garrett Boyd Morris graduated with first honor from Atlanta Girls High School yet was inadequately prepared for Vassar. Once there, however, her brilliance quickly became evident, and she was elected to Phi Beta Kappa.[4]

In order to better prepare young women for northern colleges, southern women realized they needed to open more rigorous schools and to raise standards at already existing schools. Because of her frustration with the difficulties she herself had faced, Orie Hatcher helped organize the Virginia Association of Colleges and Schools for Girls in 1906 to improve education in the state so that young Virginia women would be "universally accepted throughout the country." After meeting with officials from Mount Holyoke, Smith, Vassar, and Wellesley, Orie wanted to bring Virginia schools in line with those of the Northeast, though many of the southern individuals she worked with resisted, advocating instead that the association move more slowly.[5] Regionally, the Southern Association of College Women worked to raise the standards and classify southern schools so that students would be able to distinguish between preparatory schools, finishing schools, and genuine colleges. Founded in 1903 by Lilian Wyckoff Johnson, Celeste Parrish, and Emilie Watts McVea, all southern-born and northern-educated women, the SACW began its push to improve standards under Elizabeth Avery Colton, who had not been adequately prepared for Mount Holyoke. Under her direction, the SACW published several studies during the 1910s that classified schools according to endowment, faculty, matriculation and graduation requirements, and other factors. These efforts helped many southern students find the most appropriate preparatory schools as well as choose between southern and northern colleges.[6]

Before 1890, an option for many students who were not qualified to matriculate immediately was to spend time in the preparatory department at Vassar, Mount Holyoke, or Wellesley before entering a regular class. Mount Holyoke students were still able to take the seminary course in preparation for the college course until 1893. When Vassar opened its doors in 1865, few students tested into the college course. The preparatory department was therefore a central component of the college from its founding until the department closed in 1888. Wellesley offered a preparatory department for a far shorter amount of time, from the college's opening in 1875 only until 1879.[7] To demonstrate their high academic standards, both Smith and Bryn Mawr opened without a preparatory department. Thus, southern students who needed a preparatory department could no longer find one at the Seven Sister colleges after 1893.

Bryn Mawr College records provide evidence of how many southerners attended preparatory school or studied with a private tutor. Of 141 southern students who attended Bryn Mawr, 11 had tutors and 34 left their hometown for prep school, with 26 venturing north before college. Significantly, reports from Bryn Mawr also show how a small group of preparatory schools became responsible for sending a disproportionate number of southern students to the college. The most notable was the Bryn Mawr School, founded explicitly to prepare students for Bryn Mawr and other colleges. An astounding forty-nine BMS alumnae entered Bryn Mawr in the classes of 1886–1910. In addition, the following schools provided half a dozen or more students: Louisville Girls High School, Kentucky (eight); Miss Florence Baldwin's School, Bryn Mawr, Pennsylvania (six); St. Timothy's, Catonville, Maryland (eight); Miss Mary E. Stevens' School, Germantown, Pennsylvania (six); and Miss Patty Blackburn Semple's Collegiate School, Louisville, Kentucky (six). These six schools account for more than half of the southern students at Bryn Mawr. They highlight the large number of students from Maryland and Kentucky at Bryn Mawr and show that prep schools played an enormous role in students' decisions whether and where to attend college.

Popular northern destinations included Pennsylvania schools such as Miss Florence Baldwin's and Misses Shipleys' School, both located in Bryn Mawr itself, Miss Mary Stevens' School in nearby Germantown, and Rosemary Hall in Connecticut. Students who went to Miss Baldwin's or Misses Shipleys' probably intended to eventually attend Bryn Mawr, while other students who first went to New York or Connecticut schools may have been seeking the necessary preparation for college but had not yet decided which college they would eventually attend. Other colleges also drew heavily from local preparatory schools, such as Wellesley, which took many students from Dana Hall School and Walnut Hill School, both located nearby, and Smith College, which had the Miss Burnham School (later known as Capen School and Northampton School for Girls) across the street. At least ten southern students attended the Miss Burnham School before entering Smith College.[8]

Sue Hall must have believed that she could not find adequate training at home in Wilmington, North Carolina, to prepare her to enter Wellesley. She attended Walnut Hill School, which was only three miles from Wellesley College. Walnut Hill School was founded in 1893 by Martha Conant and Florence Bigelow at the suggestion of Wellesley president Alice Freeman in order to prepare students for Wellesley and other schools.[9] While at Walnut Hill, Sue wrote home to her parents describing various concerts, Vespers, and social events that she attended at Wellesley. She became acquainted with the teachers and students as well as the campus. Students like Connie Guion and Sue Hall had already been exposed to northern culture and therefore may have had an easier time when they started college.

Bryn Mawr's records also highlight the growing number of college preparatory schools in the South that were designed as feeder schools for the new women's colleges. Some of the most prominent southern schools included the Bryn Mawr School, which led many Maryland students to Bryn Mawr College; Science Hill Female Institute, which allowed Kentucky to dominate the southern states at Wellesley; Washington Seminary in Atlanta; the Pape School in Savannah; Girls' Preparatory School in Chattanooga; the Norfolk College for Young Ladies in Virginia; and the Ellett School in Richmond, Virginia.

One of the most notable features of many of these schools was that they were founded and staffed by graduates of the Seven Sister colleges. The diffusion of both southern and northern college graduates in schools throughout the South was extremely influential in creating rigorous preparatory schools where teachers knew what would be expected of students at the best colleges. The importance of teachers was evident even before the war, when graduates of Troy Female Seminary came south to found their own schools modeled on Troy. Troy Female Seminary was the first early-nineteenth-century permanent institution to offer a rigorous classical education similar to that found in men's colleges. Historian Anne Firor Scott found that Troy founder Emma Willard sent her graduates out to spread her teaching style and the values she taught. These graduates reached the South in fairly significant numbers. Julia Pierpont was sent by Willard from Middlebury, Connecticut, to Sparta, Georgia, where she opened a school, married, and had a child. After the death of her child and husband, she returned to Willard, who was by this time at Troy, before returning south. Pierpont moved to South Carolina, married Elias Marks, and took over South Carolina Collegiate Institute at Barhamville, the most important school for girls in South Carolina in the mid-nineteenth century. Elizabeth Sherrill, another Willard devotee, took over the Sparta school and then an academy in Augusta, Georgia. Caroline Livy left Troy to become the principal of the female academy in Rome, Georgia. Almira Lincoln Phelps, the younger sister and a protégée of Willard, was head of Patapsco Institute in Maryland.[10] South Carolina alone had ninety-three Troy graduates teaching there through 1862.[11] How many of the students (or their daughters) of these Troy alumnae and friends then went on to northern schools is not known, but the number may have been significant. Willard and her pupils, who modeled their own teaching and schools after her and Troy, endeavored to pass on to their students a sense of self-respect and a seriousness of purpose and to inspire them to intellectual training rather than frivolity. These characteristics were a precondition for college.[12] Furthermore, Emma Willard also taught students to believe in every woman's possibilities and her duty to the community, promoting the feminist values described by Scott. Her pupils included Lide Smith Meriwether, one of Memphis's leading temperance and suffrage leaders.[13]

By the late nineteenth century a wave of Wellesley, Mount Holyoke, Vassar, and other graduates were also teaching in the South. In Savannah girls had few options before 1890 for a rigorous secondary education.[14] Most went to a girls' high school or to boarding school in Virginia, Maryland, New York, or Pennsylvania. Rather than going to college, many went to finishing school, sometimes in Philadelphia, New York, or Boston. Emelyn Hartridge, member of a prominent Savannah family and a graduate of Vassar, was determined to keep students at home in Savannah for their college preparation rather than having them leave for boarding school. She returned home to start a school in 1892, sending a few graduates to college. Emelyn, however, was frustrated that most elite families still wanted their daughters to go to boarding school. After ten years she moved to New Jersey, where she founded a boarding school that attracted many Savannah students. They found her intimidating. One alumna remembered morning exercises with the "formidable, overbearing, intellectually mighty Miss Emlyn [sic] B. Hartridge standing commanderlike" in front of students. Hartridge remained committed to Vassar; she was the president of the Association of Alumnae of Vassar College and a member of the Vassar Student Aid Committee and the Vassar Club of New York.[15] Her sister Katherine, a Vassar graduate as well, taught at the school also. Meanwhile, back in Savannah, Wellesley graduate Mary Haskell took over Hartridge's school, followed by Nina Pape, another elite Savannah woman. Pape instituted many changes and focused on college preparation, happily claiming that she had one student admitted to Vassar in 1909 and one to Radcliffe two years later, and between 1915 and 1930 she sent sixteen students to Smith. Pape also hired teachers with northern college degrees.[16]

Educated themselves, many college women like Emelyn Hartridge were committed to expanding opportunities for other young southern women to get a college education. Margaret Josephine Holley, another Wellesley alumna, opened a school in Dallas from which she also sent many students to Wellesley. Like Hartridge, Josie hired her sister Frances and other Wellesley alumnae to teach at the Misses Holley School for Girls. She also retained her loyalty to Wellesley and her interest in higher education for women through her membership in the Dallas Wellesley Club and the American Association of University

Women (AAUW) and by founding a Shakespeare Society.[17] Before attending
medical school, Connie Guion taught for several years at Sweet Briar College in
Virginia. She needed the funds she earned to pay for her sister's schooling, but
she also saw her years teaching at Sweet Briar as having a higher purpose—the
education of southern women. She hoped that Sweet Briar would prepare them
enough to go north to college.[18] Jenny Nelson, the teacher who accompanied
Wellesley's first student, Anne Poe Harrison, from Virginia in 1875, decided to
leave Wellesley after teaching French there for four years and return to the South
to educate more southern women. She taught briefly in Wytheville, Virginia,
before becoming headmistress of Chatham Hall in Virginia, where she always
kept a copy of the Wellesley catalog on her desk, hoping to inspire girls to head
north.[19]

When northern-educated women opened schools throughout the South,
they stressed high academic standards and fostered networks of college graduates. The Mendenhall sisters of Jamestown, North Carolina, were Quakers who
dedicated themselves to women's education. Their father was principal of New
Garden Boarding School (which became Guilford College), where both sisters
taught. Mary Mendenhall Hobbs attended Miss Howland's in New York and
formed a girls' aid society to raise money for girls to go to college. Her sister,
Gertrude Whittier Mendenhall, who graduated from Wellesley in 1885, donated
the first five dollars. Gertrude was a favorite math teacher at North Carolina
State Normal and Industrial College. Her successor at State Normal was Virginia
Ragsdale, a Guilford College graduate who won a scholarship to Bryn Mawr.[20]
Mary Petty of Bush Hill, North Carolina, also a Wellesley alumna, joined the
Mendenhalls at Guilford College before joining the faculty at North Carolina
Normal and Industrial College. Mary Petty set up the first chemistry laboratory
in the state for women and taught mathematics and chemistry for over forty
years. Petty was also involved in the Greensboro community, helping establish
both the Woman's Club and the Friday Afternoon Club, and was first secretary
of the North Carolina Federation of Women's Clubs.[21] The Mendenhalls and
Petty were part of a community of Quakers dedicated to women's education
in the state. Mary Petty and Gertrude Mendenhall sustained each other—they
initially left home together traveling to Wellesley and later wrote joint letters
to their class as alumnae describing their work teaching the young women of
North Carolina. Other sisters and friends also taught together. Lula and Virginia Waldo, Smith College classes of 1903 and 1904, respectively, established
the Misses Waldo School in Houston, working together for a decade.

Southern college graduates hoped to inspire their pupils to the same academic achievements. Helen Jenkins, who graduated from Mount Holyoke in
1906, was principal of Thorsby Institute, an academy for the rural white poor

in Alabama. True to Mount Holyoke tradition, Jenkins stressed character development and the classics and sent many of her graduates on to college.[22] In Montgomery, Alabama, Margaret Booth, a Mount Holyoke alumna, put an ad in the newspaper during World War I saying she would prepare girls for college. After receiving over forty replies she decided to open a school to accommodate them all. Her obituary claimed that at one time she sent more graduates to northeastern women's colleges than any other southern school.[23]

Teachers improved communities both through the benefits of the education they provided in their classrooms as well as through their neighborhood involvement. Remembering the difficult three days of entrance examinations she had undergone, Mary Vardrine McBee returned to South Carolina from Smith College and in 1909 founded Ashley Hall, a school for young women in Charleston. She worked hard to earn accreditation for the school so that students would no longer have to take the dreaded entrance exams. Ashley Hall had sent its first graduate to Smith in 1912, despite a description in a 1947 *Life Magazine* article that claimed the school was founded "for girls who cherish still those amenities of feminine culture which give southern life its charm." Mary proudly told her Smith classmates that she established the first Examination Center of the College Board in South Carolina and therefore was able to send many of her graduates to college.[24] While presiding over the school for forty years, she also found time to work with several education societies and through the Charleston Civic Club helped found the Charleston Free Library after lobbying the state legislature. Mary Galbraith, an alumna of Science Hill and Wellesley, taught at Washington Seminary in Atlanta and other schools throughout the South. She recalled that Wellesley gave her a "broader outlook on life and high standard of scholarship," which she gave back to her students through teaching.[25]

The Norfolk College for Young Ladies was founded specifically to stem the tide of students who left Norfolk for other cities in the South or North for their education. School founders there, like elsewhere, wanted the school to provide an education equal to that available in the North, the standard for excellence. In 1879 a group of local businessmen calculated that fifty girls left the city to be educated elsewhere. These businessmen stood to earn a lot of money if these students spent three hundred dollars on tuition and room and board in Norfolk instead and perhaps attracted an equal number of families who would be willing to move to Norfolk in order to educate their daughters.[26] The Norfolk Collegiate Institute for Young Ladies closed, and its principal and teachers joined the new Norfolk College for Young Ladies, while nearby Leache-Wood Seminary spruced up its offerings and facilities in order to compete.

In Baltimore, concerned about young women's abilities to adequately prepare themselves for college, M. Carey Thomas and four of her friends, Mary Garrett,

Mamie Gwinn, Bessie King, and Julia Rogers, founded the Bryn Mawr School with the specific intention of preparing women for Bryn Mawr and other colleges. The school opened on September 21, 1885, only ten days before Bryn Mawr College. They designed the curriculum to include all the material required for college entrance examinations, including a strong emphasis on Latin and Greek. Before graduating, students had to pass the Bryn Mawr College entrance examinations, which were considered to be the most rigorous of women's colleges at the time.[27] To maintain such high standards, the founders chose teachers who had been educated at the best colleges, including Wellesley, Smith, Vassar, Bryn Mawr, Radcliffe, Cornell, and other top universities in the United States and Europe.[28] Teachers encouraged students to attend college, and M. Carey Thomas arranged for students to spend a day at Bryn Mawr College.[29] Not surprisingly, the connection was strong, for almost one-third of the southern students at Bryn Mawr College graduated from the Bryn Mawr School, approximately six times as many as any other school. The Bryn Mawr School did not feed only Bryn Mawr College, as at least three graduates chose Smith College over Bryn Mawr.[30]

Science Hill Female Academy in Shelbyville, Kentucky, was another important feeder school for northern colleges. Located between Louisville and Frankfort, Science Hill was established in 1825 and run until 1860 by Julia Ann Tevis and her husband, the Reverend John Tevis. In 1880 Dr. Wiley Taul Poynter bought the school, which he ran until 1939, when it closed. Poynter wanted the school to provide the same level of education as was available to the brothers of his female students and an education to southern students that their northern counterparts already had. He wrote to Wellesley, Columbia, Vassar, and Smith Colleges to find out their entrance requirements and then changed his curriculum to better prepare students to pass the entrance examinations. Poynter was successful: between 1884 and 1934 122 Science Hill alumnae earned a college degree, and an additional 257 students attended college without earning a degree. These included 111 students at Wellesley, 23 at Vassar, 14 at Mount Holyoke, 7 at Smith, and 5 at Barnard.[31]

Like many feeder schools, Science Hill had a particular connection to one school, Wellesley. Juliet Martin, Poynter's niece, was president of her class at Wellesley and a devoted alumna. She brought Alice Freeman and other faculty from Wellesley to Science Hill to speak, and Science Hill had several Wellesley alumnae on the faculty, including Nettie Garrett Pullen, a native of Paris, Kentucky. The connection was so strong that Wellesley officials, when asked to recommend a southern preparatory school, claimed that few were qualified, but Science Hill sent the most-qualified and well-prepared students.[32] Maria Daviess attended Science Hill because a preacher came to Tennessee and reported that Science Hill prepared students for Wellesley and Vassar. Her uncle decided that it would benefit her.[33] Interestingly, after this strong preparation, Daviess found Wellesley to be a disappointment. She later complained that the teachers were bad and the other students uninteresting, and she left after only one year.[34]

Students in Kentucky were fortunate to have several other excellent schools that consistently sent students to the Seven Sisters and then attracted them back as teachers. Vassar graduates Mildred Walker Anderson, class of 1897; Elizabeth Louise Parker, class of 1903; Sarah Dudley, class of 1897; Menetta Brooks, class of 1904; and Grace Kennedy, class of 1904, all taught at the Semple Collegiate School, founded by Vassar graduates Patty and Ellen Semple. Patty Semple helped found the Louisville Woman's Club in 1890 and served as its first president, while Ellen Semple became a nationally known geographer. The school was later run by principal Lucy Baird, a Bryn Mawr graduate and historian who was active both in the American Historical Association and in her local women's club. Vassar graduates Alice Bennett Parker and Lucy Belle Hemphill and Bryn Mawr graduate Elizabeth Graeme Barbour taught at Louisville Girls' High School.[35] The competition among these schools seems only to have sparked others to open schools as well. Sisters Mary and Linda Neville, both graduates of Bryn Mawr, ran the Misses Neville School in their home in Lexington from 1897 to 1908 in order to prepare students for northern colleges.[36]

Washington Seminary in Atlanta was the most prestigious girls' school in Georgia, and it prided itself on "preparing pupils for the leading colleges, particularly Wellesley, Vassar, Radcliffe[,] . . . and Bryn Mawr."[37] One of its most famous graduates was Margaret Mitchell, who finished Washington Seminary and headed to Smith College in 1918. Washington Seminary was very strong academically as well as socially prestigious.[38] After Atlantan Agnes Raoul passed her entrance examinations to Vassar, she wrote to her mother that Washington Seminary was possibly going to get a "certificate" because her exam proved its ability to adequately prepare students.[39]

Young women in Tennessee had several local options. The Girls' Preparatory School in Chattanooga began in 1905 as a college prep school, sending an incredible 266 out of the next 450 grads to college, including to Wellesley and Smith.[40] In Memphis students could choose between the Clara Conway Institute and Miss Jenny Higbee's School. Clara Conway hoped that her institute would prepare women for financial independence by training them for the best eastern women's colleges. Her ambition, which reached far above the goals of some local civic leaders in Memphis, was to create a southern Vassar or Wellesley. Her school closed in 1893 because her financial backers thought she aimed too high for her graduates. She then organized a council of women representing various women's organizations; one of the council's goals was to create a southern college for women that would be equal to the best northern schools. Jenny Higbee, originally from New Jersey, moved to Memphis, where she served as principal of the Court Street Female High School before opening her own school.[41] In Richmond, Virginia, girls attended the Ellett School (later Saint Catherine's), established by Virginia Randolph Ellett in 1890. She worked to make her school a feeder for Bryn Mawr and other women's colleges in the Northeast.

Those students not lucky enough to attend these prestigious training grounds often combined their local public school with a year or more of boarding school. Gertrude Weil attended the Goldsboro, North Carolina, public graded school, which was established in 1881, earlier than public schools were in many towns in the South. Gertrude was proud of her education there, publishing an article in the school newspaper, *Round Table*, that claimed that 125 alumni of the school had pursued higher education after their graduation, including some to the north, notably, Mount Holyoke. The school had a literary club of girls and boys and cooperated with the Ladies' Benevolent Society, preparing them for the types of intellectual stimulation and reform work many women would later undertake.[42] Following her graduation from the Goldsboro public school, Gertrude traveled to New York City to attend Horace Mann at Columbia Teachers' College for a year of college preparatory work before she entered Smith College. Her uncle Albert Rosenthal had graduated from Columbia and settled in New York, and he persuaded the Weils to send Gertrude north.[43]

Virginia Foster Durr went to New York for one year to get "polished." She attended Miss Finch's School and lived with a southern woman who had fallen on difficult economic times. Her older sister attended Sweet Briar, and Virginia returned home to attend public high school in Birmingham. She then transferred to the Cathedral School in Washington, D.C., a prestigious boarding school with many southern students. Because she read so much, including her father's library of Dickens, Scott, and Macaulay, she was "dying to go to college," and after she passed her entrance exam, her father agreed to let her go. Her mother, however, was more concerned that she make a good marriage, and she would not allow Virginia to wear her glasses in public. Virginia later speculated that her mother allowed her to attend Wellesley because she hoped Virginia would meet a husband there, while her father sent her because he feared that she would end up an old maid and need to fall back on teaching. Virginia stayed only two years because the boll weevil pushed the family into hard times, and her father was too proud to allow her to live in the self-help dormitory.[44]

Sophonisba Breckinridge was one of a number of students who attended a coeducational college in the South before enrolling at one of the Seven Sisters.

In 1880 she matriculated at age fourteen at Kentucky Agricultural and Mechanical (now the University of Kentucky), where she was one of the top three students in her class. Although the college was coeducational, Sophonisba encountered professors who did not want girls in their classes, including one who she claimed tried to humiliate her by giving her a problem he thought she could not solve in front of the school trustees. Perhaps that is why she wanted to go to Wellesley rather than a coeducational university for her bachelor's degree. "The great charm that Wellesley had for me," she explained, "was that it was made or established for me or the likes of me."[45] Had Sophonisba been at the University of Kentucky a generation later she might have had an entirely different experience with faculty. Frances Jewell McVey, a Vassar alumna and Kentucky native, returned home to teach English at the University of Kentucky and serve as dean of women. She was such a strong mentor for female students that Sarah Gibson Blanding later recalled McVey's influence at Blanding's own induction as president of Vassar College. When McVey resigned her deanship upon marriage to the university president, she recommended the then-twenty-seven-year-old Blanding to the post, a position that Blanding held for approximately two decades before moving to Vassar. Blanding treasured her friendship with McVey.[46]

Attending the right preparatory schools made entrance into a northern college much easier. Vassar, Wellesley, and Smith certified certain schools as standard preparatory schools; students with degrees from these schools would have their credentials automatically accepted. Other students had to pass entrance examinations, usually administered on campus when students arrived in September or during the spring preceding their entrance. These examinations were sometimes also administered in other cities where there were likely to be enough candidates. For example, in the late 1880s Vassar held examinations in nine cities, including Louisville. As schools began to draw students from all over the country, they followed the example of some state universities and accepted students who had certificates from certain approved schools certifying that students had sufficient knowledge of the required subjects. For a time, Wellesley accepted certificates from high schools in any state other than Massachusetts, a practice that Wellesley president Mary Woolley defended because it enabled the school to draw students from all over the country. The Association of Colleges and Secondary Schools of the Southern States as well as Smith, Vassar, and Wellesley accredited twelve preparatory schools in 1915, including the Ellett School, Chattanooga Girls' Preparatory School, Science Hill, Washington Seminary, and the Pape School.[47] Eventually, the colleges began to collaborate with other New England colleges to establish common entrance examinations and jointly choose high schools that were allowed to certify students.[48] Eme-lyn Hartridge, the Vassar alumna and Hartridge School founder, also served as president of the Headmistresses Association of the East. She worked with that group's Academic Standards Committee and represented it to the Col-lege Entrance Examination Board, positions through which she helped coor-dinate information and develop better relations between preparatory schools and women's colleges.[49]

Entrance examinations could be a very difficult and frightening experience for southern students. Mary Poppenheim, a Charlestonian at Vassar, began early on to prepare her younger sister Ida for her entrance examinations. Ida intended to join the music department, but Mary warned her that the college had raised its entrance standards because "every year [Vassar president] Dr. [James] Taylor seems to try to make things harder." When Ida took the exams in early 1888, she failed. Mary offered to teach her math when she returned home after gradua-tion, but their mother, Mary Elinor Poppenheim, suggested instead that the two travel to Paris for six months. Mary Elinor reminded Mary that even though Ida did not know her mathematics, she was good hearted and would be a good companion to Mary. Further, she asked, "Don't you think sometimes that you and Lulu [Louisa, another sister at Vassar] will have weight enough when you have graduated at Vassar to help Ida float even if she can't go there?"[50] Three years later, Mary administered the entrance examinations to both Ida and Kitty, the youngest, noting that Ida and Kitty had read 172 lines of Latin in one day in preparation.[51] Within two weeks they heard that Ida had not passed. "The postal about the Examination created a dreadful scene and panic," Mary wrote their sister Louisa. "Ida was speechless for hours and Kitty declares if Ida does not pass she will not go to College. They have both made up their minds to go to Columbia to Woman's College there if they do not pass. They are sick of all this fuss about passing and I don't blame them." Mary further revealed that Ida's geometry examination had been graded as "vague," which Mary believed was impossible. "It was either right or wrong," she declared. Louisa quickly spoke with a Vassar official and reassured her parents that the girls would pass. Her father was not surprised, as he had believed "it was the business interest of the college to get all good students they could."[52] Mary's and Louisa's strong aca-demic showing and leadership qualities (they both held many campus offices) along with their father's demonstrated record of paying their tuition bills must have convinced school officials that their young sister should be admitted.

Vassar entrance examinations also frightened Agnes Raoul, who took them in June 1899. She described them to her mother in Atlanta as difficult, writing, "I don't think there is any hope of getting through them all. Each one seems perfectly dreadful."[53] Like the Poppenheim sisters, Sue Hall took advantage of her position at Wellesley to gain information for her younger sister Jessie. Her professor Florence Bigelow recommended that Jessie take exams in algebra, geometry, Caesar, Latin prose, and German. Sue told her mother that if Jessie did extra work, she might be able to enter Wellesley straight from high school should she pass her exams but that it would be easier for her to come north and complete one year of prep school there.[54]

Colleges did what they could to recruit and attract southern students. The southern clubs, composed of southern students and honorary alumnae or southern literati, sometimes tried to generate enthusiasm for their college. For example, the Southern Club of Smith College had college president William Allan Neilson make a speech in Atlanta followed by a reception at Margaret Mitchell's home. Margaret called it the "All-South Smith Rally."[55] Dean C. Mildred Thompson of Vassar, herself an alumna from Atlanta, made it a priority to open up admissions to Vassar to students from a broad range of schools and to increase funding for scholarships for those who were qualified to attend but lacked the money. Certainly, she had in mind students like herself from southern cities and towns. In 1938 Thompson showcased Mary Clabaugh, a student from Birmingham, Alabama, who won a regional scholarship to the college.[56]

Local branches of the Southern Association of College Women (SACW) worked to stimulate interest in college through college clubs and college days. The central Kentucky club hosted a college day that included a talk by the vice principal of Science Hill as well as lantern slides of Wellesley College, while the Montgomery, Alabama, branch helped send ninety-eight girls to college with scholarships.[57] May Lansfield Keller, a Baltimore native who studied at Goucher College and was SACW president from 1910 to 1914, recalled that the SACW had a standing committee on college day for local high schools. May earned a doctorate in Germany, taught at Wells College, New York, and at the Woman's College of Baltimore, and was dean of Westhampton College in Richmond, Virginia. In 1917 she was active in the merging of the Association of Collegiate Alumnae (ACA) and the SACW and then was general director of the South Atlantic section of the AAUW for many years. "Talks were given on 'Why a Girl Should Go to College,' on the standings of various colleges, entrance requirements," she remembered. "The girls were instructed in the distinction between standard and imitation colleges, and were urged to select the best whenever possible."[58] South Carolinian Mary Poppenheim also promoted scholarships through the United Daughters of the Confederacy, which had funds available for the education of southern women at over fifty colleges, including one northern college, Vassar, due to a twelve-hundred-dollar gift from Poppenheim to promote her alma mater.[59] The Georgia Federation of Women's Clubs also realized the value of a northern education, changing its policy of only providing scholarships to students attending southern schools and working with the SACW to provide scholarships to students at Vassar, Columbia, and the University of Chicago.[60]

College clubs helped draw students to a particular college, as did feeder schools like the Bryn Mawr School and Science Hill, which pushed students to Bryn Mawr College and Wellesley, respectively. Other students chose a particular school because they were influenced by their teachers. Augusta Lantz, class of 1887 at Mount Holyoke, taught at the College for Young Women in Statesville, North Carolina, for twenty-two years. Lantz encouraged girls from Statesville to attend Mount Holyoke. She wrote to her classmates with delight when two of her students entered Mount Holyoke. Their letters, she added, "bring me in touch with college life once more."[61]

Once the first student bravely set off for college, other young women from her hometown often followed. College records indicate increasing numbers from particular towns such as Lexington, Kentucky. William Breckinridge told his daughter Sophonisba, "Your going to Wellesley turned the attention of many here to Wellesley."[62] Sophonisba was not the first student from Lexington at Wellesley. She and her family benefited from the advice of others who preceded her there. Annie Wilson, a nongraduating member of the class of 1883 from Cynthiana, Kentucky, was full of advice for Sophonisba, delivered through William's letters. The advice was of questionable value, for example, when Annie recommended that Sophonisba not walk too much because, as a southern girl, she didn't have the experience.[63]

Margaret Preston of Lexington, Kentucky, prepared for Bryn Mawr at the Miss Williams School and with her cousins, Linda and Mary Neville, both Bryn Mawr alumnae, who tutored her. Margaret's mother, "a scholar of several languages and ancient and modern literature," was educated and encouraging. She herself had written poetry as well as papers that had been well received by her women's club. Despite her mother's achievements, as alumnae the Nevilles were better positioned to help Margaret.[64] They not only encouraged Margaret to attend Bryn Mawr but supported her once she arrived on campus. When she was having difficulties with her German class, her mother contacted the Neville sisters. Mary Neville wrote to Margaret and told her not to worry. Mary regretted the worry and stress she herself had undergone and suggested to Margaret that the key to happiness was to proceed with her work but not think about it so much. Neville reassured Margaret that she was capable of good work; after all, she had passed the entrance exams.[65] Margaret's aunt Margaret Wickliffe Brown also attended Bryn Mawr.[66]

This network among family and friends was crucial to disseminating information about the colleges, encouraging southern women to apply, aiding them with entrance examinations, and then sustaining them after they arrived on campus. Barbara Adair McClung, who grew up in Atlanta, remembered that she attended Vassar because Emma Louise Garrett Boyd Morris had gone before her. "Emma Lou was a junior when I entered as a freshman," she recalled. "I don't think I should ever have gotten through without her friendship."[67] The Mitchells knew of Smith College through another family from Atlanta: Mamie Powers, who enrolled one year before Margaret and whose younger sister Maudie was friends with Margaret. Mamie claimed that both her mother and Margaret's mother decided to send their daughters to Smith because Sophia Smith had founded the school to give women equal opportunities with men.[68] Cousins and friends also paved the way for others to follow: Elsie Allen had nine cousins at Mount Holyoke between 1895 and 1935.[69] Students then nurtured these bonds when they returned home through local clubs, alumnae associations, and branches of the SACW. Lucy Prichard taught Latin in Huntingdon, West Virginia, following her graduation from Vassar. Undoubtedly feeling isolated, she discovered a neighbor from Smith College with whom she wanted to form a branch of the Association of Collegiate Alumnae (ACA). She initially despaired of finding enough other college graduates but quickly was able to locate three other Vassar alumnae and found an ACA branch.[70]

The most important influence was often an older sister. Once a young woman attended a northern college, like Mary Poppenheim, she was poised to help her younger sisters venture north as well. There were at least twenty-six southern sibling sets at Vassar, twenty-two at Wellesley, and sixteen at Bryn Mawr.[71] Emma Grant wrote that her older sister had gone to Mount Holyoke first, "so I was never at all homesick or frightened even though I came all the way from North Carolina."[72] Older sisters imbibed a strong school spirit and loyalty that they then imparted to their younger sisters. After criticizing her fellow students for their grammar, Mary Poppenheim wrote to her sister Louisa, "Now I would not write so to any one else but I think you are so soon to be a 'Vassar girl' that although you know their faults you will stand by *Vassar* forever for if you ever said this I have told you to any girl outside, I would be provoked for you must keep up the rep[utation] of the College."[73] For sisters and cousins to follow each other to college was quite typical. In a survey of nearly one hundred women college graduates taken in 1902, almost half reported choosing their school because of friends and another nearly one-tenth because of teachers, while about one-quarter were influenced by the college's reputation.[74]

Students compared schools, providing sisters and friends with insights into their impression of each college. Some southern students were able to compare colleges on their own. In 1894 Mary Haskell, a student at Wellesley, attended a lecture at Radcliffe given by Thomas W. Higginson. She recorded her reaction to the "Annex girls" in her diary, describing the students as "good looking." "An air of cultivation, good dressing and good breeding pervades the whole," she continued. "It gives the impression of a grace, a refinement, a culture and a polish about five degrees higher than that of Wellesley's. I wish I could go there for a year to get rubbed down my awkwardness."[75] Mary Comer, a Smith student from Savannah, commented on college reputations in her letters to her mother. She reminded her mother that Wellesley and Smith were rivals; thus, she was not surprised that Smith voted for McKinley and Wellesley for Bryan in mock presidential elections held on their campuses.[76] Furthermore, Vassar's apparent hold on the South angered Mary Comer. Mary asked her mother to have her sister Baby send her article to the editor of the *Smith Monthly* and to "explain how it would create an interest in Smith, and let them realize that Vassar is not the only college in the North."[77] Julia Hammond was another student who compared her own college with another. A South Carolinian at Harvard Annex, she visited Wellesley, where she was given a tour by two students from Alabama. Her first reaction was to think that perhaps she would have been better off there. Wellesley had laboratories and more science course offerings, which would have been good preparation for her goal of becoming a doctor. But she described the students negatively, writing her mother that "the girls did not seem as they all do [at Radcliffe] to be studying for something, with them it seemed only to be a way to get through college." Furthermore, she complained that the professors were shallow, and she preferred not having a roommate.[78]

Teachers, sisters, and other alumnae helped southern students determine the character and reputation of each college. Teachers at preparatory schools influenced their students both informally, through conversations and by example, and formally, through lectures and presentations on their alma mater. Eloise Whitaker's letters from North Carolina Normal and Industrial College in the late 1890s provide some insight into the reputation and reach of northern colleges. One of the professors at Normal who had a fellowship at Bryn Mawr gave a talk to Normal students on life at Bryn Mawr. She explained that the college focused on providing an opportunity for graduate students to complete original research. Eloise also marveled at a teacher with a degree from Wellesley who left Normal to teach at Bryn Mawr, claiming that the name Wellesley "means something and now she's there where they have such a high grade of teachers and plenty of them."[79] Eloise's letter also illustrates the particular reputation that each college had, an important factor in helping southern students determine where they wanted to go. Many believed that Bryn Mawr was solely intended for scholastic or academic achievement, whereas the ultimate aim of Smith (and Vassar and Wellesley) was to create a better woman, particularly one fit for service to the community, whether that was in marriage, in a career, doing volunteer work, or some combination.[80] Mount Holyoke had a unique reputation that stressed its religious character and focus on teacher preparation.

The media also played up the stereotypes of the schools. Helen M. Bennett wrote an article comparing several schools and claimed that "Smith turns out the doer; Wellesley, the student; Vassar, the adventurer; Bryn Mawr, the philosopher; Mount Holyoke, the conservative; University of Chicago, the enterprising; and the State Universities in general, the practical girl."[81] Bennett claimed to base her generalizations on the information given by students who registered with the Chicago Collegiate Bureau of Occupations. Students had to check off their interest in "education, business, Religious Work, Social Conditions, and Woman Suffrage." Smith girls were most interested in business, which Bennett explained was because they were quite efficient and organized. Wellesley, on the other hand, with its beautiful campus, inspired liberal independent thinkers, idealists less practical than their counterparts at Smith. Vassar students showed the most interest in social conditions and woman suffrage, which Bennett explained was due in part to the school's attempts to squash any discussion of suffrage, which made the forbidden fruit all the more interesting to students. Bryn Mawr, with its reputation for the most serious academics, produced the philosopher, while Mount Holyoke, with its background in producing missionaries and missionary wives, was the most conservative. Bennett argued that the campus location (such as rural or urban), certain professors, regulations, curriculum, and other factors originally influenced the type of student who graduated, and then students of the same mindset flocked to the school. Other stereotypes promoted by Mary Crawford were the rich student at Smith, the hard worker at Vassar, the religious and democratic student at Mount Holyoke, and the scholarly student at Bryn Mawr.[82]

These stereotypes derived from some truth in the particular history and circumstances of each college, although the images ultimately lost sight of reality. Mary Lyon, the founder of Mount Holyoke, was a devout Puritan Calvinist and demanded strong faith from her students, many of whom became missionaries or teachers. Founded as a female seminary in 1838 with high academic standards, the school was known also for its strict moral and disciplinary code: students daily had to self-report any infractions, admitting to their errors or declaring that they had not failed in any way that day. In the 1850s Mary Fuller exemplified the stress on religion at Mount Holyoke. Originally from Mississippi, Fuller studied at Miss Porter's in Farmington, Connecticut, from age eleven to fifteen due to a lack of adequate training available in the South. After reading the biography of Mount Holyoke's founder, Mary Lyon, she said, "I read it with the deepest of interest and begged to be allowed to go to Mount Holyoke for the religious life and training I should receive." However, after one year she left

Mount Holyoke due to poor health. Mount Holyoke may have attracted fewer southern students because students seeking a liberal arts education who had no intention of becoming missionaries or teachers may have dismissed it because of that reputation. The college may even have been associated with the education of the freedmen, as at least eighty-eight Mount Holyoke graduates taught in black schools in the South between 1861 and 1875. This represented almost 3 percent of its graduates through 1860.[83] Mount Holyoke did not have a large number of southern students. Out of 1,640 students between 1838 and 1878, only 44 were southern.[84]

Mount Holyoke was also well known for its domestic work requirement. When she founded the school, Mary Lyon hoped to attract the middle-class daughters of farmers as well as professionals, and she kept costs low by having students do the domestic work of the school. This, she argued, taught morality and self-denial. She further reasoned that if the education was high, daughters of the wealthy would come too. But southern students may have objected to the sort of work that they were accustomed to servants doing. Wellesley dropped its domestic work requirement in 1896–97, and Vassar never had one.[85]

During the 1880s, after the opening of Smith and Wellesley, alumnae and faculty began to fight for Mount Holyoke to make the transition from seminary to college by changing entrance requirements and courses and offering a four-year bachelor's degree. In March 1888 the school received a college charter and revamped its curriculum and entrance requirements; the first college students enrolled that fall. In 1893 the seminary department was dropped. In the 1890s the school also began to loosen rules concerning behavior, instituting an honor system that no longer required a daily report, lightening the domestic duties required, and adding extracurricular activities and sports. Under Mary Woolley, president from 1901 to 1937, the school finally ended its domestic work requirement in 1913 and became more interdenominational and liberal in church services—still religious but no longer known as the missionary college. A historical sketch of Mount Holyoke claimed that "the pupils were to be trained to help themselves mainly for the sake of helping others. They were to seek knowledge not merely in order to enjoy it; but rather that they might become the stronger to uplift, and the wiser to guide, anyone who needed their aid."[86] Mary Lyon herself stressed going forth to serve society and the community.[87]

Vassar College, which opened in the fall of 1865, was founded by Matthew Vassar, a brewer in Poughkeepsie, New York. Vassar's desire was to build a college that could provide an education for women, who were excluded from the best men's colleges. Vassar College, modeled after Mount Holyoke, had a large main building where students lived, attended class, and studied "as a college family." Despite the physical layout and the strict social restrictions, the curriculum mirrored men's colleges.[88] Although students sometimes went into Poughkeepsie to shop (and Episcopalian students to attend the Episcopal church), the campus was self-contained, and students were busy with a myriad of clubs, sports, and other activities. Like Wellesley, Vassar initially accepted a large number of "specials," or students who were not pursuing a degree. Most were schoolteachers who sought additional training in a particular subject and stayed at Vassar for only a year or two. Vassar did not have the same strong religious affiliation that Mount Holyoke and Wellesley began with, yet students still attended chapel twice daily as well as on the Sabbath and took a Bible class, even though the college was explicitly nonsectarian.

Smith College's original circulars stated: "The College is not intended to fit woman for a particular sphere or profession, but to perfect her intellect by the best methods which philosophy and experience suggest, so that she may be better qualified to enjoy and do well her work in life, whatever that work may be." These lines, however, no longer appeared in the catalog by 1910. The college opened in 1875 without a preparatory department, emphasizing its high standards, and its motto was "Add to your virtue, knowledge."[89] Founded with less religious influence than Wellesley and Mount Holyoke, Smith had no written rules regarding student behavior except requiring them to attend a local church on Sunday. Students also originally were intended to use the local library in order to bring the campus and the town closer together. Smith acquired a reputation of having both brainy and wealthy students, a reputation that a magazine article about the college tried to dispel by noting that the girls were not all grinds who wore "glasses and masculine collars," nor were they only concerned with "woman's rights and political economy."[90] Rather, the article stressed, Smith had societies, plays, dances, basketball (it was the first women's college to have a basketball team), and a cottage system of dormitories, where students lived in smaller groups with a housemother, rather than a large dormitory.[91]

Wellesley was founded by Henry Durant and his wife, Pauline Fowle Durant, despondent over the death of their son and determined to consecrate an institution to God's work. The original statutes governing the college claimed that "the College was founded for the glory of God and the service of the Lord Jesus Christ, in and by the education and culture of women."[92] Durant was concerned enough about the spiritual condition of his students to ask them individually about their faith on his walks across campus and to require faculty to be Evangelical Christians (a requirement that was dropped in 1898).[93] However, the college administration instead focused on establishing strong academic ideals. Like Mount Holyoke and Vassar, Wellesley opened in 1875 with a large building, College Hall, which was designed to accommodate over three hundred students, and later built smaller cottages based on the successful model implemented by Smith. Wellesley was known for its all-female faculty, which provided role models for aspiring students, and for its early embrace of science laboratories, a new methodology for teaching, including the first physics lab for women in the country.[94] Following the college motto, "Not to be ministered unto but to minister to," faculty encouraged students to embrace social work and to study the problems of poverty.

Bryn Mawr was founded by Dr. Joseph Wright Taylor, a Quaker who left money in his will for a women's college. Taylor was friends with several members of the board of trustees of Johns Hopkins University, including James Thomas, whose daughter, M. Carey Thomas, became dean and then president of the college. She exerted her strong ideas on the college for the next several decades. Thomas toured other women's colleges and was determined to make Bryn Mawr even more reflective of men's colleges. She did not want the college to open with a preparatory department and instead helped her friends found the Bryn Mawr School in Baltimore to prepare students for Bryn Mawr College. She also refused to limit the college to Quaker professors, instead seeking those most qualified in their fields. Bryn Mawr was also innovative in its adaptation from Johns Hopkins of the "group system," whereby courses were grouped and students chose from a group what they wanted to take, allowing them more flexibility. Carey Thomas was interested in training women academics and encouraged her students to take their courses seriously and to go on to graduate work. While Bryn Mawr had the social activities found at other schools, it retained a reputation for its high academic standards.[95]

Radcliffe differed from the other women's colleges because it began as the Harvard Annex in 1879, with Harvard professors teaching women separately. Arthur Gilman, the director of the Cambridge School for Girls, and his wife, Stella Scott, wanted a college for women in Cambridge. He approached Professor James Greenough, and together they recruited faculty members to teach women. Gilman carefully distinguished the women's college from Harvard by noting that Harvard had not become coeducational and that the annex was run separately from Harvard; graduates did not receive a Harvard degree but rather a diploma countersigned by Harvard officials. The women had their own building and their own endowment. On the other hand, the annex benefited from its association with Harvard, and under President Elizabeth Cary Agassiz the college grew rapidly. In 1894 the college took the name Radcliffe. Students at Radcliffe had a building, Fay House, for classes and some social activities, but they initially lived in boardinghouses and did not have the same campus living experience or extracurricular activities available at the other women's colleges until well into the 1900s.[96]

Whichever college southern women chose, once they arrived, they faced many of the same issues while adjusting to campus life. Their coursework in preparatory school and conversations with alumnae did not always prepare them for the experience of leaving their families, their communities, and their regional culture to strike out on their own as "rebels" in the "land of Yankees." They had to fight homesickness, gain independence, and adjust to rigorous expectations of scholarship. It is their experience on campus to which we turn next.

CHAPTER THREE

From Homesick Southerners
to Independent Yankees

The Campus Experience

 Raised to be dependent, southern students initially found it difficult to assert their independence while on their own at college. Mary Elinor Poppenheim cautioned her daughter Mary at Vassar, "I want to see you improve in person and manners; but . . . don't catch any Yankee ways." For Mary, Yankee ways included independence, as when she told her mother that she and her sister had successfully purchased dresses, and thus they had "become regular Yankees about taking care of ourselves."[1] Although she took to heart her mother's demands that she exhibit proper manners and appearances, at Vassar she also sharpened her ability to think independently in the classroom. She told her mother that she shocked her professors in Latin class when she offered her opinion of Dido and Aeneas. Even when her teachers attempted to change her mind, she stuck with her own judgment and noted that she frequently had a point of view different from that of her classmates.[2] Serious and steady, Mary worked as hard at maintaining proper appearances as she did at her schoolwork and ultimately began to make her own decisions about both. Mary and other southern students often exhibited the kind of independence that they associated with the North, a Yankee characteristic gained at school rather than a natural phase in their development.

This chapter explores how southern women changed while attending the Seven Sister colleges. The most striking aspect of southern women's experiences at northern colleges was the displacement that many students initially felt. Being away from home was hard enough, but being in the "land of Yankees" made it worse. As historian Daniel Sutherland wrote of southern migrants to the North in the decade after the Civil War, "a different climate, strange customs, new livelihoods, the absence of friends, a faster-paced life, occasionally hostile receptions from the northern populace . . . stacked the odds against a smooth transition to northern life."[3] Sutherland described the disorientation southerners experienced adjusting to the cold weather, northern diet, holidays, and fast pace. However, most students who remained on campus eventually adjusted and later remembered their years at school with pleasure. Most importantly, the women matured while at school. They developed independence and self-confidence, qualities that significantly affected the choices students eventually made after graduation. These qualities would be critical to the leadership they demonstrated first at school and then, after graduation, in women's organizations and social activism.

Most students were homesick, especially at first. They missed family and friends, a fact exacerbated by the long distance they had traveled from home. Students complained that they did not fit in, that the work was difficult, and that they were unaccustomed to so much independence. Agnes Raoul was nervous at the thought of leaving Atlanta to attend Vassar. Despite her excitement, she grew more anxious daily. Unfortunately, her fears were not unfounded. After her first semester she described the place as "awful, vile, and horrid."[4]

Given the distance they traveled, one might expect a lower graduation rate for southern women. However, despite their initial maladjustment, southern students were not significantly less likely to graduate than their northern classmates, with graduation rates for both groups ranging from 50 to 70 percent.[5] Perhaps this was because they were a select group of women. Daring enough to leave home for the North, many overcame obstacles and graduated.

Such tenacity was important because families and friends often did not expect students to graduate. Many left after several months because they were unhappy, homesick, or not prepared enough; others stayed only one or two years by design. At Smith College, Mary Comer contemplated whether to return, initially decided not to, and then changed her mind and remained for her junior year. Still debating if she should stay and graduate, she informed her mother that many of her friends did not plan to. Mary had to choose between going back to school or traveling to Mexico with her uncle, an alternative she said she hesitated to choose only because she feared that the trip would not take place at the last moment, and then she would have given up school for nothing.[6] At Wellesley many nongraduates later wrote that they returned home out of duty, usually after the death of a mother or to care for a sick relative. Virginian Annie Elizabeth Lee attended Wellesley for only two years despite her connections to the college's founders, the Durants. She left college to keep house for the family when her mother had a paralyzing stroke.[7] Four decades later, Margaret Mitchell quit Smith College to keep house for her father and brother following the death of her mother from influenza. Some students dropped out of school to marry, including Aida Seifert, who was born in Natchez; she left Wellesley to marry a man she met during her junior year.[8] Even students who stayed less than four years still treasured their time at college. Barbara Tunnell, who spent only one year at Smith, later claimed, "I doubt if Smith meant more to any four-year member than it did to me."[9]

The fundamental problem for many southern students was the fact that they had traveled hundreds of miles to live with strangers. The thought of his daughter attending college a thousand miles away from home so disconcerted D. E. Converse that he founded Converse College in South Carolina rather than send his daughter to New York or Washington, D.C. He wanted Converse College to be a Vassar of the South.[10] Intense homesickness struck many students who braved the journey. Kentuckian Margaret Preston was homesick, especially for her mother. Years later, she argued that it was precisely because she was so happy at home that she was miserable at Bryn Mawr. "[My] family life . . . had been too alluring," she claimed. "I nearly died of homesickness." She remembered how even the smell of the pine paneling in the buildings disturbed her. Margaret felt alone at college without her mother there to provide advice and support. Unused to being on her own, she lamented, "It sometimes seems funny to me the way I live here, doing just as I choose, with nobody asking me any questions or taking any interest. You know at home you and Keck always want to know so much about my little affairs," and again, "there is nobody here, you see, who understands me or takes a real interest in me."[11] Rather than relishing her freedom from supervision, she felt neglected and uncared for.

Despite their own sadness at being apart, most parents did their best to encourage their daughters. Kentuckian Sophonisba Breckinridge's parents were sympathetic but firm. William Breckinridge acknowledged Sophonisba's loneliness. "At Wellesley you are but one of five hundred—a new, unknown one at that, from a distant state," he wrote. He feared that she might lose her way but told her that she had her heart set on going there and now she must "conquer." Her mother admitted that if Sophonisba really wanted to come home, her father would not object, adding that she had never wanted Sophonisba to leave home to attend Wellesley. Yet Issa Breckinridge also reminded her daughter just how much Sophonisba had wanted to go to Wellesley and suggested that returning home was no panacea—Sophonisba had expressed little desire to remain at Kentucky A&M, and life at home would be "dull." Issa consistently reassured Sophonisba of her parents' love and emphasized her opportunities to learn, make friends, and enjoy nature while at Wellesley.[12] Believing that too much academic stress was unhealthy, she told Sophonisba only to "study enough to hold your own and live out of doors all you can."[13] Issa did not follow her own advice, however, and was depressed without Sophonisba at home. Finally, Sophonisba's grandmother asked Sophonisba to stop complaining to her mother. "For mercy's sake, don't write any more dismals to your Mother," she wrote. "She looks at the dark side and I think is sensational."[14]

While daughters had new experiences and schoolwork to occupy them, mothers had only their daily routine to distract them. That household chores were not enough is evident from Mary Elinor Poppenheim's lamentation when her daughters Mary and Louisa left for Vassar. After a Christmas vacation visit home to Charleston she wrote to them, "I have been trying to be busy ever since you left to kill time and try not to miss you but it is the biggest task I undertook. I think I have darned every stocking in the home, sewn on every button, fixed the blue silk for Ida, even studied the French alphabet, and yet I cannot kill time, nor fail to miss you. Today is only one week and yet it seems ages ago since you both left us."[15] Despite her sadness, Mary Elinor consistently assured her daughters that the benefits of a Vassar education were worth the sacrifice.[16]

The feeling of loss was mutual, and Mary was deeply homesick. While many, if not most, young women boarding at college and away from home for the first time were undoubtedly homesick, the plight of southern girls was especially poignant for several reasons. Students who traveled a thousand miles or more were often unable to visit their parents and commonly spent weekends and holidays either on campus or visiting the families of college friends who lived nearby. After Mary Poppenheim learned that she would be unable to spend Easter in Charleston during her first year away, for example, she tried to will herself not to be homesick. "I am not atoll homesick," she wrote. "I must not allow myself to be so." But Mary was homesick, and she could not rationalize the feeling away. She continued, "The idea of going home only put me off my center a little. I will take a sensible view of the subj[ect] and I see I will lose more than gain by going home. . . . [J]ust wait until I *do* come home, oh, won't I feel happy and be lively. . . . I will not grieve about not coming home. You must not think I will do such a foolish thing but know I will get along very nicely."[17] Mary steeled herself to endure despite her homesickness.

Furthermore, South Carolinian Julia Hammond blamed her southern culture for the homesickness she experienced at Radcliffe. She did not share her northern colleagues' devotion to their work, which she believed allowed them to leave home much more easily than she. Julia claimed, "I cannot but think they do not feel as we do."[18] She even told her younger sister to study hard at home, where she could get as good an education but would not have to endure "the pain of leaving home."[19] Julia was amazed that a Miss Ravenel of Charleston, in Boston for art school, apparently wanted to stay in the city. Julia wrote her sister that although Ravenel and other southern girls "may be willing thus to give up their home . . . I could never tarry away, there is never a land as fair as our dear home."[20] For Julia, missing home was linked to missing the familiarity of southern culture. She differentiated between southerners and northerners, who she believed had "no feeling," and criticized "Yankee" women for their bossiness. Overwhelmed by the strangeness of socializing with northerners in her Boston boardinghouse, she asked her mother to send her Bible "as a help to withstand this atmosphere of unreal things and life."[21] Only her faith could anchor her in such a strange place.

The college experience ultimately hinged on the academic experience for some and the social experience for others, depending on their personality and purpose. Students with intellectual curiosity and the capability to excel academically without undue stress generally seemed happy. Those with little interest in their coursework or who struggled to pass classes expressed the most dissatisfaction. Margaret Preston's academic difficulties contributed to her homesickness, and once she gained confidence in her work she grew happier at Bryn Mawr. At first, she believed that students were too concerned with academics, which she found stifling. Bryn Mawr was a "prison," where students only talked about their classes. This meant that there was "no broadening element" such as had been described to her by friends. With so much stress on studies, Margaret complained that she didn't like the excess "excitement" and "effort" at school. She became so unhappy that she fantasized about becoming sick and being sent home. Ultimately, her pride helped sustain her. She initially refused to give up and return home without a legitimate excuse and asked her mother not to tell any of her friends that she was homesick. Still unhappy weeks later, she wondered if she had made the wrong choice in attending Bryn Mawr and begged not to have to return the next year. Margaret complained, "I feel all the time as if I ought to like it here and be interested in the work and yet I am not." She described herself as not feeling a part of the college crowd, partly because she planned to be there only one year. She hated for others to ask her whether she was returning, because the other students found it "queer" that she did not intend to come back.

While her mother was sympathetic, she encouraged Margaret to make the best of it.[22] Sarah Preston admitted that she and Margaret's father both wished Margaret was at home, but Sarah told Margaret to try to adjust. She also advised Margaret to be social as well as do her schoolwork because "the book learning you will forget." Like other mothers, Sarah feared that if Margaret studied too hard she would not only jeopardize her health but also miss out on the social aspects of college.[23]

Margaret's academic troubles were real. In her first year she feared failing her German class. Sarah Preston reassured her that she could drop German if necessary and offered to read it with her over Christmas. Margaret was proud when she finally passed German, but she still did not want to return for her second year and was surprised when her Aunt Jessie offered to pay for it. In a letter that must have caused her mother concern, Margaret reported that a Wellesley student had walked into the lake there and committed suicide, the victim of bad grades and homesickness.

In her second and third semesters Margaret finally grew more confident as she adjusted and began to excel at her coursework. She not only mused about staying to graduate but now suggested that if she did return she would work to be one of the ten students with the highest grades, a feat that one of her friends had proposed she was capable of attaining. Margaret's pride in her accomplishments is evident in the fact that after graduation she visited Bryn Mawr several times and even ordered a class ring.[24] Furthermore, she eventually returned to college to earn her bachelor's degree in 1938.

Margaret Preston was one of many southern students who struggled academically, due in large part to inadequate preparation. Julia Hammond also was in over her head when she first arrived at Harvard Annex. She did not stay long enough to adapt. Shortly after her arrival she mailed home a copy of a freshman physics exam, writing on the back, "Examination questions answered by my class. Fearful!!!"[25] She then met with a professor of political economy who told her she was not "advanced" enough to enroll in his course, "which rather through cold water on Father, and myself."[26] She was further dismayed to find out that the thousand-page book she received for botany contained only the introductory reading. Julia struggled to keep up with her classmates, admitting to her mother that she felt lacking among so many "learned" people. Focused more on home and less on academic success, Julia hoped that even if she did not become as learned as the other students, she would still be "more fit for the delight of being your friend and daughter."[27] Julia also had difficulty adjusting to the loss of her mother as her guide. She wrote her mother that only "the thought of you will sustain me when I go out tomorrow to meet those strangers that are soon to have such an influence on my life."[28] Julia left after only one semester.

Some southerners marveled at their colleagues' focus on academics and the stress and fatigue caused by overwork. North Carolinian Sue Hall was struck by the "tired, worn look many of the girls have" at Wellesley due to the overwhelming number of hours spent at work.[29] She was surprised to find that Jessie Dagan, a southern girl, was one of the "tired" girls who worked too hard, in Hall's estimation. She described Dagan as both bright and ambitious and was struck by the fact that Dagan made up work and had been promoted ahead of her class. Agnes Raoul, on the other hand, was unimpressed with the academic opportunities at Vassar. She told her father she was more interested in

"New York, story books, dresses, and frivolous amusements" than in school-work.[30] There is little compelling evidence to suggest that Agnes was typical of southern students, despite stereotypes of the southern belle interested only in marriage. College letters suggest that this self-selecting group of women were overachievers, and most worked hard even if they struggled initially.

Whether students were driven to excel at academic work from the moment they entered college like Sophonisba or came more slowly to a love of learning like Margaret Preston, happiness in the classroom often meant satisfaction with the overall experience. While Mary Comer was not miserable at school the way Margaret was, she also needed time to develop an appreciation for her studies. Mary missed home but never became too homesick, either because she had been away from home for boarding school before Smith or because she was too busy having fun with an active social life. She described her freshman year in a paper she had to write on an interesting topic as "so deep that it almost kills me." That same year she described the cramming she did for exams, trying to fit an entire semester's work into one week. Describing her preference for "the gossip side of [history], knowing what the kings and their queens [did] and if they lived happily and so forth," over the philosophy of history, Mary was intelligent enough to pass but showed little intellectual curiosity.[31] After her first-semester exams she confessed to her mother that she had been too busy having fun to concentrate on her work, and, furthermore, she did not regret it. Over time, although Mary never stopped socializing, she grew better able to handle her coursework and significantly more interested in it. The following fall, for example, she gave up seeing Ethel Barrymore to stay home and study, she soon began to write long descriptions of her classes and the books she read in letters to her mother, and she no longer worried about her exams.[32] Although she had considered not returning after her sophomore year, she did. Mary told her mother she was very happy that she did, "for I enjoy the work so much this year. And it has opened up so many new things to me."[33] Mary developed academically at the same time she matured emotionally.

Some students excelled immediately at their coursework. In her first semester Gertrude Weil reassured her parents that her classes were not difficult.[34] Virginia Foster Durr recalled that "Wellesley was a sheer delight to me. I never felt so well or so happy in my life. I felt completely free." Virginia's delight came from her opportunity to focus on intellectual challenges rather than finding a husband, and she argued that "the main thing I learned was to use my mind and to get pleasure out of it."[35] Sophonisba Breckinridge, described by a classmate as the most brilliant in their class, wrote her father that she enjoyed her exams and that the only two she had been dreading, history and mathematics, turned out to be "lovely."[36] For the students who became intellectually engaged, learned to think, and loved to learn, college was a wonderful experience. Attending a Seven Sister college, where professors challenged students with rigorous requirements and examinations, provided an intellectual experience not easily obtainable in the South.

Colleges pressured students to do well academically, contribute to campus life through extracurricular activities, and get along with roommates and friends. Even some students who did not struggle with classes were still unhappy at school because they found it difficult to live on their own, make friends, and enjoy the social aspects of college. Margaret Mitchell felt lost at Smith. Although she could pass her courses, she was frustrated at no longer commanding a prominent role in school. "Sometimes I get so discouraged I feel that there is no use in keeping on here," she complained to her brother. "It isn't in studies, for I'm about a 'C' student—but I haven't done a thing up here. I haven't shone in any line—academic, athletic, literary, musical or anything." Like many students at top colleges today, Margaret probably felt overwhelmed as she made the adjustment from being a leader at a small school to being just one of many talented students at college. To make matters worse, she had a difficult year at Smith—during her first semester her fiancé died in battle during World War I, and then in January her mother died. Margaret acknowledged that the events of the year heightened her frustration but added, "In a college of 2500 there are so many cleverer and more talented girls than I. If I can't be first, I'd rather be nothing."[37]

Looking back on her Smith days, Margaret claimed that she had not been happy there but was lonely and a misfit, with only two friends. She blamed some of her dissatisfaction on her young age and recalled that she almost had a nervous breakdown while away at school. She remembered roaming the campus, seeking solace.[38] On the surface, however, Margaret appeared happy to her friends and had an active social life. They later remembered the famous author as having been well liked and considered lots of fun. She attended dances, dated many men from neighboring men's colleges, and once had to hitchhike back to campus after missing the last trolley, climbing the water pipe to get inside because the door was locked. Margaret had an outgoing personality and even smoked and cursed.[39] It is difficult to know whether Margaret was successful at covering her sadness or was remembered so favorably by others later because of her eventual fame. Perhaps later events in her life caused her to look back on her experience at Smith from a different perspective.[40]

When Margaret recalled her Smith days, she lamented a lack of close friends, so crucial to the college experience when one was so far from home. This was particularly true for students who were unable to travel home for holidays such as Thanksgiving and Christmas. Rather than return to South Carolina from Vassar, Mary and Louisa Poppenheim frequently traveled to the homes of their friends Minnie McKinlay in New York City and Gertie Homan in New Jersey. Louisa acknowledged the importance of friendship to her mother, writing to her about her friends. College, she claimed, had helped her to develop relationships with others. Louisa understood that in many ways the bonds forged outside the classroom were as important as the lessons learned within. She concluded that when they graduated, leaving friends would be more difficult than leaving the college itself.[41]

For students without friends, college could be a lonely place. Lucy Walker traveled to Mount Holyoke from Selma, Alabama, a distance of approximately twelve hundred miles. Addressing her former classmates in 1947, forty-seven years after graduation, she wrote, "I feel that I have no achievement to write about. My short stay at Mount Holyoke was a pleasant experience—there are names in the class books that are familiar but I did not know anyone real well. It is quite different with those of you who live near, had several years at College, and formed close friendships."[42] While many students were able to bridge the gap and form friendships, Lucy was not. The fact that she did not join her class as a freshman and spend four years with the same young women probably also impaired her relationships.

Margaret Preston was disillusioned with the social life at Bryn Mawr, griping that it was not as much fun as she had anticipated. She describes going to a college tea, like the ones "you hear about" in the media. However, the cocoa was made of cocoa, condensed milk, and hot water, which she described as "the nastiest of all nasty things." The image she had from magazines of college coeds sitting around a dormitory drinking hot cocoa and having a wonderful time did not ring true for her.[43] At Bryn Mawr she did not seem to want to enjoy herself at the many college teas, excursions, and "spreads" frequently mentioned by students. She complained that Bryn Mawr was not as fun as Linda and Mary Neville had represented it to be, but their experience there had been much happier. Linda excelled at her work and enjoyed the social aspects of school as well. She wrote her father, "Nearly all my work is over and I can take most of the time now for pleasures. I think I shall never regret coming to college. Indeed I am very glad that I came and for many reasons am sorry to see the close."[44]

Students who arrived as freshmen had an advantage over those who came later because many schools emphasized class—freshman, sophomore, junior, senior—identity for students. If students exhibited class spirit, they had a ready-made set of friends—and enemies. While classes sponsored social events for themselves and with other classes (sophomores and juniors commonly hosted freshmen at events), they also participated in more informal rituals. Mary Poppenheim described the antics of classes at Vassar, claiming that despite examinations there was still "time for Class quarrels." Mary's class of 1888, the juniors, had a fight with the seniors. The fight was surprisingly physical. Mary explained,

> They took eight of our girls and shut them up in the Senior Corridor. We were naturally very angry about it and went to their rescue. . . . These doors the S[eniors] had closed and were holding shut. There are thirty-six girls in the Senior Class and thirteen of us outside and eight inside forced the doors and got in to take our girls off. One of the eight was our president for next year. When we got in the Seniors rushed at us with window sticks and chairs and pinched, knocked down, shook and otherwise pitched into our girls. Then their President made a nice little speech where she called '88 [the juniors] a Class of "*Rowdys*" and they hissed us. We were piping mad I can tell you and we sent word to them that they must apologize.

In retaliation the juniors decided not to participate in the seniors' Class Day celebrations unless they received an apology, which they did, but not until the juniors boycotted the senior class auction. The physical nature of this fight—hitting with sticks and chairs—is shocking given the expectations for young women in any region of the country at the time. There are no other similar descriptions in any other letters in this study, nor have any been noted by any other historians, to my knowledge. Such physical violence, however, was traditionally associated with men's colleges at the turn of the century and the hazing rituals of interclass rivalry. Mary's description indicates that students at women's colleges took their class identity seriously enough to initiate class warfare of their own.[45] Competition and rowdiness were expected of college men at the time, but such actions seriously threatened the image of the womanly woman that colleges worked to produce. It appears that in this case the college ritual trumped all expectations of female behavior, although whether this was an isolated incident or a rare documentation of more frequent conduct is difficult to know. In either case, it remains shocking and virtually inexplicable.

Bryn Mawr students also identified with their class, to the chagrin of Margaret Preston. She found it difficult to establish herself socially given that students were thrown together without the rigid social hierarchy of family and name she was used to in society at home. Complaining about the college's emphasis on class identity, she claimed that she felt insignificant as a freshman. "I, for one, prefer the much maligned world where money and family and good looks count," she advised her mother. "These things seem more tangible than your years at Bryn Mawr." After two years Margaret Preston had not been converted. In the spring of 1906 she complained that she was more interested in "people and money and positions" rather than academic degrees.[46] Yet because physical appearance was also less important in the academic atmosphere of the colleges, at Bryn Mawr Margaret felt free to pay less attention to her dress than in Lexington. She told her mother that she did not need any more clothes because she rarely dressed up. "Nobody knows me," so it didn't matter the same as it would at home.[47] Margaret was less interested in money and more interested in family and status. She complained that she met too many "nouveaux riche" students at school who did not meet up to her standards of what a proper lady like her mother was. "The dean is always talking about our parents who haven't had the advantages we have had," she protested. "If I were as accomplished and good and charming as my Mother I should be satisfied. I really should like to associate somewhere with people who come somewhere near my idea of well-bred men and women, but may be that ideal is one of vanished mid-Victorian, Second Empire standards."[48]

Whether students focused on appearances and money or class year and academic performance in judging classmates, they had little knowledge of each other's family, an important marker in the South. The Poppenheims sometimes asked their parents if they knew of a student's family as they attempted to judge her. After meeting Varina Davis Brown, a fellow South Carolinian at Vassar, Mary and Louisa were reluctant to depend solely on their own evaluation of her personality. Louisa asked her father if he knew Brown's family and "what kind of people they are."[49] The Poppenheims wanted to determine the family character of their potential friends.

Forming their own codes of proper behavior in the absence of their parents was particularly vexing to many southern students. Manners mattered in southern society. The southern lady ideal demanded that southern women appear to be charming, pure, and polite. Students left home after years of instruction from their parents on proper behavior but then found themselves in new situations, having to determine how to act on their own. Women's colleges, especially in the 1870s and 1880s, left little to chance, with strict regulations on social behavior. But colleges did not regulate every social interaction, and, particularly when some rules were loosened in the 1890s, students had to mind their manners on their own.

In the 1880s Mary Elinor Poppenheim cared deeply about appearances, and she constantly reminded her daughters how to behave properly. True to the southern lady idea, their mother raised them to be pure, pious, domestic, dependent, and protected women. Thus, although Mary Elinor believed in her daughters' intellectual capacity and desired the best education for them, she also stressed that they were to be southern ladies. For her that included keeping up pure hearts and proper appearances and avoiding women's rights. Proper chaperonage was a particularly important concern to her and other parents. "You can be very particular," she advised Mary, "as you know a lady can always tell when she is with the right sort of people and if you find they are not the right kind why then leave immediately. When you have a proper chaperone you can go anywhere she approves."[50]

Unable to chaperone them herself while they were at Vassar, Mary Elinor was also concerned with Mary and Louisa's behavior around boys. Before a trip to New York to stay with a college friend she cautioned them, "I want you both to be sure and keep heart whole, don't let the flattery of any N.Y. boy or man deceive you but keep heart whole, clear head, and keen eyes. Know that men will flatter and women must be cool and sharp to sift the true from the false. 'Be wise as serpents, harmless as doves.'" In this case, Mary Elinor wanted her daughters to maintain a proper appearance and to warn them of the dangers that men posed to the chastity of innocent young women. One of the ways which Mary and Louisa could protect themselves from a soiled reputation or an unpleasant experience was to avoid contact with undesirable society. Louisa Poppenheim took this lesson to heart when she wrote her mother that a friend was taking a "night boat" by herself, which she proclaimed "rather risky." Mary Elinor agreed. Although she did not think Mable was in any real danger, she commented, "I thought a Vassar girl would be more tony and have more self-respect. Appearances must be regarded." Reinforcing Louisa's reluctance to take the same risk, her mother praised her for her decision to take "a drawing room car to go up to College when she was alone; for there is a great deal of comfort in being out of sight of unpleasant objects and the rabble. There is an inborn exclusiveness that all refined and true women should feel, and a kind of intuition that directs and guides her in the paths of righteousness and peace."[51]

While Mary and Louisa relied on their mother for advice on everything ranging from hygiene to whether or not to tip the maid, it was her constant reminders of proper manners that most influenced their personalities. They took these lessons seriously, gaining a reputation both at Vassar and at home in Charleston for their serious and proper behavior. They also continued to adhere to Victorian manners, such as maintaining an afternoon "at home" when callers could visit, well into the twentieth century. No detail of behavior or appearance was too small. Mary especially emulated her mother. She disparaged a classmate who was more interested in popularity than character. "My she is so ordinary. Isn't it strange how blood will tell and how a girl can never be a lady unless her Mother is one," she wrote home.[52]

Mary Elinor Poppenheim was especially concerned that Louisa and Mary understand how to act appropriately because she wanted them to give northerners a favorable impression of the South. She not only warned them before they visited their friends in New York of the potential flattery of New York men but also reminded them to inquire as to the proper time at which to rise in the morning. Some households found it easier when guests stayed in their rooms until an appropriate time, she wrote, though she cautioned them against sleeping too late. "I don't want the Northern people to think we Southern people are so lazy, but if the mistress requests you to take breakfast in your room don't refuse." Part of the difficulty was that she was unsure of how northerners truly acted in the privacy of their homes, asking Mary after a visit to a relative's home in New York about how northerners ran their homes and hosted guests.[53] She understood that while she based her impression of northern ways on this one visit, northerners also might judge the South based on Mary and Louisa's behavior.

Parents also worried about religion, encouraging their daughters to retain their faith while at school. Sophonisba's father encouraged her to study religion and the Bible, attend prayer meetings, and hold onto her faith while at Wellesley. Fearful that a teacher or friend would have an undue effect on her, he specifically cautioned her that she "not [to] let Miss Hayes or anybody else undermine your faith in the facts of the Bible. All you can learn these four years would not be a drop in the bucket compared to the harm this would do."[54] Jessie Hall's father also was concerned about her faith. He understood that it was difficult to remain committed to the "Spirit" while at school because the act of living with such a large number of other students was "filling the mind and heart with other things than those suggested by the Spirit." This did not mean that she had to miss out on college fun and stimulation, as he encouraged her to develop friendships with the other girls. However, he cautioned her that although it might be easier at first to try to be popular rather than stick to her convictions, ultimately, "when the girls realize that you are living according to principle and that you are no 'sham'—as they certainly will find out, then you'll have all the friends you can look after and more opportunities for doing them good than you could possibly have by yielding your convictions at first."[55]

By the beginning of the twentieth century, colleges had begun to relax their social restrictions, leaving students even more on their own to regulate their own behavior. As schools loosened the rules, students sometimes became bewildered. Agnes Raoul marveled over the fact that at Vassar she could go for a walk with an unknown man but could not have her father in her room without a chaperone.[56] By the 1910s Margaret Mitchell found a strange dichotomy of acceptable behavior on and off campus, especially regarding rules concerning the opposite sex. Apparently surprised at the behavior of some of her classmates, she wrote to her father, "I now see why Steve had objections to my coming north to college. Of course, as I haven't laid eyes on a man since I arrived, this doesn't apply to me." She found it strange that girls could have dates off campus or travel unchaperoned to New York, where presumably they were free to interact with men however they chose. However, if students stayed on campus at Smith, she complained, there were strict rules and not much to do—one could sit in a parlor, go to dinner, or take a walk with a date. An incident with a date from whom she had to reject an unwanted sexual advance may have prompted Margaret's apprehension. Despite her misgivings about behavior codes, Mitchell concluded, "Well, anyway, I love Smith, even tho it is barbarous and I wouldn't take anything for my year here. It has showed me how much nicer home is—and that there are nice places besides home."[57]

Not all southern students cared as deeply about rules, manners, and appearances. Gertrude Weil's letters home to North Carolina from Smith reference regulations that Weil considered silly. She flippantly told her mother that she had been sleighing with friends and ended up in neighboring Amherst, breaking a rule, unbeknownst to them. "Those little silly rules make me sick—as if it could be any harm for four girls to go without a chaperone to an old village that happens to contain a small man's college," she grumbled. While the more conservative Mary Elinor Poppenheim might have immediately retrieved a daughter who made a comment like that, Gertrude's mother, Mina Weil, greeted this letter with little comment. Gertrude again found herself in trouble for not having a chaperone to attend a play, which she called "pretty ridiculous." Finally, her mother felt compelled to respond. While she did not object to the lack of a chaperone, she warned Gertrude not "to meander at your own sweet will with no one aware of your goings out or incomings." Schools had already begun to relax the rules in the ten years between the Poppenheims and Gertrude Weil, and, more significantly, Mina seemed to trust Gertrude's judgment. When Gertrude no longer had to have chaperones she reassured her mother that she would not go anywhere unless it was "all right."[58]

Gertrude Weil's independent streak was just what most of the other southern parents feared. For most young women at the turn of the century, leaving home to live at college took courage. For southern students, the shock was even more intense. They had to travel hundreds of miles to a place considered "foreign" by many. Moreover, many were raised to be dependent. The experience of fear and freedom could be overwhelming. Margaret Mitchell wrote: "When mother untied the apron strings and I went away to Yankeeland on my own, I shall never forget my state of mind . . . I seemed to feel something within my innermost me uncoiling and stretching and awakening, a consciousness of myself, of power, of my own awakening personality swelling to such a point that I had to sternly restrain myself from wallowing on the soft campus grass and yelling."[59] In Margaret's case, the independence gained from her year at Smith reinforced an already fiery personality. When she returned to Atlanta, she kept house for her father and brother and resumed her active social life. When she debuted, she performed what was considered to be a risqué dance, after which she was snubbed by some women and not invited to join the Junior League.[60] Southern girls who returned home had to negotiate a new path for themselves to take the place of the freedom they had experienced at school. Walter Hines Page captured that dilemma in his largely autobiographical *The Southerner: Being the Autobiography of Nicholas Worth*. After Worth began questioning southern ways while at school in the North, on his way back south he mused, "I was now at home at Harvard; free, too, as I had not before been. Could I ever be free in the South?"[61] Surely, many a southern graduate of the Seven Sisters spoke those same words to herself as she traveled home.

Because southerners traditionally perceived the southern lady as dependent on men in the chivalrous South, these women's development of independence was a profound change. Many southern girls were not thought to be independent enough to handle life on their own at college or selfish enough to leave their families. The suffering of family members left behind was a major theme of many short stories written by southern college students; clearly, these students worried that they were being selfish.[62] Smith student Mary Comer understood that her mother, at home in Savannah, Georgia, was probably lonely without her and said she felt selfish going away.[63]

When confronted with other southern students exhibiting self-determination, Mary Poppenheim was struck by their courage. She told her mother about a student from Mississippi who had come to Vassar all by herself after never having traveled more than twenty miles from home before. Commented Mary, "That was pluck, was it not?"[64] Julia Hammond best captured the dependency dilemma of southern students. Referring to her ambition to be a doctor (or, more accurately, her father's ambition for her to become a doctor), she wrote to her mother, "I had no idea how dependent I was till I got off here by myself, and I don't exactly see how I who am so weak can strengthen others."[65]

Independence was also a part of maturation. Agnes Raoul also found autonomy away at school, which she attributed to growing older. "I never felt so much before that now I have a responsibility of my own," she wrote home, "that I have passed the age where some one else can decide all questions for me. Now I have to decide for myself so often, and I am taken for what I am, not for what my parents are."[66]

This freedom was not without its critics. Mary Comer received a letter from a male friend who attended Yale and who told her that he thought it was great that the Smith girls had such a "dandy" time, but he feared it led to too much liberty. He thought that Smith girls were too free to do whatever they wanted, which, he cautioned, developed too much independence in some girls. This, he concluded, was "the only thing I have against girls' colleges."[67]

Southern students gained independence not only through traveling and making purchases and other daily decisions on their own but also through their intellectual growth. More so than their sisters who remained in the South, students who ventured north had to fulfill rigorous academic requirements, which gave them a seriousness of purpose and feeling of achievement. Their letters indicate that they took their studies seriously.[68] All this independence was sometimes in conflict with the strong southern identity that many students felt. Informal and formal networks of southern students could assuage some of the confusion they experienced.

CHAPTER FOUR

A Southerner in Yankeeland

Southern Clubs, Yankee Ways, and

African American Classmates

 Virginian Annie Elizabeth Lee struggled to adjust to northern culture at Wellesley in the late 1870s. Her relationship to her cousin Pauline Durant, wife of Wellesley College founder Henry Durant, did not alleviate her culture shock. Annie feared that she would succumb to northern ways, for she wrote her brother that she dreamed she had taken up a Yankee accent, and her family would not let her return home.[1] After returning to Wellesley following a vacation, she lamented that she hated to return to the "Yankees." Although she did not struggle with academics, she complained about the work when she considered not being able to return home for Christmas vacation. Unhappy because she studied "from morning to night," Annie complained, "I am not going to stay up here in Yankee land ten months for anyone."[2] Furthermore, she considered herself to be an unreconstructed rebel girl. She claimed she had "no more use for [Yankees] than rattlesnakes, in fact not as much."[3] The northern history of the Civil War particularly offended Annie because she felt it was biased against the South. Northern opinions on racial matters, especially the possibility of interracial sexual relationships, turned her world upside down. Even her connections to Wellesley's founders could not shake her intense feeling that as a southerner she simply did not fit in.

Annie Lee's discomfort at Wellesley is ironic not only because of her connection to the Durants but also because the first student to enroll at Wellesley was a "southern belle" as well. Anne Poe Harrison lived with her two sisters and her widowed mother (her father died while serving the Confederacy) north of Richmond, Virginia. The girls' mother and grandmother taught them at home and then sent them to a neighbor's home, where Jenny Nelson, the aunt of author Thomas Nelson Page, taught a group of local girls. Anne and her sisters hoped to become teachers in order to support their impoverished family. Jenny Nelson began a correspondence with Henry Durant, who invited her to teach at Wellesley and bring her students with her to the new school when it opened. The Harrisons sold the family silver to pay for the trip, and Anne left with Jenny Nelson and Nelson's half-sister Carolyn Peyton Nelson. Durant asked Anne, as the older of the two girls who had traveled so far to be at Wellesley, to be the first student to sign the registration book.[4] The founders of Wellesley understood that southerners needed special attention. Pauline Durant, herself a native southerner, invited southern students to tea at her home, while Henry Durant suggested that the southern girls be given dormitory rooms with sunny windows to make them feel more at home.[5] Thus, Annie Lee and other white southern students followed in the footsteps of Wellesley's first student, Anne Harrison, as they traveled north to the college and were welcomed by the Durants.

Yet even as the Durants tried to make southern students feel comfortable in the North, the most striking fact revealed in southern students' letters is how many did not. For many, the time they spent away from the South only reinforced their southern identity. White southern students perceived themselves to be different from their northern colleagues. No matter how well they performed academically and adjusted to college life, they still believed that significant cultural differences existed between the North and South long after the Civil War. Many parents cultivated this strong sense of southern culture and identity. Some students resented northern stereotypes of southern inferiority and wanted to prove themselves. A few believed that everything northern was different, such as South Carolinian Julia Hammond, who noted that another student staying in her boardinghouse had decorated her room with "Yankee fixings" and described walking fast in the cold as "regular Yankee walk."[6] Ultimately, most southern students overcame these differences—they excelled in school and became popular enough to be elected to class offices. However, they never lost their dedication to the Southland. Their letters reveal how unreconstructed rebels and northerners got along in the decades after the Civil War during the difficult process of reconciliation. Southern students, forced to defend the South, its culture, and its racial beliefs, embraced the Lost Cause, the movement to honor the Confederacy that flourished at the turn of the century, so that they could stand with pride rather than defeat. The northern sojourn helped southern women to develop independence, as was evident in the previous chapter, but it also pushed them to cling to southern tradition. Perceived as exotic by their classmates, southern students were forced to articulate what it meant to be southern in ways that those who never left the South were not. Challenged to consider new gender roles and confronted with different racial mores, some ultimately changed, retaining their loyalty to the region by redefining southern identity around other markers of behavior. They clung to

Lost Cause histories even as they began, in small ways, to rethink their ideas concerning race and gender.

Southerners had been heading north for excitement, education, and economic opportunity for many years. Historian John Hope Franklin argued that the northern tour was like the Grand Tour of Europe, a must-see destination for many elite white southerners. "In the forty years before the Civil War," he wrote, "southerners developed the habit—scarcely short of an addiction—of going north." Although southerners complained about their economic dependence on the more developed North, they also loved the excitement of visiting its cities and learning in its classrooms. Franklin found that southern students could represent as high as one-third of the population of certain preparatory schools and colleges, including Princeton. Despite the warnings of those who opposed sending students where they might be influenced by antislavery ideology, southerners knew that the North offered a superior education.[7]

The odyssey of southerners to the North only grew after the war. Historian Daniel Sutherland estimated that about sixteen thousand southerners moved North between 1860 and 1870, and thousands continued the journey in the decades to follow. Those who left the South after the Civil War for foreign destinations—Europe, Mexico, South America—did so because they despised the idea of living there under northern rule, and they did not want free African Americans for neighbors. Those who ventured north, the "Confederate carpetbaggers," could not avoid either northern rule or free African Americans, but they believed they could find greater financial rewards than in the South. "The lure of Yankeedom radiated most powerfully from bustling, boisterous northern towns and cities," argued Sutherland. "Urban areas monopolized business and professional opportunities, the best schools, and most of the jobs."[8] This did not necessarily mean that Confederate carpetbaggers wanted to leave their beloved South but rather that they believed they had to do so both for their own financial gain as well as to benefit those left behind. "We left our hearts in the South but took our heads to the North," said one migrant.[9] "Exile," explained Sutherland, "has generally increased a southerner's regional identity and self-awareness. Only after pitting themselves against the beliefs, values, and traditions of strangers, strangers who invariably considered them provincial and inferior, did southerners—indeed, most immigrants—come to appreciate the cultural as well as the geographic distance they had traveled."[10] Southern students in the North experienced a similar sense of exile.

In the 1860s and 1870s, while their husbands and fathers sought economic opportunity, the southern women Sutherland studied found each other. They sustained themselves through friendships with other southern women and through networks of benevolent work, aiding those in need back home in the South and women and children in their new communities. Eventually, southern women in New York formed a local division of the United Daughters of the Confederacy that boasted six hundred active members by 1916.[11] These women formed a particularly insular network of southern women who promoted not just southern identity but defended the Confederate cause more vociferously than their husbands. Historians argue that, given men's common experiences as veterans of the war and their desire to build and/or resume economic relationships after the war, men had an easier time reconciling. Southern women could more easily than southern men continue to snub Yankees because they were unconcerned with political expediency. Southern women were thus considered holdouts, the rebels who refused to be reconstructed. Investing Confederate devotion in women deemphasized its power by relegating such behavior to the politically impotent and stereotypically emotionally driven women. Women, even those who had lost their faith in the cause and advocated army desertions in response to the hardships suffered on the home front, at the end of the war reaffirmed their Confederate loyalty. They blamed Yankees for their difficulties, especially if they had experienced Sherman's march. Southern women's loyalty to the Confederate cause may have been higher after the war than during it because, unlike the men, they were unable to draw on the camaraderie of veterans who, though once foes, now considered themselves equals.[12] However well settled or reconciled they became, southern men and women remained true to the South in their identity and their affection.[13]

For many students, the common college experience was not enough to overcome regional differences.[14] Thus, female students who traveled north had a particular duty to defend the South to Yankees. While a few southern students downplayed their regional identity, most self-consciously thought of themselves as southerners, if not unreconstructed rebels. Growing up listening to stories of their parents' experiences during the war, students had strong ties to the Confederacy and took particular pride in defending both the Confederacy as well as southern culture more generally. As Fred Hobson argued in *Tell about the South*, southerners have had a "rage to explain" their differences from the rest of the nation. While for some, slavery and overt racism was a burden, a source of guilt and shame, for others the southern past was a noble civilization they preferred to celebrate. Southern students, too, as representatives of their region, shared that rage to explain.[15] While their presence in the North and their relations with northerners may have enabled some to work for reconciliation between the sections, an increasingly popular notion, they did so on their own terms.

While at Bryn Mawr in the early 1900s, Kentuckian Margaret Preston commented frequently on the strangeness of northerners and their ways. Margaret believed northerners were cold and correct in comparison to friendly and hospitable southerners, and her years at school only reinforced these images. When she visited a college friend's home, she described the house as plain, the girl's parents as nice but plain, and a card party with boys in attendance as awkward. After a visit to another friend whose family, she complained, never laughed, Margaret concluded, "Northerners don't seem to know how to make a show as we do."[16] Ten years later she still felt the same way. On a visit to the North she wrote her future husband, "The Lord has certainly been good to me to cast my lot in the South. I wouldn't live up here for anything. These Northerners all seem so cold and unaffectionate and worse than either, the men seem so very unchivalric in their attitude to women."[17] Neither a college education nor embrace of the woman suffrage movement could induce Margaret to give up her expectation of chivalry. To Margaret, the contrasting images were not just stereotypes but lived truths. Northerners and southerners were just different people. She once asked her mother to send her the proper clothing for an occasion to be spent with a northern family, commenting, "For the people up here think Southerners queer anyway, and really we are different."[18] That sense of difference was part of what had made her so intensely homesick for her family and southern society. Margaret experienced being the "other" for the first time at Bryn Mawr, a sense of displacement that acutely limited her ability to fit in. She and other southern students constantly compared their ideas and culture to that of the North, with the South always coming out on top.[19]

Margaret's disorientation, like that of other students in this book, had not changed much since the antebellum era. In 1854 Paul H. Hayne wrote that he longed to return home to the South because in the North "I am *not at home*. I feel as an alien, and sojourner in the land." In the 1860s and early 1870s Confederate carpetbaggers expressed a similar sense of exile. "I feel most infernally out of place in this Yankee country," wrote one in 1868, "and am most anxious to return to my home and people." Like Margaret, another wrote, "The people are alien to me, their ways are not my ways nor their thoughts my thoughts."[20] Sectionalism had not ceased in the decades that had passed since the war.

Southerners brought with them an identity forged in the southern past. Virginian Annie Elizabeth Lee was particularly distressed by the history of the South taught in the North. She considered presenting a history book with a more southern point of view to the college library to teach the "truth" to her northern colleagues.[21] Such a donation would have echoed the work of the United Daughters of the Confederacy and southern women's clubs, which promoted the Lost Cause telling of southern history through regulating books in schools, library donations, essay contests, and public monuments to the Confederacy.[22] Through the Lost Cause, southerners attempted to assuage defeat in the Civil War through honoring Confederate soldiers and the ideals for which they fought. As the movement grew, adherents celebrated a Lost Cause version of southern history that proclaimed slavery just and slaves happy. Despite attempts by northern students to sway southerners' views on the war and slavery, rebel girls stuck to the Lost Cause myths. Well before the Civil War such sectional rivalry was already evident. In 1852 Eleanor Crawford signed Eliza Austin's class album at Mount Holyoke, "Ell from the 'Old Dominion' has not yet been convinced that slavery is a sin!"[23]

North Carolinian Connie Guion was also raised on the Lost Cause, recalling not only that her father taught her that "damn Yankee is one word" but that her grade school reinforced his lessons with its celebration of southern songs and holidays.[24] Connie was the only student from North Carolina at Wellesley during her tenure in the 1890s, although she was particularly friendly with Carrie Nelson of Warrenton, Virginia, the niece of Jenny Nelson, who had taught at Wellesley when it opened. Every Sunday Carrie, a member of an aristocratic southern family who had fallen on difficult economic times after the war, took Connie to see Pauline Durant, the wife of the college founder. Connie wrote to her mother, "Mrs. Durant is a Southerner and I'm crazy about her." When Carrie graduated, Connie was awarded the Durant scholarship.[25] Margaret Mitchell had the same loyal devotion to the South. Her roommate later recalled,

> When topics took more serious turns, you could pretty safely depend that Peggy would get them around somehow to the Civil War, for her indignation over Sherman's March to the Sea was just as much a part of her as her [flashing] eyes or her joyful laugh. She would sling you off a well-rounded tabloid description of the Second Battle of Bull Run with the same eager sparkle that another girl might tell you about last night's bridge hand. . . . Whenever she got mad enough at her roommate to call me a "Damn Yankee," I knew our home life was threatened![26]

Annie Lee, Connie Guion, and Margaret Mitchell reflected well the reputation southern women had developed for their intense support of the Confederacy and refusal to forgive the North or abandon their Confederate nationalism. The girls believed it was their legitimate role to continue to support the Confederacy, evident in their unabashed enthusiasm for all things southern. They met and exceeded any northern stereotypes of their devotion to the cause. They did so in defense of their families' service to the Confederacy. The fathers, grandfathers, and uncles of these women were almost without exception Confederate veterans (when their veteran status could be determined). Gertrude Weil, Sophonisba Breckinridge, Margaret Preston, Emma Garrett Boyd Morris, Helen Keller, Louisa and Mary Poppenheim, Agnes Raoul, Emelyn Hartridge, Julia Hammond, Connie Guion, Josie Simrall, Sue Hall, and Annie Lee all had relatives who served the Confederacy. Only Linda Neville had divided loyalties—her father was sympathetic to the Union, while her mother's family supported the Confederacy. While undoubtedly some southern students at northern colleges, especially those from states like Kentucky and Tennessee, had family members who supported the Union, it does not appear from this study that those southern women predominated the southern population at northern women's colleges.[27]

Lost Cause southern identity was infused with pride as well as the bitterness of defeat. Southerners honored the Confederate cause not only to assuage their defeat in the Civil War but also to combat the national stereotype of southern poverty and backwardness so prevalent at the turn of the century. Southern social welfare reformers wanted to improve living conditions in the South for many reasons, not the least of which was to honor the Lost Cause and prove the superiority of southern civilization. Many students also wanted to prove themselves against misconceptions that demeaned their intellectual capability. Both southerners and northerners had strong images of each other. According to Mary Gude, an Atlantan attending Radcliffe, "The New England girls never get over wondering at what they consider our queer ways. You feel as if you were being studied all the time, and when you would say the most ordinary things they would suddenly become convulsed with laughter at a phrase or an expression." Mary Gude found that the stereotype of southern girls was that they were attractive but "are engaged to five or six men, and that they don't do anything but frivol away their time."[28] Southern students who were serious about their academic career had to prove that they were capable of intellectual achievement and fight the image of the southern belle, whose sole ambition was to attract a husband. Virginian Vassar graduate Orie Latham Hatcher feared that the generalization of southern women as lacking "adequate mental discipline, sense of order and restraint, dispassionateness of judgment, and in general a steady, quiet, impersonal efficiency" was true of all southern women—except those with substantial contact with the North. She blamed southern men for women's deficiencies.[29]

Brilliant Kentuckian Sophonisba Breckinridge was also subject to the misperceptions of others at Wellesley in the 1880s. A classmate from Ann Arbor insulted her, probably implying that southern women either were less capable or did not work as hard as their northern counterparts. While both of these were wildly inaccurate descriptions of the brilliant and intense Sophonisba, the comment rankled her. She complained to her father, who wrote her back at length. He acknowledged that her classmate's comments about southerners reflected commonly held ideas in the North, which he claimed "were . . . in part the result of provincial ignorance . . . but like all prejudices it also has a foundation in truth." The truth encapsulated in the stereotype was that "the culture of the South has always tended to elegance of manners, grace of conversation, polish of the lighter accomplishments; and our ladies as a rule have not sought a severer training." William Breckenridge reasoned that this was because before the war women had not worked for wages but rather ran the home and entertained guests and visitors. He appreciated the qualities such a vocation developed in them ("they were—pure, chaste, brave, attractive, elegant") and thought that the only characteristics they lacked were those needed by women who lived in a "severer climate, the harder life and a different society." But, he suggested, "in all essentials, the true ladies are alike everywhere"—it was only subtle differences that separated them. Rather than disavowing the image, William Breckinridge attributed it to the past, acknowledging that before the war southern women had been less educated and more charming. The differences between regions, however, he believed were incidental and irrelevant to determining whether one was a true lady. Sophonisba's father's advice was to treat the incident with good humor.[30]

B. Frank Hall was more direct and less politic in his advice to his daughter Jessie, at Wellesley nearly twenty years after Sophonisba. He was quite proud of her achievements and assured her that her professors would recognize her talent. Harking back to the Civil War, Frank Hall asserted, "These Northern Yankees are just getting a few more lessons about the make up of our Southern Yankees. In the war we didn't mind matching up 1 against 2. They have been claiming superiority in intellect and mental vigor; but I think some of our people can match—if not outclass them on their own grounds."[31] For Frank Hall, southern students had to battle the belle image if only to prove to Yankees that southerners were equally capable and intelligent despite their loss in the Civil War. He almost seemed to forget that the South lost the war in his enthusiasm for southern ability. Students played an important role in aiding reconciliation. They were ambassadors from South to North in the immediate postwar period and the only southerners that many northerners knew.

The typical image of the southern belle also marked her as lazy. While at nursing school in Baltimore, Julia's sister Katharine Hammond received advice from a Mrs. Reid, who told her she had to do well because she was a southern woman. Mrs. Reid suggested that it was difficult for any woman to work professionally but that southern women had it even harder. Katharine complained that Mrs. Reid blamed southern women themselves, claiming that their difficulties came from their "indolent Southern nature."[32] Even school officials believed the clichés. When Sophonisba Breckinridge attended Wellesley students had to do domestic chores. Sophonisba claimed that as "I had manners and as I was

Southern and Southern girls were supposed to be lazy, I was a show student for inquiring parents skeptical about the domestic work required of all students." Apparently, Sophonisba was meant to reassure parents that even a southerner who was used to servants at home could handle the domestic work requirement.

Julia Hammond was also insulted, in her case by what she perceived to be the snobbery of northerners. While at Radcliffe she complained, "These people are so wonderful to me in their perfectly quite unapproachable conceit. They think if only a little of Massachusetts could be carried South every thing would be all right."[33] Given that the Civil War had ended only sixteen years earlier, some tension between northern and southern students is not unexpected.

Southern students had to take care and not become like the enemy. Sue Hall captured this undercurrent of unease when she told her mother that she hoped her aunt "won't have to disown me for too much of a Yankee."[34] Like Annie Lee, she worried that if she changed too much while in the North she would no longer be accepted when she returned home.

Some students actively defended and explained southern culture, especially southern ideas of womanhood. When a teacher encouraged Mary Haskell of Columbia, South Carolina, to write an article for the *Wellesley Magazine*, she welcomed the opportunity "so that I might do something for the South, by collecting such materials of history, customs, localities, ideas as might be available someday." The work was well worth the effort. "I felt better," she explained, "and nobler, willing and longing to so something for *my* people, the South." Mary Haskell was also glad that her friend Louise was at Harvard Annex, where they could each specialize in different subject areas, both "for the sake of our Southern people." Thus, Mary was able to conceive of her education as something not just for herself or indeed her hometown but in fact for her entire region.[35] This understanding that they were representatives of their region, along with a sense of duty to the South, would later inform southern women's social activism when they returned home.[36]

Many parents carefully nurtured their children's southern identity. They risked sending them to college in the North, knowing that, due to career choice or marriage, their daughters might not return to the South.[37] Thus, it was essential that they continue to nurture the Lost Cause in their children while at college just as they had done when the girls were growing up in the South. At Vassar in the 1880s, not only were Mary and Louisa Poppenheim a thousand miles from home in Charleston, but they were in the North, a foreign country of sorts. Their mother, Mary Elinor Poppenheim, fostered in them pride in the South, which enabled them to strengthen their identity as southerners rather than lose it while away from home. For example, she explained to them her feelings of loyalty to Jefferson Davis, who was making a public appearance in Savannah. "We may be stripped of all possessions," she wrote, "but the Southern heart and head remain true still, and that they have not taken; nor *cannot* take."[38] Mary Elinor also shipped palmetto trees, the state tree of South Carolina, to Vassar so that Mary could graduate under their shadow. Mary Elinor wrote to the girls that she was "real proud of the South and of S.C.," a pride that she attributed to the poverty that those of her generation experienced during the Civil War.[39]

Mary Elinor may have been comforted to know that the assistant lady principal at Vassar College was Mrs. Nancy Bostick DeSaussure, a fellow Charlestonian. DeSaussure had been hired after the death of her husband due to her connections with Miss Morse, a former family tutor who had since become an administrator at Vassar. DeSaussure shared Mary Elinor Poppenheim's desire to pass southern pride and Confederate tradition to her children. She wrote a book about her days in the antebellum South that she specifically directed to her granddaughter as a way to teach her her own benevolent view of slavery and the horrors of Reconstruction. The book describes the kindness of the white DeSaussure family to their slaves and compares the well-being of slaves on plantations to the lack of civilization exhibited by blacks on their own in Africa.[40]

Mary Poppenheim, for her part, took her mother's feelings to heart. She advised her mother to read the latest edition of the *Century Magazine* because it had many articles on the Civil War. "One article is on Mrs. Stowes 'Uncle Tom' and one on Sherman's march to Savannah," she wrote. Mary also preferred the *Atlantic Monthly*, which she noted had featured an article on southern colleges, and "it always has some thing about the South and is not a bit partial to the North."[41] The *Century Magazine*, the *Atlantic Monthly*, and other popular magazines of the time commonly printed articles that romanticized the South and portrayed a benevolent plantation system and cavalier southern gentlemen, making the Lost Cause version of history more and more popularly accepted by northerners as well. Mary had a reputation with her classmates for her love for the South. Her class prophecy, written in 1888, noted, "She had never 'like a cat,' become attached to College, and her return to her 'father' and the Sunny South with which she was identified in our minds, had removed the only things about which she complained: first, that she must be away from home at all, and second, if she must be away, to be North."[42] Mary Elinor was obviously successful at fostering the girls' southern heritage despite the distance, for Mary later became the national president of the United Daughters of the Confederacy (UDC).[43] She coedited a collection of reminiscences of the war, including her mother's stories of her leadership of a soldiers' aid society and how the family sought refuge during Sherman's march through South Carolina. As president of the UDC, Mary had the opportunity to address the New York division, which she described as being "on the firing line." Perhaps recalling her own experiences in the North, she told members that southerners especially appreciated their work: "We have a much easier time, I know, to get members and to do our work than you have up here." She expressed her gratitude to those southern women who supported the UDC "where it is so much needed."[44]

Other parents also cultivated strong sectional feelings. Jessie Hall's parents sent her clippings on Southern Memorial Day and Civil War history that were imbued with Lost Cause sentiment while she was at Walnut Hill School in Massachusetts preparing for Wellesley. They also sent support and suggestions for the Southern Club at Wellesley.[45]

Sectional feeling was particularly evident during national political debates and elections. Even before the Civil War students took strong sides in sectional debates. At Mount Holyoke Ann Edwards, class of 1859, avoided any discussion of slavery with her southern roommate—they wrote compositions for and against the Fugitive Slave Acts side by side in silence. However, in 1854, after the passage of the Kansas-Nebraska Act, which allowed the possibility of slavery in territory formerly guaranteed to be free, northern Mount Holyoke students were in mourning. They tied black badges on doorknobs, closed the blinds, and hung mourning draperies. Ann's southern roommate tore hers off the door. The southern girls also did not attend a faculty-student assembly. Southern attendance at Holyoke fell off during the war and Reconstruction and then rose again in the 1880s.[46] Well after the war, however, students and their parents still put regional identity first when it came to national politics. Like most mothers, Issa Breckinridge rarely commented on politics. Yet she told Sophonisba that she was happy that her children would live under Democratic and southern rule "after years of domination and humiliation" following the election of 1884.[47]

Because of the real and/or perceived differences between southern and northern students, southern students had formal and informal networks. They sought each other out, befriended one another, and helped each other through the rough times. One Mount Holyoke student remembered that "Alice Sparks and I were the two Southern girls of '88 . . . , a tie that bound us from the beginning."[48] Even though they were from different states, it was their southern regional identity that took precedence. Agnes Caldwell also described herself and Louise Eginton as the southerners at Wellesley who procured southern food and, ever the proper southern hostesses, shared it with friends.[49] Knowing that there would be southern students at Wellesley when she arrived made Sue Hall more comfortable. While still preparing at the Walnut Hill School, Sue Hall spent a day with two Wellesley students, one of whom, she excitedly told her mother, was a southerner. She also was part of the group of southern students in the 1890s (all twenty-six on campus) who were invited to the Wellesley president's home, because Julia Irvine's "people" were from eastern North Carolina.[50] Annie Lee was friends with the southern girls because she complained that "Yankee" girls had no manners, adding, "Some of them I like very much but the majority I almost hate."[51]

At Wellesley differences among southerners seemed to disappear, and they even sometimes found that they had connections to each other. Sue Hall met a southern Wellesley student who knew Sue's sister-in-law Margaret. Sue also asked her mother if she knew Jessie Dagan of Charleston. "We had a nice 'southern' chat to-day which was refreshing to us both," Sue reported after talking with Jessie. That fall after dinner with Jessie Sue was again ecstatic. "Well we had a regular feast,—she knows so many N.C. girls and has lived in Charleston a little while, and is a true Southerner. We talked and talked."[52] It is striking just how important and comforting it was to a student from North Carolina and a student from South Carolina to meet and talk "southern" with each other. It highlights how foreign the North must have felt to these students and how essential a link to the South, and therefore to home, was. Despite the common experience of college, southern students still felt intensely different from northern students.

Sophonisba Breckinridge made a particular effort to meet all the Kentucky girls, in part because her father had encouraged her to remain loyal to friends from home. He explained that he treasured his Kentucky friends with whom he had bonded at school and served in the war. He feared that Sophonisba would lose that opportunity by going to school out of state.[53] Friends made at college while living together and sharing similar experiences during a time of intense growth had the potential to be some of the closest and most long-standing friends one made. Because students at the Seven Sister colleges came from around the country, it would be difficult to remain in touch after graduation. *Godey's Lady's Book* editor Sara Josepha Hale cautioned against sending students to a different region for this reason. She argued that the differences in customs would be too great, and it was not wise for a student to make friends she would later lose touch with.[54] Although southern students sometimes stayed in the North and otherwise kept up long-distance friendships for years, forming relationships with their fellow southerners while at college still gave them an extra sense of comfort. The Poppenheim sisters therefore made a special effort to seek an introduction to fellow South Carolinian Varina Davis Brown. Students also realized that their parents would be reassured to know their daughters had the company of other southern young women. Agnes Raoul reported to her parents in Atlanta when she met fellow Atlantans Barbara Adair and Daisy Stewart and a girl from Savannah at Vassar.[55] Parents who feared that their daughters might be too influenced by Yankee ways encouraged and were glad to hear about the southern network.

Agnes Raoul also joined the "much talked about Southern club" on the same day on which she told her mother that school was going better for her and she felt less homesick.[56] While the timing may have been a coincidence, it is likely that the more formal network of Southern Clubs assuaged homesickness for many southern students. While teaching at Vassar, Lilian Wyckoff Johnson organized one of the first college Southern Clubs with students Ida and Christie Poppenheim (the younger sisters of Mary and Louisa Poppenheim). Ida served as first president; alumnae Mary and Louisa were associate members; and Thomas Nelson Page, the well-known southern writer, was an honorary member. Johnson then helped to organize other clubs at Smith, Holyoke, Barnard, and Cornell.

The Southern Clubs primarily offered an organized opportunity for southern students to locate each other and socialize without having to rely on chance meetings. The club provided a place where southerners were free to be themselves without the judgment of northerners; they established a formal community among the southern exiles.[57] Occasionally, Southern Clubs did more than build community through socializing. They cultivated southern heritage by working on projects, such as purchasing books for the library. Johnson also appealed to several Southern Clubs to support her plan for a southern women's college that would rank with the best northern schools. Southern Clubs inspired the formation of the Southern Association of College Women when Johnson and others planned this intercollegiate union of female southern college graduates in 1903.[58] College yearbooks list the Southern Club as one of the extracurricular campus groups and often feature drawings of stereotypical negative images of African Americans.

Sue Hall's letters provide an intimate view of the Southern Club of Wellesley, begun in 1900. At the time of its founding, the Southern Club was the only regional club at Wellesley. Sue told her parents that a senior from Texas was the motivating force behind the club and that they were planning the club's colors, badges, rules, and agenda. She asked for suggestions for a badge, discussing a particular badge from the Confederacy featuring a stork feeding her children, and she asked who would have worn it. The club adopted her parents' suggestion of a cotton boll for an emblem. Sue also learned that the colors of the Confederacy were red and white and its flower was the red rose—new information for her. A month later she wrote, "You will be interested to know that our Southern Club is materializing. Plans have been accepted by the Academic Council (powers that be) without a murmur." She did not specify why southern students had worried that their plans would not be accepted—perhaps they feared being accused of resisting Reconstruction or more simply not being taken seriously. This was the case at Barnard, where the day after students formed the Southern Club, New Yorkers formed the Greater New York Club to promote interest in New York among Barnard students and in Barnard among New Yorkers. In its constitution it mocked the Southern Club, noting that Greater New York Club associate members did not have to be New York natives but had to show "Greater New York spirit" by "being fully competent to surpass in argument any member of the Southern Club." This yearbook shows that although many students had pride in their regions, southerners seem to have been the most intent on nurturing their unique identity.[59] While they took their regional identity seriously, other students did not.

Sue Hall noted that there was infighting among the southern students at Wellesley concerning the club's admission requirements, which were southern birth, parentage, and residence. Apparently, those of southern ancestry and parentage but who lived in the North wanted to join. Sue asked her parents' help in publicizing the club by having a notice printed in a periodical called the *Messenger*. They supported the club by sending southern food, which everyone enjoyed.[60] Sue's younger sister Jessie also joined the club when she arrived at Wellesley, and Sue sent her her pin.[61] As with Southern Clubs at other schools, Thomas Nelson Page accepted the Wellesley Southern Club's invitation to become an honorary member.

While the club had colors, a badge, and other rules, its essential function was to promote friendship among the southern students and to nurture their sense of southern identity. In many ways the club took on some of the same functions as a chapter of the UDC: members promoted Confederate history, honored Confederate heroes, and fostered fellowship among Lost Cause devotees. The Wellesley Southern Club celebrated Robert E. Lee's birthday and decided to donate a biography of Lee to the college library. The biography was undoubtedly meant to teach northern students the correct or true history of the Confederate side of the war.[62] When Connie Guion arrived at Wellesley, she promptly joined the Southern Club, which she described as "a small, enthusiastic group devoted to being proud you were a Southerner." According to her, the students sang "Dixie," eulogized Robert E. Lee, and ate southern food.[63]

At Vassar the club also donated books on southern history to the college library. Southern Club president Emma Garrett Boyd Morris directed her donation to history professor Lucy Salmon, who told Emma, "I have wished to use the money as wisely as possible and in such a way that the members of the Southern Club would share equally with the Department of History in the enjoyment of the books." Salmon ordered a book by John Fiske on Virginia and Mrs. Goodwin's *A Colonial Cavalier*, which the library put on restricted circulation for members of the Southern Club.[64]

Gertrude Weil's papers include a circular from the Smith College Southern Club touting its scholarship for southern students. That club was founded "to promote friendship and good feeling among its members at the College, and to make Smith College and its interests known in the South."[65] The Smith 1907 yearbook shows that the club had thirteen members, including those identified as from Tacoma, Washington, and Philadelphia.[66] Thus, at Smith entrance requirements for the club were less strict than those at Wellesley, allowing southern transplants to retain their southern identification.

The Southern Club had long-lasting meaning for students at Smith. In 1916 twenty graduates from around the South (eight in person and twelve by telegram) founded a Smith College Southern Club, with officers from the classes of 1896, 1897, 1907, and 1913. Such a show of sectional identity years after graduation is surprising. Perhaps these graduates felt that the Smith Alumnae Association excluded them and that they wanted to hold alumnae meetings closer to home. They sent a representative to the meeting of the Alumnae Council (whether this was just a way to send greetings or they wanted to make more of a statement is not known).[67] In 1935 southern students at Smith revived the old Southern Club, which they described as having flourished before World War I. The club's purpose was social, "to get the members of the faculty and the students who came from south of Mason and Dixon's line better acquainted, and to keep alive among the members of the club, while living in the North, the traditions and customs which have made the South so distinctive a section of our country and have contributed so greatly to our national culture." A professor from the Department of History, Mr. Hildt, and students from Savannah, Birmingham, and Chapel Hill decided to organize and find out if there was enough support among the other students and faculty. The club, like the original, did not require dues and planned little more than one or two dinners a year for students and faculty to meet and socialize.[68]

Southern students who joined the Southern Club and otherwise self-consciously identified themselves as southern developed reputations based on their sense of place. Class prophecies for southern students often mentioned their sectional identity. Like Mary Poppenheim, who "like a cat" had never become attached to the North, Lucy Prichard was designated "an extreme Southerner [who] hated cold weather" and in her prophecy would travel to the North Pole to reform Eskimos.[69]

Despite the fact that Sophonisba Breckinridge made Chicago her permanent home soon after enrolling at the University of Chicago, her friends still considered her a southerner. May Cook, a Wellesley classmate from Illinois who suggested that Sophonisba go to the University of Chicago, remembered Sophonisba's southern accent, her charm, her manners, and her deep attachments to her kin, noting that she paid for her nieces' and nephews' education. Nationally known reformer Jane Addams referred the letters she received from southerners to Sophonisba for her advice. Sophonisba continued to inspire other southern women while in Chicago. Elizabeth McCrackin, a southern woman influenced by Sophonisba while they were at the University of Chicago, explained that although she was living in New York and Boston, "I am above all, a Southerner forever at heart; and as one of my girls would say, you have made a way." Sophonisba never lost her southern accent, and she returned frequently to Kentucky. Attached by her love for the state as well as for her brother, Sophonisba often spoke in Kentucky, wrote for her brother's newspaper, and had some financial investments in the state. She did not seek to cut herself off from her southern identity.[70]

Alumnae records show a continued loyalty to the South on the part of many women. They directly identified themselves as southern both while at school and afterward—their sojourn to the North only strengthened their feelings for the region. May Jackson claimed to be a direct descendant of Stonewall Jackson on her alumnae questionnaire for Mount Holyoke. Anne Audubon Wetzel returned home to Tennessee, and even though she moved around, she always returned to Tennessee and wrote about her experiences in the mountains of Appalachia.[71] Helen Keller, a Radcliffe alumna, remained a southerner at heart, although she never returned to Tuscumbia, Alabama. She proudly noted her father's and grandfather's Confederate service and her grandmother's relationship to Robert E. Lee in her 1903 autobiography, *The Story of My Life*. In 1929 she spoke to the Alabamians in New York meeting as a "representative of the South." Interestingly, because Keller developed relatively progressive views on issues such as child labor and race (e.g., donating money to the NAACP), her family and friends from home blamed—probably accurately—her ideas on northern influences.[72]

Many other women developed careers—paid and unpaid—that demonstrate their continuing southern sense of place. Most commonly, they joined the flood of southern writers publishing fiction and nonfiction that supported the Lost Cause.[73] The Vassar college prophecy for Varina Davis Brown, named after the wife of Jefferson Davis, claimed that she would organize a system of schools in the South.[74] Instead, after a year of teaching at Anderson Female College, she turned to history and in 1931 published *A Colonel at Gettysburg and Spotsylvania*, a history of her father's role as colonel of the Fourteenth South Carolina Regiment, which he led into Gettysburg.[75] Barbara Tunnell of Smith College wrote articles, poems, and stories on southern architecture and gardens as well as regional fiction. In 1949 she published *Southbound*, the story of a blonde white southern woman who was the daughter of a black woman and a white man. While at Smith, which she described as meaning so much to her, she was already writing about southern homes and gardens for magazine readers in love with the "glamour of the old South." Frances Jewell McVey, a Vassar alumna and former dean of women at the University of Kentucky, wrote articles on southern cooking and culture for magazines and newspapers, including the *New York Times*. Although *Atlantic Monthly* editor and writer Florence Converse remained in Massachusetts, living with Wellesley professor Vida Scudder, she did not forget her native New Orleans and in fact set her first novel there. *Diana Victrix* features two northern, college-educated women who travel to New Orleans for rest.[76] Mildred Thompson, the Atlanta-born Vassar graduate who became dean of Vassar, was a historian who studied the South and her native Georgia. Her books included *Reconstruction in Georgia* (1915), *Carpet-baggers in the United States Senate* (1920), and *The Freedman's Bureau in Georgia* (1921).[77] After twenty-five years as dean of Vassar she retired and returned home to Atlanta, where she taught briefly at the University of Georgia and worked to improve education for southern women. One of her former students and colleagues in the history department at Vassar recalled that Thompson was secure in her identity as a Georgian, which "gave her a sense of identity and belonging which was very real and tangible to her" and the confidence to represent the nation in work for the United Nations.[78] As is discussed in chapter 2, many southern graduates expressed their loyalty to the South by returning home specifically to improve southern educational opportunities, especially for girls.

Grace Richmond was one of the few southerners whose college letters show she was reluctant to identify herself as a southerner. Although she grew up in Tennessee, neither her mother's nor her father's family was originally from the South. Theodore and Harriett Burgett Richmond moved from Indiana to Athens, Tennessee, in 1865 before settling in Chattanooga in 1870. Grace entered Vassar College in the fall of 1881 along with another student from Chattanooga, Alice Watkins. When Grace first encountered Mrs. Nancy Bostick DeSaussure, the assistant lady principal and author of *Old Plantation Days*, Grace reported to her parents that she and Anna B. Wheeler, her roommate, forgot that DeSaussure came from Charleston. DeSaussure asked if they were northern or southern (perhaps Grace's accent gave her away). Grace wrote, "We assured her in rather stronger terms than we would have used if we had remembered her that we were northerners."[79] Grace also complained that DeSaussure, her daughter Nannie, who was an art student at Vassar, and Sara Cecil, a student from Danville, Kentucky, "rave about the South until one would think it a perfect paradise." Despite her lack of southern pride, Grace still felt at home with her fellow Tennesseans.

She roomed with Alice and made a point to socialize with other students from Tennessee.[80] M. Carey Thomas, the president of Bryn Mawr, also did not seem to identify herself as a southerner. She grew up in a southern city, Baltimore, but socialized exclusively within the Society of Friends there. Her biographer argues that her journal gave little indication of southern distinctiveness.[81]

White southern students became acutely aware of their southernness when race issues surfaced. Like antebellum southerners who defended slavery when they traveled north, these women in the 1870s through the early 1900s defended southern racial mores.[82] They left home at a time when race relations in the South became more violent with the dramatic rise of lynching in that region and when white Democrats disenfranchised African Americans and instituted Jim Crow segregation laws to formally divide blacks from whites. Southern students encountered a variety of attitudes toward African Americans from their northern classmates, from equally racist to quite liberal. Their letters reveal that southern students were not monolithically against the presence of black students at their schools, despite the claims of college presidents who refused to admit African Americans so as not to antagonize southern white students. The most racist white southerners probably never went north to school because they knew that some schools were integrated, or they chose Vassar, which was not, thus perhaps helping to account for its high numbers of southern students. Some students did refuse to eat with or otherwise interact with black students. Yet, particularly by the 1910s, others were more curious than offended by the presence of black students, and some later credited their experiences in the North with challenging their racist beliefs and eventually leading them into the civil rights movement. The college experience was particularly significant because southern autobiographies reveal that most white southerners did not begin to understand the significance of race until their adolescence. It was at that point that they observed the difference that race made in economics and often began to assert their white privilege through taunting or demeaning blacks, often despite warnings from well-to-do white parents to treat blacks well.[83]

In the 1870s most southern white students were not yet ready to begin to think differently about race. Virginian Annie Lee had several encounters at Wellesley with teachers and others over their racial mores. Her racist attitude rubbed the help in the dining room the wrong way, with one black cook spilling soup on her. When one of her friends asked why she referred to him as "the cook" and not "Mr. B.," she did not reply. Later she told her brother, "That nigger and I are forever quarreling." Annie then asked for another cook to serve her and noted that this one, although African American too, was polite because he was a southerner.[84] Annie was also shocked by the actions of her white northern teachers.

Miss Gage went to a "colored dress ball" given by the waiters at a Boston hotel and then reported that not only was there no "fearful smell" in the crowd
of black men but that she almost fell in love with a handsome mulatto man.
Annie responded, "What do you think of that? . . . I do think these Yankee[s]
will kill me yet! Now wasn't that silly in Miss Gage—or rather disgusting."[85]
Her reaction to Gage's relatively liberal racial views was one of many instances
in which northerners who did not share the same racial attitudes challenged
southern students.

Tennessean Maria Daviess was similarly taken aback by race relations at
Wellesley in the 1890s. Maria complained that after a black woman gave a speech
on Negro education, the woman ate with the Wellesley president at her table. Maria recalled that she froze, unable to take her place, when the president
quickly saved her by calling for a "Yankee" to take her place at the table. Yet
Maria served the woman coffee, explaining that she could serve her but not
eat with her because of her belief in the strict inequality of social relations between the races.[86] In her autobiography Maria referred to herself as an "unreconstructed" southerner.

Some white students refused to eat with blacks or take classes with them, and
they subjected blacks to slights—both subtle and blatant—for several decades.
A 1928 African American graduate of Wellesley, Jane Bolin Offut, recalled that
the school rule was that each table had to be filled before students could start
sitting at a different table. When she sat down to eat in the dining hall, southern
white students would stand outside and wait until her table was filled and then
sit elsewhere. She and Clarissa Scott Delaney, Wellesley class of 1923, were not
chosen for senior societies, although they were eligible. Clarissa Scott Delaney
was the daughter of Emmett J. and Eleanora Scott. Her father was secretary to
Booker T. Washington, and she followed Portia Washington to Massachusetts,
first to Bradford Academy and then to Wellesley. Clarissa's classmates remembered that she endured many slights from both northerners and southerners
because, as one northern student said, "it was just not done to fraternize with
Negroes!" Southern white students also refused to use the same bathtub as
Katherine Hamilton, another black student. Clarissa bore the insults because
she wanted to obtain the best education possible and had an underlying desire
to uplift her race.[87]

While Annie Lee and Maria Daviess reacted with horror to what they perceived as northern violations of the racial codes they had grown up with, many
students were called upon to explain that code for the first time. Classmates
sometimes asked southern students for their opinion on racial matters, including disenfranchisement and domestic servants. At least one fellow student
viewed Sue Hall as knowledgeable about the debate over disenfranchisement

because of her southern background. She consulted Sue for a paper on whether there should be "an educational qualification in the South" for voting privileges. Sue decided to give the student an article written by a Mr. Mannington but noted that she did not know of any articles written specifically to address the question. "Isn't that what the white people approve," she then asked her mother about the educational qualification, "rather than disenfranchisement? I find that Mass. has none, and this was quite a surprise." Her father sent some information in reply, but Sue's letters do not reveal his viewpoint.[88] Her comments are intriguing. She seems to have had a naive understanding of white oppression of African Americans. She understood that many southern whites discussed educational qualification rather than outright disenfranchisement, but did she understand that this was effectively the same thing? And if she did, then why was she surprised to find that Massachusetts did not have such a qualification?

Southerners were often eager to give their opinion on racial matters, a point underscored by the many articles about race written by southerners and published in northern magazines at the time. On occasion, however, even when they had little to say, northerners sometimes still considered southerners to be expert witnesses. When Sue went to visit her friend Clara King in New Jersey over a break, she attended a literary society meeting where there was a discussion of the "Negro Question in the South. We had [a] long and tiresome (to me) discussion, in which I was of course interested, but took small part. However, the next day comes out a short report of the meeting in both the local papers, stating that I had given the Southern point of view in the discussion!"[89] Again, Hall's comments are tantalizing. Why was the discussion tiresome to her? Was she simply fatigued from her journey? Was she offended by the northern interpretation, or did she find the question so obvious as not to require such a long discussion? Whatever her views, they were positioned as the southern opinion.

Although letters from college generally contained few comments about race, references to domestic servants indicate racial attitudes. As they did with other topics related to race, southerners considered themselves experts on how to deal with black servants. Moreover, their image of African Americans as loyal but often incapable servants and never social equals highlights the at best paternalistic attitude displayed toward individual blacks. Josephine Simrall noted that she heard a talk on the domestic problem, given in part from the point of view of the servant, which she found food for thought for when she would be in charge of a home. An article suggesting a "cooperative" plan for servants struck her as good in theory but as impractical, "especially with the negroes." Like Mary Elinor Poppenheim, who complained about the poor work of a house servant but commented, "She is a negro and that covers all," Josie understood that there were often difficulties between servants and mistresses, and she wanted to avoid them. However, although the details of the cooperative plan are not apparent, the mere use of the word "cooperative" hints that it probably struck a nerve with Simrall as being too suggestive of equality.[90]

Gertrude Weil's views on race are also contradictory. Although she would later help lead the North Carolina Commission on Interracial Cooperation, as a student at Smith in the late 1890s she saw no reason to challenge the black mammy image, which presented African American women as happy taking care of white children, with little concern for their own families or for the possibility of moving beyond service to a white family. Gertrude wrote home asking for a feather for a mammy costume and was thrilled to hear famed southern author George Washington Cable read stories on mammy and the war. In fact, she did not hesitate to take the part of a black woman in a play; she played a servant, "nigger Chloe." Notably, northerners made up the audiences for these performances and readings, an indication of how successful Lost Cause adherents were in promoting their point of view, especially through magazines and books.[91] On the other hand, the Home Culture Club, which Cable helped lead, was interracial; historian Sarah Wilkerson-Freeman points out that Gertrude Weil did not reveal this in her many letters home that describe her enthusiasm for the club. Perhaps her later work on interracial relations was also foreshadowed in her response to a debate on the question: "Shall the Federal government give aid to the negro in keeping his right to vote?" Gertrude's own opinion was negative, although she open-mindedly acknowledged that "the affirmatives made their points tell stronger."[92]

As perceived experts on disenfranchisement or black servants, southern white students sometimes had their ideas about race and equality challenged by white northerners. The presence of African American students in some of the colleges was even more significant. Mount Holyoke and Vassar hesitated to admit African American students, ostensibly because they did not want to offend southern students. In 1900 the president of Vassar wrote in response to a query from Spelman Seminary regarding placing its graduates there that the college would not admit black students because of the presence of white southern students.[93] Vassar College was reluctant to admit black students because of its academic reputation and affluent alumnae—and its large southern population. In March 1919 the college received applications from the two daughters of a light-skinned, mixed-race alumna who had graduated from Vassar by passing as white and whose race was not discovered until after graduation. The admissions committee met and agreed that since Vassar had no official policy concerning race and admissions, the two girls would be admitted as students provided their credentials were sound. One of the daughters, "whose physical appearance gave no obvious sign of racial origin," matriculated and graduated. Only two other black women were admitted before the 1940s, when some alumnae began to push for Vassar to accept a small number of black women.[94] Schools remained segregated, ostensibly because of their southern white students, just as in many other contexts northerners deferred to southern racial codes rather than standing up for racial justice, ranging from the formal end of Reconstruction to the segregation of national organizations like the General Federation of Women's Clubs. African Americans repeatedly lost in the struggle between reconciliation and racial justice.

By 1913 Mount Holyoke was making a similar argument.[95] The official policy there, voted in 1845, was not to accept black students. However, at least two black students were unknowingly admitted in the 1880s and 1890s. Once their racial identity was discovered, they were allowed to live in single rooms on campus. Mount Holyoke did not have many black students before the 1960s, but in the late 1920s it did attract more southern black students, especially from Atlanta and Washington, D.C., due to connections with Dunbar High School in Washington and Spelman College in Atlanta.

Bryn Mawr, due to the personal beliefs of M. Carey Thomas, its president and a native of Baltimore, did not admit black students until after 1922. Despite her lack of identification as a southerner, Thomas had grown up in Baltimore, a segregated city, where most of her contact with African Americans was with servants. Occasional meetings with prominent blacks such as Frances Harper and Booker T. Washington did nothing to change her prejudices, and she remained overtly committed to Anglo-Saxon superiority. Her hostility extended as well to Jews, whom she refused to hire at Bryn Mawr and spoke disparagingly of. At Bryn Mawr one black student enrolled after Thomas's retirement but left after one week under mysterious but undoubtedly negative circumstances. Bryn Mawr did not graduate a black woman until 1931 and did not allow black women to live on campus until 1942. Only nine black women graduated from Bryn Mawr before 1960.[96]

Wellesley, Radcliffe, and Smith were relatively more welcoming to black students. Wellesley, founded in 1875, quickly began admitting black students. Harriett Alleyne Rice was Wellesley's first African American graduate in 1887. Although Rice acknowledged many difficulties in her life and career because of her race (she obtained a medical degree from Women's Medical School of the New York Infirmary in 1893), her experience at Wellesley was positive, and she kept in touch with the school, even returning to give a lecture on her experiences during World War I. Although there were only three black students in the nineteenth century, in general Wellesley was considered by many African Americans to be a relatively hospitable place for African American students. The school allowed black students to live on campus and did not officially segregate housing until 1913, presumably when larger numbers of African American students began to apply. Radcliffe also admitted black students early on, with the first graduate in 1898. They were not allowed to live in campus housing but participated in extracurricular activities. Segregated housing was not much of an issue initially because most students came from the Cambridge area. Radcliffe graduated far more black students than any of the other Seven Sisters until the 1940s and 1950s, with one or more in every class by the 1910s. Smith College's first black graduate, Otelia Cromwell, was in the class of 1900. Like Radcliffe, Smith did not allow black students to live on campus until 1913, after the NAACP got involved when African American Carrie Lee was admitted to Smith from a predominantly white high school and placed with a white roommate from Tennessee. When the southern student protested, Lee lived in a professor's home until the trustees amended policy later that year.

Just because schools did not wish to admit black students did not mean that there were no black students. In 1897 Anita Florence Hemmings graduated from Vassar College. Shortly before commencement, *New York World* newspaper described her as "one of the most beautiful young women who ever attended the great institution of learning. Her manners were those of a person of gentle birth, and her intelligence and ability were recognized alike by her classmates and professors." This description is noteworthy because it was her exotic beauty that seems to have caused the problems that almost led to her not graduating. Her roommate accused her of "passing" for white. When Vassar officials realized they had unwittingly admitted an African American student, despite all her achievements (Hemmings was apparently an "impressive" student and choir soprano), the school board called a special meeting to decide whether or not to let her graduate.[97] If Hemmings wanted to attend Vassar, she had to "pass" as white; it was the only way she could attend Vassar at the time.

Those African American students who attended northern women's colleges openly were mostly northerners. The act of leaving the South, where there were few opportunities for women's higher education with quality academics, and enrolling in a prestigious northern women's college such as Wellesley was profoundly political. Few southern African American women had the means or opportunity to do so. Most who went north for education attended either junior colleges or small schools, went to Oberlin in Ohio, with its history of integration, or did graduate work.[98]

Portia Washington, who spent a year at Wellesley, was a notable exception. Born in Alabama in 1883, she was the first child of Booker T. Washington. After four years at Framingham State Normal School in Massachusetts, she returned home at age sixteen to attend Tuskegee Institute, where she completed the dressmaking course and worked on her musical training and German-language skills. Armed with this less than adequate college preparation, Portia entered Wellesley College in the fall of 1901.[99] Why she chose Wellesley is not clear. Portia herself admitted that she was probably accepted at Wellesley on the basis of her father's influence rather than her academic potential.[100] She apparently was more interested in furthering her music studies—not a strong subject at Wellesley—than earning a bachelor's degree, but she was not accepted to a school with a stronger music curriculum and thus ended up at Wellesley.[101] Prepared or not, Portia entered Wellesley as a "special" student, which meant that she was not working toward a degree but rather working on a particular subject area, music (this was a common practice for women who were teachers and wanted to do extra work in their area).

Like other African American students, Portia was sometimes shunned socially. She did not live in a dormitory but instead boarded off campus and took meals with several well-known liberal professors. While some accounts accused Wellesley of bowing to southern white student demands that blacks not live on campus, Portia, her father, and Caroline Hazard, president of Vassar, defended Wellesley, stating that special students never lived on campus. In a widely reported interview given shortly after her arrival at Wellesley, Portia pointed out that a fellow black student, Charlotte Atwood, lived on campus and ate in the dining hall without undue attention. Despite Atwood's blackness (and Booker noted that Atwood was darker skinned than Portia), Atwood was, Portia claimed, in a way invisible. Atwood was able to "pass" as a Wellesley student, her race insignificant.[102]

But Atwood's presence was in fact noted by white students, especially southerners. The simple fact was that African American students were very visible. Portia at first denied that fellow students took notice of her blackness. "I certainly have not had the slightest reason to feel that there might be such a thing as a color line here," she said, explaining that people were very nice to her. Yet Portia also subtly accused both southern and northern white women of segregation. Because white southern students were few in number, Portia and other African American students dealt primarily with northern white students, some of whom exhibited as much or more prejudice as their southern counterparts. Portia carefully said, "College girls of the North are as a class inclined to be a bit selfish and rather thoughtless when they are themselves having a good time of the students who are not quite so much 'in it' as they." Perhaps this was because southerners, she maintained, were friendlier than northerners. Although everyone was kind to her, she queried, "I have wondered a little why the very fact of common interest in an Alma Mater should not be a stronger bond from the very first than it seems to be here." In other words, was Portia Washington in fact asking why northern white students did not fully accept her? Portia tried to deny the existence of a color line, yet she admitted to receiving subtle snubs from both southern and northern students. She understood that northern white women had to sort out their own conceptions of race. Despite the North's greater opportunities for blacks, segregation and prejudice were strong. Northern white students confronted their prejudices daily as they decided whether or not to talk to her, to eat with her, to befriend her.

Portia did not perform well academically and withdrew after only one year, causing further controversy, covered in the *New York Times* and other newspapers. The *New York Sun* reported that Portia had created problems between northern and southern students and was "a thorn in the flesh to the faculty" because of the publicity and interviews she gave. The president of Wellesley denied such accusations, and Portia's father eventually explained that Portia withdrew because she needed a regular seminary course as better preparation for her musical studies.[103]

Some white southern students resented what they saw as false racial toleration on the part of northerners. Atlantan Mary Gude argued that northerners professed interest in Atlanta University, but "they admit very frankly that they don't care for [blacks] to move into their neighborhood." White southerners, she implied, were not only more honest about their racial prejudices, but they lived in closer contact with African Americans.

Yet Portia defended Wellesley by noting that any snubs she received in the North were from southerners, because white southern women had to be educated out of their prejudices. Their adherence to the color line was, she said, "a thing beyond their control." An article in the *Indianapolis Freeman* based on the same interview claimed that southern white students ignored their black colleagues but did not antagonize them either; they were "neutral."[104]

As Portia's comments suggest, there were "neutral" southern white students who did not want to jeopardize their own education to remain at an integrated school. They did not verbally or physically abuse African American students but simply tried to avoid them, thus sidestepping questions of social equality or having to concede that African Americans were their intellectual equals. Many white southern students ignored black classmates, perhaps because not dignifying them with acknowledgment meant that whites did not have to face the idea that blacks could be either as intelligent or part of their social circle. Other white students came from more liberal families and expressed curiosity rather than animosity. Taught to be civil to African Americans, these white students tried to maintain their ideas about white superiority despite the nagging doubts caused by the presence of a black student in the same classes at the same prestigious college.

Gertrude Weil met two black women who came from Hampton, Virginia, to study at Harvard. She described them to her mother as "very nice and intelligent," suggesting that her mother would not have been offended to hear this appraisal.[105] Years after graduating, Gertrude served on the North Carolina Commission on Interracial Cooperation. She later asserted that her interest in race issues was similar to her interest in woman suffrage. "I have never understood why we must talk and talk about it," she said. "It seems not a question for people to grow eloquent about. It is so obvious that to treat people equally is the right thing to do."[106] Perhaps Gertrude's time in the North pushed her to embrace such a radical notion.

Other white southern students expressed a similar interest in the African American students in their own schools. Sue Hall employed three exclamation points after the news that the freshman class had a black student. "Oh by the way, there's a colored girl in the Freshman class!!!" she wrote to her mother. "Break the news gently to Annie. Elizabeth sprung the startling announcement upon me—I have not seen the girl yet. I am curious to see her, of course and I don't know just what to do about an introduction! I shall not seek one, but shall certainly not be rude to her."[107] Sue was clearly unsure how to conduct herself with a black colleague. Her racial upbringing had taught her not to seek an introduction and the friendship or equality it implied. Yet, like other middle- and upper-class white southerners, she did not want to lower herself by behaving rudely to the African American student.[108]

This attitude mirrored Issa Breckinridge's instructions to Sophonisba. In 1884 Issa wrote to Sophonisba asking her to explain her interactions with African American students: "Tell me about the colored students,—are either in your class, are you thrown with them in any way, and how do you treat them? I hope there will be no necessity for you to come in contact with them in any way, but I have no fear of contamination or of your not doing what is becoming a lady." Issa told Sophonisba that other Kentucky mothers were more concerned about the African American students than she was. "I have enough faith in your good breeding and good sense and true ladyhood that I have not concerned my self about it," she continued. "It is a hard thing for people raised with our prejudices to ever treat them as equals—but they can do you no harm and I can trust you to treat them properly." Despite her professed lack of concern, Issa was glad to hear from Sophonisba that she had no interactions with them.[109] Like Sue Hall's, Sophonisba's parents expected her to avoid the students but not to treat them rudely.

Sophonisba's father also focused more on her education than on the problem of African American students at Wellesley. She remembered arriving on campus for her first day with another family from Kentucky, May Stone and

her parents, and seeing a "handsome, handsomely dressed couple of the negro race with an attractive daughter likewise approach the door." Mrs. Stone
asked Sophonisba's father if he thought it was all right to allow her to go to
Wellesley given the presence of this classmate, and he said, "She got on all right
with the boys [while a student at Kentucky A&M], I think that she will get on
all right with the colored." His attitude was not surprising, as he had already
demonstrated relatively liberal opinions on several race issues, including opposing disenfranchising African Americans through the literacy and other tests and
working for Lexington public schools for black children. He also lost an election in 1868 running for county attorney when he acknowledged that he would
accept Negro testimony in court. Both her grandfather and great-grandfather
tried to eliminate color as a qualification for voting in the late eighteenth and
mid-nineteenth centuries in Kentucky.

Yet William by no means considered blacks to be equal to whites. Sophonisba
understood that although he did not oppose her attending college with black
students, it did not mean she had to treat them as social equals. She recalled
when the Jubilee Singers from Fisk performed at Wellesley, Wellesley president
Alice Freeman invited them to dine in the dining room. "Some were placed at
our table," she remembered. "I found no difficulty in serving them. . . . My own
food I could not swallow," echoing Maria Daviess' reaction. When Sophonisba
wrote to her father about the incident, he told her that Freeman's inviting them
to eat was "temporary fanaticism produced by the anti-slavery agitation before the War, and by that War, and being temporary and harmless, it is to be
treated with forbearance. . . . The problem of the colored race in America is a
very troublesome one. But to a gentleman or lady there need be no personal
embarrassment."[110] This attitude mirrors the focus on good breeding stressed
by Issa.

The student who entered Wellesley on the first day of school with Sophonisba
and May Stone was Ella Smith, who later became a friend of Sophonisba. During
their time at Wellesley Ella wanted to invite as many people to the Junior Prom-
enade as everyone else could, but her classmates wanted to restrict the number
of invitations she was allowed. They argued that she could "claim equality in Educational matters but not social matters." Rather than refuting their argument
for inequality, Sophonisba sided with Ella by arguing that "every experience at
Wellesley was educational." Years later, when Sophonisba was at the University
of Chicago, a black student named Georgiana Simpson attempted to live in a
dorm during summer school. When she was told, Sophonisba first asked Georgiana to leave, and when she refused, Sophonisba had a change of heart and
instead spoke on her behalf to the white southern students. Four chose to leave.
Sophonisba also defended Georgiana Simpson to the university president, who

then insisted that Simpson leave despite Sophonisba's argument. Sophonisba also was an active member of the NAACP, worked with the National Association of Colored Women, aided the black Wendell Phillips Settlement House, and obtained two scholarships to the School of Civics at the university for African American women.[111] Her history of American women, *Women in the Twentieth Century: A Study of Their Political, Social and Economic Activities*, may have been one of the first modern books to consider the activities of African American women alongside white women. Breckinridge included the National Association of Colored Women and other African American women's organizations in her discussion of women's clubs and paid attention to race when discussing work opportunities for women.[112]

In her autobiography Sophonisba recalls several incidents in regard to race; all were related to her experiences at Wellesley or at the University of Chicago. Clearly, going to college in the North was extremely significant in shaping her ideas about race. She and other white students were put in the position of having to consider social equality for the first time. Furthermore, having black students as classmates was evidence of their intellectual ability that belied southern stereotypes. Sophonisba's Wellesley classmate made her think about race in ways that the blacks she encountered in Lexington could not, because in Lexington she primarily met African Americans in service positions. Whether or not they wanted to admit it, going to school with black students clearly and significantly changed how some white southerners thought about race. African Americans entered college parlors in ways they could never enter the living rooms of white family homes.

School authorities also challenged the racism of some southern white students. When Margaret Mitchell discovered that she was in a history class at Smith in the 1910s with a black student and she supposedly told the teacher off, the teacher refused to change her class. Margaret claimed she would go to the dean, to the president if necessary, and get it changed. Somehow she did. Margaret later claimed that Professor Dorothy Ware flunked her even though the dean approved the transfer. Margaret called Ware a hypocrite, asking if Ware "had ever undressed and nursed a Negro woman or sat on a drunk Negro man's head to keep him from being shot by the police." Mitchell's mother blamed the incident on the fact that Ware's family had been to the South to teach blacks and had not been well received by white southerners.[113] Margaret grounded her refusal to take a class with an African American—an act that suggested social equality—in her familiarity with blacks, an ease she believed was only possible within a white supremacist society.

Likewise, Virginia Foster Durr moved on campus for her second year at Wellesley in 1922. "The first night, I went to the dining room and a Negro girl was sitting at my table. My God, I nearly fell over dead. I couldn't believe it. She wasn't very black, sort of pale, but she was sitting there eating with me in college." Virginia immediately left the dining room and returned to her room, where the head of the house came to question her. When asked why she refused to eat with a black student, Virginia said only, "Because I'm from Alabama and my father would have a fit. I just couldn't dream of it." The housemother told her that if she refused to eat with the black student, then she was breaking the rules of Wellesley College, and she would be asked to withdraw. Reluctant to leave Wellesley, where she was having the time of her life, Virginia finally decided that as long as her father did not find out, she could remain.

For Virginia Durr, it was "the first time that my values had ever been challenged." She tried to explain herself to a northern classmate who asked her why she hugged her cook at home but would not eat with a fellow student and found herself unable to explain the logic of race etiquette so deeply ingrained in her. Such challenges did not immediately cause a change of heart concerning her racial attitude. That change came more slowly, but it began with this first doubt. Virginia was pleasant and polite to the girl, whom she eventually came to see as perfectly well mannered and sharing her southern distaste for improperly cooked grits. "But it was the first time I became aware that my attitude was considered foolish to some people and that Wellesley College wasn't going to stand for it."[114]

According to Virginia Durr, she was not the only southerner to have this revelation. They all realized that they broke taboos when they dined, swam, or otherwise interacted with African American students. The discomfort over breaking with southern tradition paled in comparison to the overall college experience, and they hoped that by not calling attention to their action they would not be called to task by other southern students or by their families and friends at home. Virginia claims that none of them did any "soul searching" at the time.

Virginia obviously did do some soul searching soon after graduation. She later volunteered with the Democratic Party, working to get rid of the poll tax that disenfranchised so many women, poor whites, and African Americans. She joined Church Women United and helped integrate its prayer meetings, a practice that ended when the women were harassed. Her husband, Clifford, who worked for FDR's New Deal government, joined the Southern Conference for Human Welfare, and the couple was accused of being Communists. Virginia, called to appear before the Senate Internal Security Subcommittee, wrote a statement saying that she was in contempt of the committee because it was a kangaroo court and, when called to the stand, refused to plead the Fifth. Instead, she simply refused to answer questions, remaining silent and powdering her nose. Clifford was one of the lawyers called when Rosa Parks was arrested for refusing to give up her seat on the bus in Montgomery, and the Durrs supported the bus boycott.[115]

Virginia Foster Durr was one of several white southern women active in the early civil rights movement who credited her college experience with moving her toward activism. For some students, exposure to northern mores pushed them to challenge long-held assumptions about social hierarchy, gender, and race. Adolphine Fletcher Terry, a native of Little Rock, Arkansas, and member of a prominent family, graduated from Vassar College in the early 1900s. Both her mother's concern for African Americans and the northern culture she was exposed to at Vassar "led her to vow upon her return to Arkansas that she was NOT going to be a southern lady." Although she was always active in civic affairs, her opportunity for leadership came during the Little Rock desegregation crisis, where she led the Women's Emergency Committee to Open Our Schools and helped resolve the crisis.[116]

Wellesley alumna Lilian Wyckoff Johnson started a cooperative community center and school in Grundy County, Tennessee. She later gave the lease to Myles Horton, founder of the Highlander School. The school initially focused on labor issues before becoming a training center for civil rights workers in the 1950s. By that time Lilian had moved to Bradenton, Florida, where she continued her activism into her eighties. Partially inspired by her experiences with Horton and the Highlander School, she cofounded the Bradenton Community Welfare Council, composed of African American and white women's organizations, which established an African American Youth Center, among other projects.[117] Orie Latham Hatcher's Baptist parents had set an example of cooperation with black Baptists. Her father wrote a biography of John Jasper, a black minister, and her mother served as a trustee of Hartshorn Memorial College for black women in Virginia. Although she did not have fellow black students in her classes at Vassar (nor did she teach them at Bryn Mawr), she later worked to expand her vocational bureau's efforts to include black women.[118]

C. Mildred Thompson, a Vassar alumna from Atlanta, was influenced not by the experience of African American colleagues but by the academic rigor demanded by history professors such as Lucy Salmon. Thompson got her doctorate at Columbia University, eventually publishing her best-known work, *Reconstruction in Georgia, Economic, Social, and Political, 1865–1872*, in 1915. Although she studied with William A. Dunning, she was more sympathetic in her appraisal of African American Reconstruction political influence than Dunning and most of his followers. She judged the Reconstruction government administration to be "not entirely bad, even quite good in some members." She was forthright in admitting the violence of the Ku Klux Klan and concluded, "In its largest sense, Reconstruction in Georgia meant a wider democratization of society." In comparison to other works produced by southern white historians of the Dunning school, she showed moderation and judgment. By the early 1960s Thompson was anxious for younger scholars to continue the work she had started in order to better understand the economic plight of African Americans and the civil rights movement.[119]

Obviously, not all northern-educated women embraced progressive racial ideas. In the 1950s one Wellesley alumna wrote her classmates to say that she hoped the next president would be a Democrat who believed in segregation.[120] Why some women became more tolerant while others did not is not clear. For some, religion may have been significant. Histories of white women involved in the early interracial movement show that many Methodists were inspired by their church's antislavery history and connections formed through organizations like the YWCA. Episcopalians in South Carolina were motivated in addition by a sense of noblesse oblige, while Jewish women like Gertrude Weil may have been more open to interracial cooperation.[121]

Few southern women were as brave as Virginia Durr and Adolphine Terry or as interested in challenging southern race mores. This was particularly true of the first generation of southern students in the 1870s and 1880s, although by the 1910s even this wall was beginning to crack. Seeking a liberal arts education to improve themselves as women, southern women at northern colleges did not intend to discard southern racial beliefs. By the early twentieth century a northern education had the potential to challenge even this bedrock of southern society. Whether or not they began to think differently about race, they returned to the South as different women, more independent and more curious about the world around them. Although still loyal to the South, many rethought the necessity of marriage and embraced social activism. Despite the continued conservatism of the South, graduates of northern colleges found it easier to challenge the status quo on gender issues than on race in their own lives.

Mary, Louisa, Ida, and Christie Poppenheim, Vassar College, ca. 1880s.
Special Collections, Vassar College Libraries.

Louisa Poppenheim performing in Trig Ceremonies, Vassar College, 1889.
Special Collections, Vassar College Libraries.

Mary Vardrine McBee, founder of Ashley Hall, Charleston, South Carolina. Property of Ashley Hall Archives.

Margaret Preston in her wedding dress, 1917. PA60M150: Item #365, Preston-Johnston Family Photographs, University of Kentucky.

Linda Neville and her patients from Children's Free Hospital, Louisville, Kentucky. PA61M158: Item #126, Linda Neville, Charles Kerr, and Neville Family Papers, University of Kentucky.

Margaret Preston, Bryn Mawr student, in her cap and gown. PA61M158: Item #248, Linda Neville, Charles Kerr, and Neville Family Papers, University of Kentucky.

Vassar College's main building, as viewed through the gate, 1865.
Special Collections, Vassar College Libraries.

Student room, Vassar College, 1878. Special Collections, Vassar College Libraries.

SOUTHERN CLUB

For any but a Southern girl
To join this Club, 't were vain ;
But the line of demarcation
Is not exactly plain.

1900 ELIZABETH GRAHAM, *President*
1901 ISABEL M. HULL, *Vice-President*
1901 VIRGINIA L. NISBET, *Secretary and Treasurer*

MEMBERS

Kentucky	.	.	10	North Carolina	. .	4
Georgia .	.	.	8	District of Columbia	.	3
Missouri	.	.	7	Texas . . .	.	2
Tennessee	.	.	5	Arkansas . . .		1

Total 40

HONORARY MEMBERS

James Lane Allen

John G. Fox, Jr.

Thomas Nelson Page

Mabel Werne

128

Southern Club, from the Vassarian Yearbook, 1900.
Special Collections, Vassar College Libraries.

Gertrude Weil, at the far left, with North Carolinian suffragists.
Courtesy of the North Carolina Office of Archives and History,
Raleigh, North Carolina.

Student room in College Hall, Wellesley College, 1881.
Courtesy of Wellesley College Archives.

Sophonisba Breckinridge.
Courtesy of Wellesley
College Archives, photo
by Pach Bro's.

College Hall, Wellesley College. Courtesy of Wellesley College Archives.

Students doing domestic work, Freeman Hall, Wellesley College, undated.
Courtesy of Wellesley College Archives, photo by Partridge.

Dr. Connie Guion.
Courtesy of Wellesley
College Archives, photo
by Carolina B. Rice.

Virginian Annie Poe Harrison,
the first student to register at the
newly opened Wellesley College.
Courtesy of Wellesley College
Archives.

CHAPTER FIVE

After College

The Marriage and Career Dilemma

 Kentuckian Sophonisba Breckinridge had strong and lasting career aspirations that her family only reluctantly supported. Sophonisba was a slight woman who weighed a mere ninety pounds, but her flashing eyes and mass of dark hair hinted at her intense personality. A brilliant student at Wellesley who stood out for her intellect among her peers there, Sophonisba well reflected her name's meaning: "a woman who conserves wisdom." Driven to hard work and inspired by her father's career, Sophonisba wanted to become a lawyer. In 1887 she wrote him for guidance, plaintively asking, "I wish you would think so as to be very clear on the subject . . . as to what you want Sophonisba to do when she gets her B.S. degree. I know it will be decided for me but if I knew what I thought I was working towards it would make it easier for me to decide what electives to take next year, etc."[1] Sophonisba unsuccessfully asked her father to allow her to work in his law office after she graduated. She later complained that Wellesley, with its strong liberal arts curriculum, did not prepare her for a career other than teaching. Reluctantly, Sophonisba briefly taught after graduation but gave it up due to illness. She kept house for her father after her mother's death, eventually read law books, and passed the bar, but, unable to build a thriving law practice, she drifted, depressed and restless for several years.[2] A visit to May Estelle Cook, a Wellesley friend who lived in Oak Park, just outside Chicago, changed Sophonisba's life. Cook introduced her to Marion Talbot at the University of Chicago, where Sophonisba decided to enroll. She eventually earned her doctorate, taught, and became a nationally known reformer.[3]

In some ways Sophonisba, who struggled for almost ten years before she resolved her postcollege dilemma by forgoing marriage and housekeeping for her father and becoming instead a professional and an academic, was typical of many southern students who sought a classical education at one of the Seven Sisters. Their education challenged their intellect and opened up their world, but it did not necessarily prepare them for a career other than teaching. Unwilling to teach or otherwise work for wages and loath to settle into a domestic routine notable only for its social opportunities, students struggled to find a meaningful occupation for their time. The majority of southern students who attended the Seven Sister colleges at the turn of the century returned to the South to live after graduation. Due to unique southern cultural and gender norms and fewer job opportunities in the region, many southern students chose neither marriage nor paid employment but instead served their communities through volunteer work.

Southern students at northern colleges married at approximately the same low rates as their northern colleagues, rates that were considerably lower than those found at southern colleges and among the general population. The college experience, including exposure to northern women and northern culture, liberal professors, courses focused on social welfare, extracurricular leadership opportunities, and intellectual stimulation, promoted independence and self-confidence in southern women. Many felt freer to reject the assumption that they would marry. The cultural incompatibility between northern men and southern women further complicated their marriage options. Some women feared the possibility that they would have to live in the North if they married a northerner; such a choice threatened the bond of the southern family.

At the same time, many were also unwilling to work for wages or become professionals. Northern-educated southern women worked for wages at slightly lower rates than their northern colleagues though at higher rates than their southern counterparts. Opportunities were still limited; nationally, while approximately 90 percent of men over age sixteen worked from 1870 to 1930, the percentage of working women increased only from 14.8 to 25.3 percent in that same time frame. Women also formed less than half of the professional class of workers in the country.[4] Those women who wanted to become professionals had to face obstacles concerning their training, access to jobs, and disapproval from family, including husbands. Women of ambition had to overachieve in order to overcome the barriers. They also sometimes sought separate enclaves (such as teaching at a women's college or working in a field such as social work) or other innovative methods of creating a place for women in the field.[5] Most students who worked chose teaching, especially because they wanted to give back to southern women, but the South's relatively small industrial base prevented women from securing jobs in offices and retail establishments that were more readily available in the North. Furthermore, elite white southerners did not believe it was proper for white women, especially married women and certainly not mothers, to work outside the home. It was not until the 1910s that students began to consider combining marriage and career rather than choosing between the two (or neither). Southern white women had to carefully consider the decision to work for wages.

Given the social taboo against women's employment, these women lent their leadership skills instead to women's organizations and volunteer work. By founding women's clubs, leading the movement for woman suffrage, and initiating progressive reforms, they changed communities across the South. Many also became feminists. Affected by such regional factors and culture, their situation was unique. Because so many southern students came from small towns, the exposure to progressive ideas at northern colleges was even more significant. Their letters reveal just how much the college experience shaped their life choices.

Marriage

In their studies of single women, historians Virginia Lee Chambers-Schiller and Trisha Franzen found that many women who remained single did so because they desired an independence they thought impossible to obtain in marriage. Some women wanted financial autonomy; they moved out of their parents' home and established a household on their own or with a friend. Others wanted to pursue a career, an option they did not believe was possible as a married woman.[6] The large number of college graduates who remained single and had careers suggests that these women found fulfillment in their work and perhaps did not feel the need for marriage. Others were involved in significant relationships with mothers, sisters, female friends, or lovers that made marriage superfluous. Finally, some women grew less interested in marriage as they grew in self-confidence and intellect—they may have feared that they could not pursue their intellectual curiosity in the role of a wife. Those who did marry may have made their marriages more equitable, perhaps because they married when they were older, perhaps because they had developed feminist beliefs. Not all single women consciously chose not to marry. Some women stayed single despite their initial expectations—they were stymied by a lack of suitors, for example.

College interfered with marriage plans for many female college graduates at the turn of the century. The percentage of college graduates who married ranged from about 40 to 65 percent from the 1880s to 1915, in comparison to approximately 90 percent for the general female population.[7] Between 1875 and 1915 southern students generally married at the same rate as their northern classmates or at a slightly lower rate. At Mount Holyoke 53 percent of all graduates married, while 55 percent of southern graduates married; 61 percent of all Smith graduates married, compared to 57 percent of southern graduates; and at Vassar 64 percent of all graduates married, in comparison to 61 percent of southern graduates.[8]

Marriage rates at southern liberal arts female colleges were higher. According to Pamela Dean and Gail Apperson Kilman, from the 1890s through 1911 the marriage rate for graduates at Randolph-Macon was 61 percent, at Wesleyan, 82 percent, and at North Carolina Normal and Industrial College, principally a training ground for teachers, the rate was 68 percent. Even though these numbers are lower than those of the general population in the South at the time, southern colleges emphasized marriage. One historian argues that some southern students who had female, northern professors had trouble relating to them and instead connected with married alumnae who seemed to fit their aspirations better.[9] Furthermore, colleges like Sophie Newcomb had the reputation of preparing charming women for marriage to Tulane graduates; its commencement speakers emphasized the eligibility of educated women.[10]

Attending college changed not only the likelihood that women would marry but also the age at which alumnae married and the number of children they had. While the majority of alumnae married within five years of graduation, a sizeable minority of southern graduates waited over ten years, as high as almost 16 percent at Wellesley.[11] Many students also were already in their late twenties or older when they started school, suggesting that they began school after already deciding not to marry rather than that college influenced their decision.[12]

For southern students, the choice of whether or not to marry or to work did not show any correlation to whether a student returned to the South or stayed in the North to live. The number of students who felt freer to seek employment or stay single in the North was probably offset by the number of students who stayed in the North because they had met and married a northerner.

The relatively low numbers of college women marrying caused much public controversy at the turn of the century, replacing the earlier debate over the supposedly negative effects that college wreaked on the health of young women. In 1885 the Association of Collegiate Alumnae (ACA) released a study that found that only 27.8 percent of college graduates married. This number was so low because it included very recent graduates, women who eventually married. The numbers also probably reflect the lower marriage rates of the Northeast (ranging from 60 to 70 percent).[13] Women and educators at women's colleges rushed to defend female college students, arguing that many college women would still choose to marry even if later in life, that their marriages were stronger and less likely to end in divorce, and that they married at similar rates to their social class.[14]

Further studies sought to investigate why the numbers were so low. A survey of female college graduates predominantly from the Seven Sister colleges revealed that twenty-two out of one hundred believed their ideas about marriage changed while at school. One alumna asserted that college "raised one's ideals of what it should be, and made a poor choice impossible," while another contended that she grew to understand that marriage "should not be one's sole ambition." Whether due to these changes in mindset, increased independence and higher ideals, or more simply to their lack of contact with men while at women's colleges, alumnae were more likely to conclude that their chances for marriage decreased rather than increased with a college education.[15] At Mount Holyoke, as the school transitioned from a seminary to a college and grew more academic, one student claimed that the bachelor's degree replaced the degrees most familiar to students there: FFOM, Fit for an Old Maid; FFMW, Fit for a Minister's Wife; and FFM, Fit for a Missionary. Mount Holyoke graduates, it seemed, did not marry unless it was to a minister.[16]

After 1900 concern over the seeming epidemic of single college women grew in light of arguments about race suicide and the possible sexual "deviancy" or homosexuality of some of the single women. Harking back to Edward Clarke's emphasis on the deleterious physical effects of college on women, some even complained that college destroyed women's beauty. Wellesley College responded by hiring more male teachers in the 1930s to offset the perceived influence of a predominantly female and single faculty.[17] Under president Henry Noble Mac-Cracken Vassar began to offer domestic science courses, moving slightly away from the emphasis on liberal arts and more toward training for marriage and motherhood.[18] Even M. Carey Thomas, who was so dedicated to women's scholarship, concluded that some of Bryn Mawr's students were more interested in marriage than an academic single life; in response she encouraged graduates to work and marry rather than choose between them.[19] By the 1910s college women married at a higher rate, closer to that of the general population, socialized more, and were less "intense" than the first generation of college women who had struggled just to justify women's higher education.[20] The marriage rate increased from the 1880s to the early 1910s at both Vassar and Smith. At Smith, the percentage of all graduates marrying rose from 47 percent in the 1880s to 67 percent between 1910 and 1915 and from 33 to 70 percent for southern graduates in the same time period. Mount Holyoke marriage rates stayed approximately the same.

No single explanation for the large numbers of unmarried women appears in the letters and alumnae surveys of northern-educated southern college students. The college experience itself changed a lot of women, whether by limiting their opportunities to date suitable men or by shaping their beliefs concerning marriage. Practical questions affected some women. Whom and when would they marry? Southern or northern men? Would they remain in the North or return home? Philosophical questions concerned others. Was marriage necessary for women? Could they find happiness in a life of books or a career instead? Did feminism and marriage mix?

Some southern women who chose to go to the Seven Sisters left home already more interested in books than boys, and, furthermore, they were comfortable with that preference. Tennessean Grace Richmond had already developed a reputation for bookishness before she left for Vassar—her mother wrote her that a Mr. White said she "cared more for books than anything else." Grace seemed to understand that this precluded marriage. She described herself to her brother Chester as twenty-five and already an old maid.[21] Josie Simrall, a Kentuckian at Wellesley, also assumed that her studies and teaching goals destined her to remain single. She wrote to her mother, "Perhaps when I get to be a comfortable old maid—well through with all the sciences and language and all my other duties—I shall have time to spend another winter in the 'Sunny South.' "[22]

Whether they arrived at school prepared for single life or not, the heady experience of intellectual challenge and the focus on the mind and ideas rather than debuts and dances certainly redirected many young women. Virginia Foster Durr, a Wellesley alumna from Alabama, "realized for the first time that women could be something. This was the real liberation that I got at Wellesley. I realized women didn't have to marry to be somebody. . . . I realized that women could be happy without getting married, they could use their minds and accomplish things."[23] It was far less likely that Virginia would have come to that realization at a southern college that emphasized training for marriage rather than training the mind.

The example set by women faculty of single, independent, smart, and contented women was influential as well. Wellesley, in particular, had an all-female faculty for decades. Many faculty members encouraged graduates to give up marriage for paid work and provided an example of successful single career women through their own experiences.[24] Other students encountered single female teachers while preparing for college. Clara Conway, founder of the Clara Conway Institute in Memphis, which prepared students for northern colleges and drew teachers like Lilian Wyckoff Johnson, a Wellesley alumna, prepared her students for the possibility of an independent single life. Conway often quoted George Eliot to her students, telling them, "Only an independent woman could give her hand with grace and dignity. . . . She can afford to wait until the king shall come and if he doesn't she can live her own life in her own way."[25]

Sometimes what students read at college was also influential. Atlantan Agnes Raoul wrote to her sister Mary that after reading *Middlemarch* and some of Thackeray's works she concluded: "If you want to be happy, don't get married." She suggested that the books ought to be given to those considering eloping.[26]

Given that these were favorites of many college students at the time, it is not hard to imagine the discussions about marriage that the books engendered in many college dormitory rooms. That marriage and career were on the mind of Georgiana Goddard King is evident in her short story "Free among the Dead." The story centers on two roommates, Sydney and Esther, who were to room together again when they returned to Bryn Mawr for graduate school. Sydney, however, marries and does not return. When Hilda, a third friend, hears of Sydney's marriage, she says, "Oh Dear! I'm rather sorry. I always believed in her, you know. She might have done things." Esther replies, "Presumably one can do things with a husband." "Ah, she can't. And, she won't," says Hilda. Significantly, Georgiana King described Sydney as having many obligations to her parents and siblings, while Esther, who continued in school, was orphaned with "no near relations." The story highlights the dilemma that southern students experienced when they tried to balance family—including husbands—with college and career.[27]

Because students were expected to choose between marriage and career, society and even many educators encouraged them to develop their femininity and sexual attractiveness in lieu of a career. Marriage was to replace aspirations for self-support. Southern education reformer Celeste Parrish, herself educated at Cornell University, resisted the messages that many, including commencement speakers, gave, "in which students were solemnly warned against being 'mannish' in any way, by which the male speaker usually meant harboring expectations of advanced careers or self-support."[28] Most frustrating to Parrish was the tendency of men to define womanly qualities as those they themselves desired in a wife, thus stressing women's natural selflessness and dependency. A woman's dependency in turn shored up a man's independence and mastery of his household, even if it no longer included slaves. Parrish tried to convince young women that they had choices: they could choose marriage and motherhood, or they could choose to stay single and have a career without damaging their femininity. She defended the unmarried from accusations of abnormality or mannishness and called upon women to examine themselves, their skills, and their desires and to choose accordingly. "She may love a good man and be his wife and the mother of his children," she wrote, "or she may, for good reason, refuse both wifehood and motherhood. She is never the mere minister to a man's sensual pleasure. She may be a man's friend and companion, his helper and co-worker. She is never, voluntarily, his dependent or his plaything."[29] Celeste Parrish's call for independence and choice appealed to many southern women, but undoubtedly other southern women would have rejected her ideas as unrealistic. Those best placed to help Parrish redefine the "womanly woman" in the South were the select few who had been awakened to the many possibilities for women while studying in the North.

Although South Carolinian Vassar alumnae Louisa and Mary Poppenheim seemed interested in some of the young men they met while they were young, neither sister married. Louisa's classmates at Vassar considered her a social butterfly, in her prophecy recalling her "social triumphs recorded in the Edgefield papers" and predicting that she would become a "social queen in the nation's capital."[30] Yet, at the age of twenty-nine, Louisa accepted her role as a single woman and did not seem to regret it. She gave a toast to marriage at the South Carolina Federation of Women's Clubs convention in 1899, an organization she helped found. In it she described marriage as a negative experience for women, as "that Sargasso Sea wherein float so many wrecks of rosy-hued dreams of maidenhood." Louisa admitted that some women were successfully able to negotiate marriage, but, she quipped, "every married woman thinks her case the exception." She noted that she, as "an old maid," was the most appropriate person to give the toast. A married woman might have painted a more positive picture of marriage that would have tempted the single women who were necessary to women's clubs. Louisa concluded her toast by insinuating that men gave only their names and their money to women, while women centered their lives on men.[31] Linda Neville, a Bryn Mawr graduate living in Lexington, also suggested that single women were better suited than married women for social activism in women's clubs and other organizations. After decades of activism for the blind in Kentucky, Linda wrote that she had no hope of finding a successor who was healthy, passionate about the cause, financially independent, "and if I dare say it," she added, "with freedom from such a potential encumbrance as a spouse."[32]

Other women also seemed comfortable enough with their single status to joke, although it is difficult to tell if Mount Holyoke alumna Elizabeth Veach was reconciled or bitter when she told her class only four years after graduation, "I am still the same old maid, and am likely to stay so." Connie Guion felt the pressure to marry (or become an academic or professional). In her fifth reunion Wellesley yearbook, she wrote to her classmates, "I somehow feel as if I were casting a blight on [the class of 1906's] silvery name when I sign myself as old, simple Connie M. Guion—still an old maid with no addenda."[33] But others were more explicit in their embrace of career over marriage. Dorothy Burdick, who became a doctor, rejected the negative associations of an "old maid," writing about herself, "Status—Single, old maid, spinster, or professional woman,— last preferred." Students like these likely drew support for their choices from their fellow classmates who made similar decisions. For them, professional work provided personal fulfillment.[34]

Remaining single was a viable option for many because they did not need to support themselves financially. Students were expected to return home and live with their parents until they married, and single women often ended up spending the rest of their lives in the family home. Mary and Louisa Poppenheim lived in their parents' home in Charleston, first with their parents, then with each other after their parents died. They lived off their inheritance and investments until the Great Depression, when they took in boarders. Others wanted to marry because they feared having to support themselves. Virginia Foster Durr sought a mate because she believed old maids were poor.[35]

For many students, parents were the ultimate source of advice and influence when it came to important decisions like marriage. Sophonisba Breckinridge's parents sent her mixed messages concerning marriage, career, and a woman's happiness. At Wellesley she focused on her classes, not her social life, to the extent that Sophonisba had little interest in attending her brother's parties at Princeton, claiming she did so only to make her brother feel loved.[36] While her mother, Issa Breckinridge, constantly wrote to Sophonisba about women's duty, morality, and proper behavior, she apparently felt some frustration with her own life and feared for Sophonisba's as well. She suggested to her daughter that there might be more to life than marriage and motherhood. Issa wrote to Sophonisba that she didn't know what to do with herself: "Indeed it seems to me I have outlived my usefulness—Ella Grown [Sophonisba's sister]. You and Desha and Robert gone—so good for nothing as to be no account—I wonder what's to become of me."[37] She further complained that life as a southern lady encompassed too many "stupid old tea[s]" and that life at home was "dull and stupid and if you were at home you would give your eyes to be at Wellesley."[38] On the other hand, Issa told Sophonisba that if she maintained her health and strength, she could "*be and do all that God ever wanted women to do!*" By her own example, Issa did not believe that God intended women to step much beyond a traditional role of mother and housewife, although she admittedly was unhappy in that role.[39]

Sophonisba was also very close to Alice Freeman, president of Wellesley College. While Freeman believed fervently in women's intellectual ability, when she was pursued by George Herbert Palmer, she resigned her position at Wellesley to marry him. Sophonisba was a senior at the time, and Freeman's decision to give up her career for marriage must have affected her. Sophonisba later dated two men quite seriously, both of whom she admits in her autobiography to having loved, but she did not marry either of them. She remained close to her family and maintained lifelong friendships with Edith Abbott and Marion Talbot. Although Sophonisba moved in with Abbott later in life, there is no evidence of a sexual relationship between them. Sophonisba's unpublished autobiography does not reveal why she did not marry either of the men she dated, but it seems likely that her time at Wellesley, where she flourished in her academic classes, developed leadership as class president, and lived among liberal, feminist professors, led her to reconsider marriage. Influenced by her mother's frustration, Freeman's choice, and her own intellectually stimulating career as an academic and reformer, she may have feared that marriage would interfere with her happiness.

In the South another prominent educator and Vassar alumna, Frances Jewell, gave up a promising career for marriage. Frances was a member of the English department and dean of women at the University of Kentucky when she resigned to marry the university president, Frank L. McVey. Raised in Lexington, Frances was known by her friends for her concerns for everyone else—they even illustrated her photo in the yearbook with a bleeding heart. After marrying McVey, she continued her interests in the university and in women's higher education, hosting numerous social occasions at her home and serving a variety of positions in the YWCA, the Southern Women's Educational Alliance, the Women's Club of Kentucky, the AAUW, the Kentucky Illiteracy Commission, and her alma mater as a member of the board of trustees of Vassar College. Despite having given up her own career to marry, during the Great Depression Frances defended the rights of married women to work. She praised Kentucky's decision not to pass legislation firing married teachers and pointed to many married women's financial support of their families.[40]

Margaret Preston's experience at Bryn Mawr also affected her, although she did marry. When Margaret first left Lexington society for Pennsylvania, she (and her mother) prioritized her social life. Besides complaining about Bryn Mawr's negative effects on the beauty of its students, Margaret missed her mother intensely. She described visiting boys as "fearful" and wrote her mother, "I don't think I shall ever do much in society, [f]or I am not at all attractive to casual people. Only a few like me. The thing I want is to be with you." Still hoping to leave Bryn Mawr early and return home, Margaret changed her tune about her social life, telling her mother that she did not want to return for a second year because she would be twenty and wanted to spend some time in society while she was still young.[41] In her second year, as she began to prosper academically, Margaret talked less about society and more about her classes.

Margaret's correspondence with her eventual husband, Philip Johnston, reveals a much more mature woman who married relatively late (at age thirty-two) and was confident about herself and her relationship. Johnston respected Margaret's literary interests, and she viewed him as understanding when it came to woman suffrage and feminism. When Margaret shared with him her experience trying unsuccessfully to convince a man about suffrage, she called the man "unenlightened."[42] Johnston, however, was "enlightened" enough to respect Margaret's desire to eliminate the word "obey" from her marriage vows (although their Episcopalian priest refused their request).[43]

Margaret's feminist views on marriage came from her experiences at Bryn Mawr as well as from the example of her mother and her grandmother. Living at home with her parents, with whom she had a close relationship and where she was financially secure, she had the freedom to marry for love and friendship rather than out of desperation. Margaret's mother, a suffragist, may have used birth control, an indication that she also sought some measure of control within her marriage. Margaret's paternal grandmother set an example of a woman in an unhappy marriage who asserted her power by no longer sleeping with her husband and threatening divorce.[44] Her unwillingness to suffer a bad marriage may have strengthened Margaret's resolve for a more equitable marriage.

Margaret's marriage of equal partners can also be more directly attributed to her time at Bryn Mawr. She learned to be self-reliant and became more confident in her intelligence and ability. Other college graduates believed that their education taught life skills rather than professional skills. Thus, even if they did not do professional work, their college degrees had prepared them for marriage and motherhood. Aphra Phelps of Louisville, Kentucky, said of her years at Wellesley, "My majors of Chemistry and Math haven't proven very useful," although she did consider a professional career before she married. Rather, Aphra claimed that her "years at Wellesley gave me a broad outlook, taught me to be self-reliant and happy. I'm sure I was a better mother because Wellesley gave me cultural refinement and tolerance."[45] Such skills went a long way toward making for happier and, in many cases, more equitable marriages.

Many students, whether or not they eventually married, had difficulty dating because they were not attracted to northern men. Mary Poppenheim described two northern friends to her mother as "very nice but not a bit like our Southern men." In another letter home she explained that southern men were more charming, while northern men were too hurried to enjoy life.[46] Some students also wanted to avoid moving north if they married a northern man. Mary's mother was concerned about a Mr. Buckingham from Poughkeepsie who seemed to be romantically interested in Mary. She told Mary and her sister Louisa that if Mary married him, their father declared that he would move his business to New York and only spend winters in the South.[47] Separation seemed to be unthinkable to both daughters and parents. Ironically, some northerners called for just such interregional romances between northern men and southern women as a means of promoting reconciliation between the sections in the late 1870s and 1880s. They hoped to win over unreconstructed southern women with romance, an approach not likely to appeal to some rebels. They might have been more approving of male southern authors who wrote stories of southern men who won northern women over to southern racial ideology. In either case, reconciliation would be achieved because women were expected to adapt to the culture and ideology of their husbands.[48]

Despite returning to the South after graduation, Mary and Louisa did not find any eligible southern gentlemen, and perhaps with their northern education, intelligence, and seriousness they intimidated prospective suitors from Charleston. Even as their intellect helped them to fit in at college, it marked them as different at home. Mary and Louisa were too young to have read Sarah Morgan Dawson's 1873 column in the *Charleston News and Courier* on the problems educated women faced, but the sentiment she described still lingered. "There is nothing less in demand in the woman-market than brains," Dawson wrote. "The woman who would be friends with the average mankind must reduce herself to a state of semi-imbecility. . . . A learned pig is more respected and admired" than a learned woman, she concluded. Millicent Carey McIntosh, daughter of M. Carey Thomas's sister, said that in 1885 "her mother was so embarrassed at being a student at Bryn Mawr College 'that when she saw her friends on the streets of Baltimore she would cross over to the other side so that she wouldn't have to speak to them.' "[49] Author Margaret Mitchell must have experienced a similar discomfort with her intellect. She created in Scarlett O'Hara a heroine who was smart, who could do figures in her head, and who chafed at having to act dumber than the men with whom she flirted.

Some college women argued that they were no less interested in marrying than other women, but they had more trouble finding the right man. Furthermore, college graduates were more likely to marry college-educated men and thus had a smaller pool of men from which to draw.[50] Vassar students asserted that men were not attracted to intelligent women and joked that potential suitors rejected so many of their invitations to dances on campus that they eventually had to bribe a younger brother to attend, in the meanwhile spending a small fortune on rejected invitations.[51]

Vassar graduate Daisy Lee Worthington, from Louisville, Kentucky, tried to deflect attention away from the women and toward their potential suitors. Responding to an article written by a male Brooklyn high school teacher against higher education for women, in part due to their biological destiny to be mothers and the low marriage rates of college women, Daisy took issue with his arguments. She rebutted that women who did not marry worked instead "for the general betterment of society" in a myriad of ways. She also suggested that some men feared women who were educated because they might not want to take a vow to "love, honor, obey, bow down, and worship them."[52]

Marriage rates were also low because between the ages of sixteen and twenty-two (including those who attended the preparatory department first) college women were in a single-sex setting rather than making their debut into society. Mary and Louisa Poppenheim entered the marriage market later than their peers who did not go away to college. Mary graduated a few months before her twenty-second birthday, and Louisa graduated at age twenty-one. While at school, Mary took offense when a friend implied that she was destined to be an old maid even though she had just recently turned twenty-one. Mary complained to her mother:

> In talking of the marriages which seem to be the all absorbing topic in Charleston at present she said she was afraid that she and I would be left out if we didn't take care. Now I think she is decidedly cheeky to bracket me with herself. I wish her to remember that she has been on the market three years while I have not so much as shown my nose there for five minutes—Besides I think it lots more respectable not to offer yourself for bidders than to offer yourself and have no bidder.[53]

Perhaps Mary was so insulted because she realized that when she did finally enter the matrimonial market she would be almost twenty-two, or perhaps she was reevaluating whether she wanted to marry at all. Her use of the phrases "on the market" and "offer yourself for bidders" indicates that she resented women's lack of power in choosing a spouse and regarded married women as akin to chattel. Her years at Vassar opened her mind to the possibilities of achieving happiness through her own activities and her family rather than through "selling herself" into marriage.[54]

Like Mary Poppenheim, South Carolinian Julia Hammond did not seem attracted to northern men. Julia did little socializing with men while a student at Radcliffe, telling her mother early on that she had not even met "my first grown man of Cambridge," probably a reference to Harvard University. When she finally did meet Harvard students, she was unimpressed, describing them to her father as "rather rough young fellows."[55] Radcliffe helped Julia to reconsider marriage. She noticed that college girls were "sensible, plain-looking" but admired the girls who "had other thoughts in life than getting married," including a fellow student who postponed marriage for study and another who taught "not because she was obliged to, but because she wished to."[56] Ultimately, the devotion to her family that made Julia leave Radcliffe and return home after only three months at school also prevented her from marrying her lover for many years. Like Margaret Preston, Julia had a strong bond with her mother. She remained at home for the rest of her life, turning down a marriage proposal from someone she loved because she did not want to leave her mother. However, she secretly kept in touch with him, and when her mother died she finally felt free to marry at the age of fifty-one, just three weeks after her mother's death.[57]

Some women felt less pressure to marry if they had a significant relationship with another woman, a mother, sister, or female lover. Virginia Lee Chambers-Schiller contends that the use of the phrase "my earthly all" between sisters, which was more commonly used between spouses, indicates the intimate nature of the emotional relationship that some single sisters developed. She argues that many sisters viewed their relationship with each other as a type of marriage, an intimate and committed relationship that society recognized as legitimate.[58] Chambers-Schiller and historians of siblings in the antebellum South postulate that sibling relationships supported personal growth in a way that marriage could not precisely because there was no gendered power relation.[59] Mary and Louisa Poppenheim's relationship with each other is only one example of college graduate siblings who lived together. Other sisters also worked together, especially as teachers at the same school, including Mary Vardrine McBee and Estelle McBee. Mary founded Ashley Hall preparatory school in Charleston in 1909 and brought her sister Estelle to live with her and teach at the school. The two lived together until Estelle passed away in 1964. Mary and Linda Neville also lived together after graduation from Bryn Mawr, caring for their ailing father. For over ten years they taught together in the Misses Neville School in their home in Lexington, and when Mary developed cancer, Linda cared for her for two years until her death.[60]

Other women formed lifelong committed relationships with other women. Historians have hesitated to call these relationships lesbian, in part because the women themselves did not but also because it is difficult to determine whether the relationships included sexual physical contact. Whether or not they were sexual, the women lived with each other, sometimes bought property together, and otherwise dedicated themselves to each other. Connie Guion, a doctor originally from Lincolnton, North Carolina, lived with classmate Ruth Woodhull in New York City for decades. South Carolina Radcliffe alumna Abby Winch (Winnie) Christensen lived with her friend, Miss J. G. Morse, for two decades. New Orleans native Florence Converse, a teacher, writer, and author of two histories of Wellesley, lived for years with Professor Vida Scudder and both of their mothers.[61]

These relationships sometimes followed "smashes" or "crushes," which the young women experienced with other students while at school. The rules governing students' social life, which prevented free intercourse with men, also encouraged women to develop intimate relationships with each other. Decades earlier, Bessie Lacy, a North Carolinian who attended Edgeworth Female Seminary in the late 1840s, developed an intimate friendship with another female student that her courtship letters to her eventual husband demonstrate she was unable to replicate with him.[62] The ideal of separate spheres for men and women led women to experience some of their most important moments (such as childbirth, illness, and death) in the company of other women, and nineteenth-century women lived in a "female world of love and ritual."[63]

At women's colleges in the late nineteenth century, students romanced each other: they sent each other flowers, gave each other chocolates, wrote poetry, and otherwise exhibited many of the behaviors associated with romantic love. Student smashes caused great jealousies and heartaches when they ended and otherwise occupied students so thoroughly that Vassar professor Maria Mitchell believed they interfered with students' studies.[64] Grace Richmond, the Poppenheims, and Margaret Preston all describe smashes in their letters, with little thought to their propriety.[65] Most parents and administrators did not exhibit concern, primarily because until around the 1920s they considered smashes harmless and unlikely to lead to anything but a heterosexual marriage. When psychiatrists and psychologists rejected the supposed passionlessness of women and instead recognized their sexual enjoyment and when they began to consider homosexuality a disease, smashes lost their innocent character. Furthermore, in 1897 Havelock Ellis criticized love between women because it increased women's independence from men, thus threatening marriage.[66] Given these concerns, smashes became less common.

Although the marriage rates of southern students at northern colleges were considerably lower than their counterparts who stayed home, many, of course, did marry. Some met husbands while at school; thus, for them the experience enhanced rather than limited their opportunity for marriage. Mary Howard's mother-in-law was shocked to hear that her sister, Ellen Howard, married a professor at the Presbyterian Theological College of Pittsburgh. "Did you ever hear of anything so amazing?" Sarah Bruce wrote her son. "That unattractive, ugly girl—that no one ever thought would have a lover—to marry in this surprising way." Bruce explained that Ellen met Professor Wilson, an educated and well-to-do man from a good family, while at Vassar. She became friends with his sister and visited the family. Bruce concluded, "Mary made a splendid stroke when she sent this ugly sister to Vassar."[67] By widening their circle of acquaintances, the college experience could therefore also have a positive effect on women's marriage chances.

Career

The majority of college graduates from the Seven Sisters worked for wages at some point after their graduation, often before marriage. Yet despite their low marriage rates, southern graduates worked for wages at slightly lower rates than their northern counterparts. For example, at Vassar, 61 percent of total graduates between 1875 and 1915 reported paid employment at some point after graduation, while only 45 percent of southern graduates did.[68] Furthermore, southern students attended Mount Holyoke and Bryn Mawr—schools where upward of 80–90 percent worked—in far smaller numbers than Wellesley or Vassar—

where far fewer had careers. The two schools most popular with southern students, Vassar and Wellesley, wanted to provide a liberal arts education for their students rather than training them for paid employment. Vassar taught a few education courses after 1898, but the school did not want to create a different curriculum for future teachers.[69] College choice clearly factored into graduates' ultimate decision concerning work. But the most significant reason why southern graduates reported less paid employment was that they did not think it proper for women to work outside the home for wages.

Because employment rates for women varied according to class, with many middle- and upper-class married women shunning paid employment unless it was financially necessary through much of the nineteenth century, it is difficult to compare alumnae work rates with those of other women of their social class. One survey taken in 1900 attempted to address this difficulty. Mary Roberts Smith surveyed married college graduates, asking them to answer questions concerning themselves and their sisters, cousins, and friends who did not attend college. She found that nearly three-quarters of college women worked outside the home before marriage, while only approximately one-third of their relatives and friends did.[70] Another survey of socially prominent women represented in the 1914 *Woman's Who's Who of America*, of which 40 percent were college graduates, found that 68 percent of women reported paid employment at least for a time.[71]

In comparison, graduates of southern liberal arts colleges like Randolph-Macon rarely worked for wages. Randolph-Macon faculty and founders believed that most students would marry and only a select few would work for wages; even this admission—that a small number might teach or otherwise work—was considered radical and kept quiet, unlike at schools such as Mount Holyoke and Wellesley, which were proud of their teacher training programs. T. H. Gaines, the president of Agnes Scott College, called homemaking "the greatest vocation in the world for women" and told Orie Latham Hatcher of the Southern Women's Educational Alliance that the college had "no present intention of introducing any other vocational subject." Graduates of the new normal and industrial colleges established for women across the South were more likely to become teachers.[72] These schools were created for daughters in farm families who needed to earn money to support themselves and their families. Offering preparation for wage work, however, was controversial. Winthrop College in Rock Hill, South Carolina, was founded for teacher training. It was later renamed the Industrial and Female College and began to offer domestic science for women to utilize not as teachers but in their personal lives as mothers.[73]

Economic status determined whether or not many women would work. Changes in the southern economy following the Civil War meant that increasing numbers of elite women were more likely to work in order to provide extra income to their families. In 1883 the school superintendent in Alabama claimed that "members of the most elegant and cultivated families in the State are engaged in teaching."[74] But these women, given the elite class status of those students who traveled north, could afford to choose a classical education over a vocational one, and many did not desire a professional career. While some southern alumnae valued the economic independence they achieved as professionals and worked to ensure better employment opportunities for women of all classes, others benefited from their parents' prosperity and were less concerned with economic independence. Women like Louisa and Mary Poppenheim and Gertrude Weil could afford to commit themselves to volunteer work and stay single because their parents' wealth supported them. Not beholden to husbands, instead they had to be careful not to risk their parents' disapproval, at least until their parents' death.

Parents generally provided the most significant influence on a graduate's path following graduation, particularly for a woman unused to economic self-support. Female college professors at Wellesley had parents who pushed them to succeed, to go to college and graduate school, and to have a career. Historian Patricia Palmieri calls them "designated daughters," as opposed to "dutiful daughters." Their parents saw them as pioneers and took pride in their contributions to the community.[75]

Most prominent southern families, however, wanted their daughters to return home and resume their domestic duties rather than work for wages. When Virginia Foster Durr took a job at the county bar association library in order to help support her socially prominent but economically struggling family, her parents were embarrassed. Her mother told her friends that Virginia took the job because she wanted too many dresses.[76] Parents of the middle and upper class still did not want their daughters working unless they were financially obligated to do so.[77] Belle Kearney, the Woman's Christian Temperance Union leader from Mississippi, was unable to attend a northern college because her once-wealthy family could not afford the tuition, yet she never considered working for wages to pay her own fees because her "family would have considered it an eternal disgrace for me to have worked publicly." Anne Walter Fearn, a Mississippi debutante who broke the mold and attended the Woman's Medical College of Pennsylvania, recalled that her family believed she would be a "sacrilege against womanhood" if she became a doctor. Ultimately, they came to support her, but not before her mother reminded her not to disgrace her father's name and threatened to disown Anne.[78] Mary Elinor Poppenheim did not want her daughters working either. When Ida initially failed the entrance examinations to Vassar, Mary Elinor suggested that she travel to Paris to learn French, commenting, "Who knows but maybe some day she might be able to support herself by teaching French, if she should ever have to work for her living by teaching Music and French. Which I hope may never be her fate, or the fate of any of our dear daughters to have to work for their living." From 1899 to 1913 Mary and Louisa Poppenheim owned and edited a journal for women in women's clubs and the UDC entitled the *Keystone*, but this was not a profit-making enterprise for them. Their work for the *Keystone* was voluntary, a fact they proudly noted. Advertising and subscriptions raised enough money to print and mail it, and they did not receive any wages.[79] Linda Neville's family was wealthy enough that she did not need to work for wages, and her father envisioned more study for her instead. "After so much studying," he told her, "you will not be content to remain idle . . . you will enjoy advantages in continuing the study of Latin." He proposed that she study at home for a year or two and then either attend graduate school or edit a book.[80]

Orie Latham Hatcher, the Vassar graduate and education reformer, knew her native Virginia well. In writing an article for the *Nation* in 1918, Orie admitted that (along with Charleston, South Carolina, which she referred to as "a small world unto itself") "nowhere else in the South . . . has a certain conception of what a woman should be and do persisted so fervently as in Virginia." Women in Virginia traditionally were social, gracious, sensitive, and delicate, and they belonged in the home, where they could be protected from the public realm by men. Women worked outside the home only when they needed the money— and the "socially genteel" sought teaching positions because the schoolhouse most nearly resembled the home itself. Women, she argued, avoided work outside the home, occasionally doing sewing or taking in boarders but most often seeking financial support from a male relative. Orie Hatcher, however, saw change occurring even in Virginia, where the impoverishing circumstances of the Civil War, the suffrage movement, and increased access to education gradually were enabling and encouraging women to do more work outside the home. Yet, she concluded, in Virginia these changes in women's roles were taking place successfully only because some level of "that certain delicacy of femininity . . . remained one of the chief assets of woman of the new era as of the old."[81] Virginia, it seems, was not as unique as she proposed, and her explication of the expectations of femininity held firm in the entire South.

College graduates sometimes struggled in the confines of the home, keeping house and caring for children. One Vassar alumna who spent her postgraduate years traveling, volunteering with her local women's club, and caring for her children wrote to her class nine years after graduating, "Mrs. Blatch's lectures sometimes come to my mind and the vigor with which she condemned, as an economic waste, an educated woman being nursery maid. But I am hoping it is not all waste, and that the baby will turn out to be something extra fine from having been brought up with such intelligent care." Eleanor Belknap continued to struggle with her intellectual development and her baby's development. The following year she had changed course, now subscribing to the theory that less intelligent mothers were better. She admitted that her women's club was "too social. I often long to do some real *deep* thinking on some purely intellectual subject . . . but fearing there may be something in this theory that the stupider you are the better mother you will be, I refrain."[82]

When students considered what to do after college, many felt the "family claim" or duty to return home and aid their own families. They especially wanted to spend time with their mothers, from whom they had been separated during college. In describing the family claim, reformer Jane Addams argued that new graduates returned home from school eager to use the knowledge and skills they had acquired for a greater purpose—service to the community. But they encountered parents who insisted that instead they submit to domestic duties. Addams contended that women who abided by the family claim ultimately were unhappy because their experiences, and thus their expectations, differed from those of their parents. Parents (through college) exposed daughters to the poor and suffering and taught them to be selfless, yet when those daughters felt a "social claim" to aid the needy in their community, parents asserted the family claim to prevent them from leaving home to teach, live in a settlement house, or organize workers. In consequence, Addams wrote, "the daughter loses something vital out of her life to which she is entitled. She is restricted and unhappy; her elders, meanwhile, are unconscious of the situation, and we have all the elements of a tragedy."[83] Furthermore, parents belittled their daughters' interests. Addams believed that parents saw a girl as "carried away by a foolish enthusiasm, that she is in search of a career, that she is restless and does not know what she wants." Parents, she thought, blamed their daughter's dissatisfaction on anything but a justifiable urge to do more. They interpreted her desire to participate in affairs outside the family as pitting her will against that of her family. For Addams, the solution to the inevitable clash between the family claim and the social claim was for girls to do what they needed to do and for parents to support their interests and recognize them as individuals.[84]

Jane Addams wrote about the family claim and the social claim so convincingly because she herself had experienced the clash between them. After her graduation from Rockford Female Seminary in Rockford, Illinois, Addams drifted without purpose, suffering physical and mental illness as a result of her frustrations. When she founded Hull House, a settlement house in Chicago,

Addams forthrightly admitted that settlement houses fulfilled the need for college women to be useful as much as they served the interests of the beneficiaries of their programs.

Like Addams, Sophonisba Breckinridge also suffered from bouts of depression between her graduation and her decision to attend the University of Chicago graduate school. She regretted choosing to attend Wellesley. She claimed that she "never forgave" herself for going there instead of staying at home and attending Kentucky A&M University, which would have provided her with a "more honest and simpler" life. Why did she doubt her decision so deeply? Perhaps because her mother became ill and died shortly after Sophonisba's graduation from Wellesley while Sophonisba was traveling in Europe with her sister. Furthermore, while she was a student her parents constantly pushed her to be dutiful, loving, and unselfish. Her mother, Issa Breckinridge, told Sophonisba that she loved her for being dutiful rather than for being smart. While parents like the Breckinridges wanted their daughters to be educated, they hoped college students would not abjure virtues such as duty to family and selflessness—virtues traditionally ascribed to women.[85]

Given these values, Sophonisba's family sent her contradictory messages regarding her career aspirations. Sophonisba considered teaching but was not enthusiastic about it. When her Latin teacher took her aside and told her that teachers who knew Latin were always in demand, she wrote her mother, "This seems coming to the point as to supporting myself, don't you think?" But as her graduation grew closer, Sophonisba considered several options, including following her father into law. "Sometimes I think I want to double mathematics and go on studying it always," she wrote him, "and then I am sure I want to work in your office."[86]

Sophonisba later concluded that her father's desire that she be capable of financial independence came in part from his experience of having to support his mother after the Civil War—he realized then that a southern woman without a man had a difficult time. William Breckinridge told her, "You ought to look squarely in the face that if I die, you will have to make your own living; and if I live you may have to do so anyhow. God preserve you . . . from the aimless, worse than aimless life of the young girls you would associate with here." However, he did not want her to teach or otherwise languish in a low-paid "women's" job, suggesting, "I trust you will like chemistry and the science—such as pharmacy and in electricity, botany and such sciences there is a great field of profitable and [?] work for women; less onerous and more attractive than the needle, the school room and the store."[87]

Two months after asking her father's guidance on a career choice, Sophonisba more directly asserted that she wanted to become a lawyer. She asked her father to let her work in his office after she graduated.[88] In her unpublished autobiography she wrote that she never thought she would have to teach, but she did want to be a lawyer. Yet Wellesley did not prepare her for that career. "I reasoned in such a stupid way," she complained, and she chose Wellesley and a liberal education over the University of Michigan and professional training. After graduation she concluded, "I was no nearer earning my living when I came back than when I had left home four years before." Sophonisba reflected that it was "pitiful" how little her Wellesley education had prepared her for professional employment.

Sophonisba's first foray into employment did not last long. She considered attending law school when the family moved to Washington, D.C., after her father was elected to Congress, but the only school in D.C. that admitted women had night classes, held at a time when she felt bound to be helping out at home. Instead, she taught briefly. Her brother was aghast that she was teaching in order to earn money and positively scandalized that she intended to ride a bicycle to school. Undaunted, she gave up the bike but not the teaching. Sophonisba may have first ridden the bicycle during her days at Wellesley, when, inspired by a passion for athletics and exercise, college students played basketball, golf, tennis, and other sports. Combining exercise and outdoor recreation, bicycling was a national passion in the 1890s, especially for women, who enjoyed the freedom and excitement of bicycling. Sophonisba's mode of transportation must have symbolized her independence to her brother.[89] Eventually, however, despite the exercise, she was weakened by a severe case of influenza and quit teaching. Sophonisba then returned to her original desire to become an attorney. Although she backed out of attending law school at the University of Michigan for financial reasons, she read law books and then passed the bar in Kentucky.[90] She always said that it was her tears that helped her finally overcome her father's and brother's objections to her career choice.[91] Unable to attract clients, Sophonisba gave up her legal career and drifted aimlessly. Looking back, she described herself as confused during the years she spent between graduation from Wellesley and beginning graduate work at the University of Chicago.

After May Estelle Cook took her to the University of Chicago, Sophonisba entered graduate school in political economy. She worked in the residence halls and as an assistant to Talbot and then taught after receiving her doctorate and her law degree there. She never returned home to Kentucky to live, although she stayed in close contact.[92]

Sophonisba found that, as a graduate student, the fact that some women married jeopardized the rest of the female students. She told her father that she was unlikely to get the higher five-hundred-dollar fellowship because the administration believed that women took them and then got married and dropped their career. "A good many officers of the University are down on the women fellows for marrying off so, and I don't blame them," she wrote.[93] Sophonisba also struggled to find employment in academia. After receiving her doctorate she did not receive a position in the economics or political science departments and only received a faculty position as an instructor when the University of Chicago created a new department, the Department of Household Administration, under Marion Talbot. This department was intended to provide a place for women to study the home and make a more scientific study of housekeeping. Sophonisba eventually found a more suitable place for herself by helping to create the Chicago School of Civics and Philanthropy and by delving into social reform, marrying her academic studies with her concern for the larger community.[94]

Sophonisba's father ultimately came to understand her. In 1902, the year after Sophonisba received her doctorate and while she was in law school, William Breckinridge wrote a column in the *Lexington Herald* called "The Problem of the Daughter." In it he argued that many college-educated women—and their fathers—began to question why they needed to marry, why they could not get certain jobs. "The father at length begins to question the system in which his circle of society prepares a daughter exclusively for marriage and to be a costly and pleasing plaything in her father's or her husband's home," he wrote. William understood that women wanted to be themselves and that they developed a social consciousness that made them interested in the world around them. The father, he concluded, "becomes more sympathetic than disapproving."[95]

Sophonisba Breckinridge spent part of her career studying the progress of women, publishing *Women in the Twentieth Century: A Study of Their Political, Social and Economic Activities* in 1933. In it she explored women's activism outside the home in both volunteer and paid positions. Sophonisba argued that women's lives had changed due to their own involvement in the nineteenth-century antislavery movement and changes in industrial working conditions for women.[96] Using data from the census and Bureau of Labor statistics, Sophonisba contended that women still faced many barriers to high-paying occupations due to lingering prejudices that earlier had been manifested as doubts about women's physical capabilities. She pointed out that the growing number of women workers raised some significant questions, notably, if "the access of women to the satisfactions of life must either require celibacy or continue to be vicarious or indirect through a husband, or whether . . . her participation in productive life and in domestic life be individual and direct." Thus, she concluded that the rise in the number of native-born women working signified "growth of more independent and self-respecting attitudes on the part of women."[97] Sophonisba's research topic and her conclusions were influenced by her own experience. After drifting restlessly for years, she found that she needed to be employed despite her family's initial disapproval—and they eventually came to understand her. Her study shows her commitment to identifying the needs of working women and helping other women find satisfaction in the workplace that she herself enjoyed.

Ellen Churchill Semple, an 1882 graduate of Vassar, also drifted for nine restless years before she found her calling as a geographer. Graduating as class valedictorian although she was only nineteen, Ellen returned home to Louisville, where she taught. Unfulfilled, she first began a program of self-education and then returned to Vassar for a master's degree. She traveled to Germany to study with the anthropogeographer Friedrich Ratzel. Initially forced to listen to lectures from a chair outside the classroom, she was finally allowed by the university to study formally with him. After study in Germany, she and her sister Patty, also a Vassar alumna, founded the Semple Collegiate School, where Ellen taught history for two years. Ellen returned to the University of Leipzig in 1895 and several years later wrote *American History and Its Geographic Environment*, a standard college textbook for many years. Ellen also pioneered field study in geography, riding a horse throughout Appalachia. She remained loyal to her home in Louisville and to Vassar, claiming that English and Latin classes trained her to write well and understand the ancient world, while the student body influenced her with its cosmopolitan makeup. Ellen Semple reflected, "I owe Vassar much."[98]

Like Sophonisba and Ellen, Margaret Mitchell suffered from the blues after leaving Smith College. Margaret's mother, May Belle, died young while Margaret was still at school. May Belle, a suffragist, left a somewhat cryptic message in her last letter written while she was ill with the influenza that would kill her. She wrote, "Give of yourself with both hands and overflowing heart, but give only the excess after you have lived your own life." May Belle seemed to be suggesting that Margaret put her own happiness first, but she quickly stepped back from such a bold assertion. "This is badly put," she continued. "What I mean is that your life and energies belong to yourself, your husband and your children. Anything leftover after you have served these, give and give generously, but be sure there is no stinting of love and attention at home." May Belle then advised Margaret to go ahead and marry rather than stay single in order to care for her father. "Care for your father when he is old . . . but never let his or anyone else's life interfere with your real life," she wrote. What did her mother mean? That Margaret Mitchell needed to live for herself first and then her husband and children? Or that she had to live for her husband and children before she could aid others like her father?[99]

Her mother's death forced Margaret to abandon Smith after only one year, returning home to Atlanta to run the household. Her friend Courtenay Ross claimed that Margaret never complained about having to leave Smith.[100] Yet she expressed a longing to be back in school even if she did not overtly rebel against her situation. She corresponded with Allen Edee, an Amherst College student whom she had dated. When he asked if she had any plans to visit him in New York or Northampton, she replied that she could envision the school year getting under way and the girls returning. "And oh! how I miss it!" she lamented. "Housekeeping in the day and flirting o'nights is all right, but I miss the comradeship and the mischief and the 'always something doing' atmosphere, my school days are over, I fear." Admitting that she knew she needed further education, she wondered, "Lord knows how I'll end up." Margaret was adamant that she did not return to Atlanta to find a husband, nor did she quit school to debut. "Debut! My God, Al!" she scoffed. "Giving up college and forever all dreams of a journalistic career to come home and keep house and keep my family and home intact and take Mother's place in society was about the only unselfish thing I can remember having done in my life. . . . Debut! Poo! Poo!"[101] Margaret believed that she had changed during her year at school, which perhaps explains why she felt depressed; she told Allen Edee that "there is something missing in my life." In July 1920 she tried to figure out a way to get back to school: "More than ever is the call for more schooling, more than ever the desire to know if I'm worth anything is strong. . . . I feel like a dynamo going to waste." Margaret told Edee that although she had decided she had to find a way to get back to school, she had not told her family yet because she feared they would strongly object. Her brother had even argued that "college was the ruination of girls!"

Margaret finally sought employment after visiting a friend in Alabama who worked for the newspaper there. Upon her return to Atlanta she applied to the *Atlanta Journal* Sunday magazine for a job writing feature stories. Not surprisingly, her father did not approve of her getting the job. She had wanted to take business courses to learn to type, but "Dad wouldn't let me," she recalled. "That was in those days beyond recall when nice girls didn't work—and before I stopped being a nice girl and became a reporter." Furthermore, Margaret investigated professional women for the magazine and found scarcely any in Atlanta. Male editors and reporters resented women reporters. She frequently wrote about the dilemma facing southern women who wanted to work and marry, querying young women about their ambition. Many wanted to work before marriage, citing independence and pay as the chief appeal of a career, but even these young women believed that their work experience would ultimately make them better spouses and stay-at-home mothers—none envisioned working once they had children.[102] Like her subjects, after her marriage in 1925 to John Marsh, Margaret quit the magazine as soon as her husband made enough

money to support the family. But she was frustrated by the role of society debutante and matron. She kept reading and eventually decided to write a novel that
would become *Gone with the Wind*.[103]

Pressure to fulfill the family claim also came from other suitors and husbands who made it difficult for women to pursue professional careers. Mary
Chase became interested in biology at Wellesley while dissecting cats with Professor Mary Alice Willcox. Willcox encouraged Mary to study in Zurich, but her
parents would not allow her to go to Europe. According to Mary, she attended
medical school in Philadelphia but transferred to New York because she found
herself with too many beaux, one of whom she married. After her marriage she
and her husband decided that their small town did not need two doctors, so
he practiced and she did not. Mary, however, found enjoyment in her domestic
role, and when she looked back in 1938 she claimed that she did not regret her
choices.[104]

Unlike Sophonisba and Margaret, who challenged their fathers and brothers when they started working, Josephine Simrall had her parents' approval
when she left for college intending to teach in academia. When Josie apolo-
gized for spending so much money, she reminded her father that she hoped
"someday—and soon too—to be a source of income rather than outlay." Josie
certainly managed to make ends meet for herself. After teaching at Sweet Briar
in the Department of Psychology and at the University of Kentucky in English, she served the University of Cincinnati as dean of women for many years.
She also became involved in her community, organizing a College Club and
a Woman's City Club, and she was a member of the AAUW and her church
women's group.[105] When Sue Hall's graduation from Wellesley approached she
feared she would not be able to land a teaching position. "I shall be disappointed
if I don't get a place and am glad my friends think I will," she told her parents.[106]
While Jane Addams's explanation of the tension between the social claim and
the family claim was accurate for many, for others the family claim did not have
to mean a choice between social work and domestic drudgery. In their cases, the
backing of their family could legitimate their work and protect their reputation
as proper middle-class women.[107]

With the support of her father, Wellesley alumna Lilian Wyckoff Johnson
mixed professional aspirations with voluntary social reform work. She initially
sought a professional career because she wanted to follow her father's dreams
that she work to open a college for southern women, teaching in various positions until she abandoned the idea for a college and instead helped establish the
West Tennessee State Normal School in Memphis. Educated first at Wellesley,
she then attended the University of Michigan and studied abroad before she received her doctorate from Cornell. She also taught at the Clara Conway Institute

and at Vassar and was president of Western College for Women in Oxford, Ohio. Exhausted, she left Ohio and returned home to Memphis, where she taught at a local high school. Through the Nineteenth Century Club, Lilian worked to establish a normal school in Memphis, lobbying the state legislature and working to build public support for the school. A local newspaper claimed, "She stepped out ahead of the crowd to meet the human needs she saw. Many followed the example she set. Others who did not were at least inspired by her courage, her selflessness, and her zest for living." Lilian eventually became interested in rural community cooperative reform and after her retirement to Florida worked to improve race relations.[108]

Southern students themselves expressed a range of attitudes toward employment. While some battled parents to pursue the careers of their dreams, many clearly found the idea of women working for wages distasteful. Neither Mary and Louisa Poppenheim nor Margaret Preston intended to work for wages. Despite her growing studiousness, Margaret did not envision herself with a career, asking her mother why she was studying at Bryn Mawr to begin with: "Surely you don't think Aunt Jessie wants me to, do you, in order to fit myself for teaching or anything like that?" she queried.[109]

Julia Hammond apparently went to Radcliffe with the thought of being a doctor, encouraged to do so by her father. Hammond, however, was far too attached to her home and family to pursue such a career. Her initial impression of a female doctor she met in Cambridge was positive but revealed Julia's struggle to reconcile family with career. After meeting Dr. Helen Morten, she wrote her mother describing the labor and selflessness that the medical profession demanded. "But this life does not as you think break up family ties, but rather binds them closer," she continued, describing how Morten cared for her invalid sister and supported two other sisters. Julia also must have been considering the propriety of female doctors, for she described to her mother several days later what Morten wore and reassured her mother that Morten was a refined lady.[110] Julia, however, was unwilling to make the sacrifices necessary to become a doctor. Within several months she was at home with her mother. Back home in South Carolina she chose housekeeping over paid employment.

By far the most acceptable, and available, work for those who wanted to earn a living was teaching. The vast majority of graduates from the Seven Sisters who worked taught at one point in their career, including over 70 percent of southern graduates from Bryn Mawr, Mount Holyoke, and Vassar.[111] Tennessean Mary Galbraith was inspired by the "broad outlook on life and high standard of scholarship" she gained at Wellesley College to give something back as a teacher.[112] Many taught their entire lives, eventually becoming principal or headmistress or founding a school. Others taught for less than five years after graduation and then quit teaching to marry, including at least eighteen southerners from Vassar alone. Loula Rhyne, class of 1888, returned to North Carolina from Mount Holyoke to teach at Statesville College for three years, then quit teaching to marry and have children.[113] Some students began teaching a year after graduation because they had become bored or frustrated with life back home dedicated to housework and social life only. Alice Sparks, class of 1888, from Nashville, went home for a year after Mount Holyoke to get "acquainted again with my family" before moving to Georgia to teach at Dalton College. After resting for one year after Mount Holyoke, Eva Stanley, class of 1892, declared herself bored and took up teaching.[114] Still others taught, usually to earn money, before embarking on a later career, including Connie Guion of Wellesley, who taught for five years to put her sisters through college before attending medical school and becoming a doctor. Frances Veach returned home from Mount Holyoke to Danville, Kentucky, where she taught at her alma mater, Caldwell College. She wrote to her classmates that she was happy to be there because, "first of all, it is near home and in Kentucky. Anyone who ever saw me board a Western train at Springfield [Massachusetts] knows how much that means to me."[115]

In addition to the many southern women who returned home to teach and were dedicated to sending more southern students to their alma mater, several notable women became significant education reformers. Orie Latham Hatcher, a classmate of Mary Poppenheim at Vassar, gave up a promising career in academia at Bryn Mawr to return home to Virginia and improve educational opportunities for southern girls. After her graduation in 1888 she taught for several years at Miss Belle Peers's School in Louisville and then at Richmond Female Institute, where she helped its president, Dr. James H. Nelson, plan its transformation into the Woman's College of Richmond. After teaching at the new college she received her doctorate in English at the University of Chicago and eventually became an associate professor of comparative and English literature at Bryn Mawr. While still living in Pennsylvania, Orie helped found the Virginia Association of Colleges and Schools for Girls in 1906. This association surveyed women's schools, evaluating educational standards. Her career changed direction in 1914, when she met with fellow Richmond activist Mary Cooke Branch Munford and others who sought to provide southern women with "reliable information and sound counsel regarding education, occupational choices and training." The group organized the Virginia Bureau of Vocations for women, and Orie left Bryn Mawr to become its first president. She found that schools prepared women for teaching and homemaking and little else in terms of paid occupation, and she wanted to serve southern women by helping their education prepare them for employment. As the scope of the bureau grew, it became known as the Southern Women's Educational Alliance and then the Alliance for Guidance of Rural Youth. The alliance first focused on broadening educational opportunities for southern women and providing information to girls about their professional options. It helped open the Medical College of Virginia to women and published many pamphlets and the book *Occupations for Women*, written by Orie Hatcher. The alliance was a clearinghouse through which schools and organizations worked with Orie to provide information to students and help them obtain the necessary funding for their education. In the mid-1920s the alliance shifted its focus to training educational and occupational guidance counselors for rural youth, including both boys and girls.

Orie Hatcher was the guiding force of the Alliance for Guidance of Rural Youth. She was inspired by her mother's example as well as by the opportunities for women that she witnessed firsthand in the North. When her mother graduated from Fluvanna Institute in Virginia, her senior thesis, "Independence of Thought," claimed that "if women could not do as they chose, they might think as they chose and get ready for action." Orie herself managed to reconcile her northern influence with her southern roots. She always stressed the southern personnel behind the alliance and convinced southern society women to support her causes. At the same time, she realized the relatively radical nature of her work, which she understood "went a great deal beyond public sentiment and understanding." The first thing she had to do was convince southerners that it was proper for southern women to work outside the home—no easy task. "We are here," she wrote, "to counteract the tradition that any educated woman who must earn her living must choose between teaching and stenography, and to show her that there are really hundreds of other possibilities from which to choose." An "importer" of ideas from the North concerning education and employment, Orie sought to improve both and to convince colleges that they could provide vocational guidance even as they retained their high standards of a liberal arts education. Her personality and dedication were so inspiring that she convinced other bright young women to work with her for little or no salary.[116]

Julia Strudwick Tutwiler was another educator dedicated to improving educational opportunities for southerners. Her first desire to better the community came during the Civil War, when she wanted to nurse soldiers. She begged her father to allow her to do so, but he refused her request, instead asking her to teach at his school, Greene Springs Academy. After a year at Vassar in 1866 and additional training in Germany, Julia taught first at Tuscaloosa Female College and then at Livingston Female Academy, where she was coprincipal. She worked to convince the Alabama legislature to establish a normal department at Livingston, which eventually became known as Livingston Normal College. Julia also was instrumental in the University of Alabama's decision to admit women.

But not only was Julia interested in normal training and the college course for women, she also worked to establish an industrial school for girls with the idea that women needed technical training to be better homemakers as well as to have job skills to earn money—revolutionary ideas in late-nineteenth-century Alabama.[117]

Many southern women at northern colleges continued their studies in graduate school, receiving a doctorate and embarking on a career in academia, with a sizable number of students eventually serving as a college dean or president. In addition to Josephine Simrall, dean of women at the University of Cincinnati, and Lilian Wyckoff Johnson, president of Western College for Women, Mount Holyoke alumna Mary Ashby Cheek was president of Rockford College, and Vassar alumna Frances Jewell served as dean of women at the University of Kentucky before her marriage to the university president. C. Mildred Thompson, an Atlantan who graduated from Vassar in 1903, returned there to teach history in 1907 and became the dean of the college, a position she held for twenty-five years. While a student at Vassar, she was on the debate team that beat Wellesley in Vassar's first intercollegiate debate and was elected to Phi Beta Kappa. After retiring from Vassar, she taught briefly at the University of Georgia and was asked to serve as dean of women at the Free University of Strasbourg. Thompson also represented the United States at the United Nations Education Conference in 1945 and at the Conference of Allied Ministers of Education in 1944, and she helped draft the charter of UNESCO. Thompson encouraged Vassar students to pursue careers, even suggesting that the first female president of the nation might be a Vassar graduate. She told students that they did not have to choose between marriage and a career and reminded those concerned with childcare duties that children grow up.[118] Georgiana Goddard King, though she never earned a doctorate or became an administrator, made a name for herself by pioneering research in Spanish art and culture. Born in West Virginia and raised in New York and Norfolk, Virginia, she received her bachelor of arts in 1896 and master of arts in 1897 from Bryn Mawr College and returned to teach there from 1906 to 1935. Described as a "tradition and a cult" as a teacher, she also published many books on Spanish art, architecture, and literature. Her best-known book, *The Way of St. James*, was a "combination of art criticism, literary criticism, travelogue, and adventure, written in her highly personal literary style."[119]

Career options outside of teaching were limited though growing by the early twentieth century.[120] In 1885 Jane M. Bancroft suggested that more career opportunities were becoming available. Although there were already too many teachers, she argued that women were still needed to teach science, to act as principals or superintendents, and to teach pedagogy. She then suggested medicine, pharmacology, civil service, law, architecture, and journalism as appropriate fields for women to begin to enter in larger numbers.[121] In the South, middle- and upper-class women found teaching to be the most reputable job, with writing (fiction or journalism) another option. There were few other acceptable positions for "ladies" and, with industrial growth lagging behind that of the North, even fewer opportunities in business and retail.

Although Mount Holyoke was well known for encouraging graduates to become Christian missionaries to foreign lands, Wellesley also produced a surprising number of southern students who dedicated themselves to missionary work. Jessie Hall spent thirty-four years teaching at a girls' school in China before being forced to return home during World War II; Cornelia McGhilvary spent fifty-one years in Siam (Thailand), where she ran a boys' school with her husband; Nellie Ferger was a principal in a girls' school in India from 1918 to 1956; and Martha Cecil was a missionary to China for thirty-six years. Martha Cecil had been president of the Christian Association at Wellesley and credited the Wellesley motto with impacting her lifework.[122]

A small number of southern women from northern colleges became doctors or attorneys. North Carolinian Connie Guion became a distinguished physician in New York City, garnering many honors, including the naming of a building at New York Hospital after her. Connie said later that she gained much more than the foundation in science necessary for medical school while at Wellesley. The Durants encouraged her to believe that women could do anything, and she made friends and broadened her interests.[123] Sallie Borden, a Mount Holyoke alumna, felt the same compulsion to serve the South that many teachers did, and after she became a physician she opened a clinic to serve the poor and African Americans in Goldsboro, North Carolina.[124] Jennie N. and Mary Browne, Bryn Mawr graduates, both became doctors, while their sister Ethel received a doctorate in zoology. The three sisters were daughters of another Bryn Mawr graduate, Jennie Nicholson Browne, supported woman suffrage, and were active in the DAR, Colonial Dames, College Club, Social Service Club, and American Medical Association.[125]

Many other southern women sought a life in letters, another field of employment that, like teaching, was socially acceptable for proper women. Josephine Pinckney and Beatrice Witte Ravenel, two wealthy Charleston natives, attended Radcliffe before writing poetry and novels. Beatrice attended Radcliffe for five years in the 1890s and was one of the editors of the *Harvard Monthly Magazine* while there. There "she made a vivid impression on her contemporaries as a forceful, strong-minded young woman rather contemptuous of the niceties of polite society." Described as "the most brilliant student at the Harvard Annex," she kept company with young poets and intellectuals in Cambridge. Her earliest poetry showed glimpses of a rebellious woman, asking in an 1894 poem,

"Is your self like a hot-house, too troubled and warm," and questioning the gender of God in another. She returned home from Cambridge, married, had a daughter, and wrote virtually nothing until 1918, when she began publishing again. While many of her editorials and short stories reflected prevailing ideas in Charleston society, Beatrice Witte Ravenel continued to express her iconoclastic ideas and gave voice to the silenced in her poetry. Josephine Pinckney was a descendant of noted plantation owner and author Eliza Pinckney and was the first student to attend the Ashley Hall School, founded by Wellesley alumna Mary McBee. After some European travel, Josephine attended summer school at Columbia University in New York, took classes at age twenty-four at the College of Charleston when it first allowed women, and two years later completed her formal education with one semester at Radcliffe. Already a published poet, she went to study with professors from Harvard whom she believed could help her improve her skills in composition and literary history. Both authors were dedicated to Charleston, a prominent backdrop for much of their writings, although Josephine's writing explored the end of the aristocracy there. Josephine also helped found the Charleston Society of the Preservation of Spirituals and restored a home in the city. She also contributed a chapter, entitled "Bulwarks against Change," to the *Culture in the South* collection of essays debating southern identity in the modern world. In it, she argued that southern character was marked by conservatism and the importance of the family, which resisted "the forces of steel and electricity" as long as possible, although her novels seem to indicate that steel and electricity ultimately won.[126]

Other southern women took up the pen writing newspaper columns. Nell Battle Lewis was a Phi Beta Kappa graduate of Smith who came from prominent North Carolina families. Although she later claimed that Smith "provided nothing to kick against," her biographer argues that she lost the provincialism of many southern women through her exposure at college to a variety of people and issues. Nell was active in the North Carolina Federation of Women's Clubs and the North Carolina League of Women Voters, where she worked with Gertrude Weil. She initially worked against child labor, illiteracy, and farm tenancy and was a proponent of women's rights and the social welfare of women and children. A southerner through and through, Nell believed that women in the South needed the freedom and education that chivalry precluded. She wore riding breeches (i.e., pants) to her first job interview and got a newspaper job through her father's connections. Adopting the cultural dress of the flappers, Nell smoked, cut her hair, and even commuted to work on her bicycle.[127] Hired to write on society news and women's issues, she later initiated a weekly column called "Incidentally." Writing in a flamboyant style reminiscent of H. L. Mencken, Nell crusaded against many aspects of southern culture. A member of the Association of Southern Women for the Prevention of Lynching, Nell was considered by some to be a racial liberal, even though she never questioned Jim Crow, abandoned her support for states' rights, or changed her view of Reconstruction as a tragically marred mistake. Furthermore, she struggled with the image of the southern lady as someone to be worshiped on a pedestal. Historian Darden Pyron contends that Nell understood that "the Lady *was* the South: both represented society, culture, order, continuity, the old way, the past, tradition, and—within the special context of the Civil War in particular—death. To break this chain of connections, then, was to be an individual and live." But, Pyron cautioned, when women considered their own status, they threatened to undermine not only their own sense of self but also the entwined southern racial and sexual hierarchy.

Nell Battle Lewis herself wrote, "The whole of my sentimental attachment is to the Old South order. . . . I almost feel [as] if I had stuck a knife in a friend's back. But I can't help it—no, I just can't! . . . For I cannot feel that I should sacrifice either to sentiment or to false patriotism an estimate of the old regime as it related to women." Yet Lewis based her idea of the new woman on more traditional beliefs—that woman's primary role as mother and housekeeper should inspire her to social reform to better the home. [128] She decided to enter the male-dominated political arena, starting law school, running for the state legislature, and supporting Al Smith's presidential campaign. The loss of these two campaigns, the stress of her leadership in a textile strike in Gastonia and her legal representation of female delinquents accused of arson at the state's female detention home, and personal financial difficulties led to her physical collapse and a nervous breakdown. Eventually, she could no longer "reconcile her dedication to social reform with her devotion to white supremacy." She dropped her crusade for social justice, relatively liberal racial attitudes, and emergent feminism, becoming a reactionary conservative and staunch anti-Communist. [129] Nell was apparently unable to reconcile the contradictions within her beliefs and her liberal concerns with the conservatism of the region.

Unlike the experiences of those students who left for college already determined either to work or not to work, Gertrude Weil's experience perhaps best captures an uncertain middle ground. Gertrude went to Smith for an education, not job training, but she and her parents were broad minded enough to consider what she should do if she had to earn money. They also wanted her to be busy and productive after graduation without having to leave home. Gertrude's mother, Mina Weil, asked her what career she would choose after college if she had to choose one "as a necessity." Mina was quick to reassure Gertrude that she wanted her daughter to come home but commented that Gertrude would have to readjust to living at home after years away from it.[130] Gertrude replied that, along with many fellow students seeking jobs, she had already begun to consider what she could do. She first proposed "some sort of designing—book-covers designing," which she could presumably do from her parents' home. But if she were to live away, she continued, then she wanted "to teach in one of the slum schools of New York. . . . I haven't much experience in making myself useful or in saving other people trouble and care—it might be good to begin experimenting."[131] Gertrude's mother wrote a long response:

> I think just now we are selfish enough to want you at home for awhile . . . and I think if you look for it you can find something to do for the needy class here. We have no manual training of any sort in our graded school, so it seems to me if you can arrange to teach some drawing and sewing perhaps to the lower grades, the school would be the better for it, and you too. I want you to have some regular work once you get home, or you will be lost after 15 years of knowing what each day held for you. Make some inquiries concerning book designing, for this sounds like pleasant work and I would just like to know you could really earn if necessary—I have a horror of a helpless girl—a dependent one.

Despite her concern for Gertrude's need for stimulation and useful service to the community, Gertrude's mother did not want her to leave home. She also did not necessarily believe that such work would ruin Gertrude for potential marriage: "I hope you can give some time systematically to woman's work, making clothes and cooking, for as a rule these are the necessary qualifications for a good home-maker."[132] Her mother's suggestions caused Gertrude to consider starting a sewing class for children.[133] Gertrude was not ready to return home immediately and instead spent some time traveling, including to Europe with friends from college. She shared the same ambivalence as Margaret Mitchell toward the expectation that elite southern white women needed to prioritize their social life. Gertrude wrote home from Europe, "I'm afraid I was never intended for a sporty life. This dissipation is too much for me. . . . I have made many observations of Society—some of them tickle my sense of humor almost to the laughing point." Not only did Gertrude feel as though she was wasting time, but she had a hard time believing that some women found fulfillment in that kind of social life alone. "How a girl can do nothing but this and look forward to nothing but this is beyond my understanding. . . . I couldn't tell you all the Silly things that Society uttered that evening. I suppose this is what girls grow to womanhood for," she concluded.[134] When she finally returned to Goldsboro, where she remained the rest of her life, she taught sewing to mill women but found her niche as a leader in the state Federation of Women's Clubs, the woman suffrage movement, the Commission on Interracial Cooperation, and other volunteer reform associations. Her choice—volunteer work—was a common compromise for southern women.

Despite the professional success of Sophonisba Breckinridge, Nell Battle Lewis, and the other professional women, the mixed messages southern students received from parents and other family members regarding the appropriateness of paid employment left many women reluctant to work for wages unless it was financially necessary. However, they, too, experienced desires to change themselves and their communities and to do more than attend teas. In short, they sought to change the role of the southern lady. Margaret Preston, Mary and Louisa Poppenheim, Linda Neville, Gertrude Weil, and hundreds of other southern graduates therefore carved out new roles for themselves as activist women rather than as professionals or wage earners. The influence of their college education on their social reform efforts is evident in the next chapter.

CHAPTER SIX

After College

The Activist

 North Carolinian Gertrude Weil's favorite class during her senior year at Smith College was Some Problems of Poverty: The Unemployed; the Employment of Women and Children; the Housing of the Poor; Social Settlements, taught by Professor Charles F. Emerick.[1] Through this and other courses Gertrude came to believe that poverty for women could not be alleviated until women had full rights. She therefore embraced woman suffrage. Gertrude's education was not limited to the classroom. She traveled to New York City, where she visited settlement houses and had tea at the Friendly Aid, run by Mary Simkhovitch, who had spoken at Smith. When Gertrude witnessed poor neighborhoods, she compared the reality of poverty to the descriptions she had read in Jacob Riis's 1892 book *The Children of the Poor* while in class at Smith.[2]

Yet Gertrude's family was wealthy, and when she returned home to Goldsboro, North Carolina, she was initially unsure of how to translate her newly found passion for justice into action. Traveling with little serious aim made her restless; she sought work with more meaning. Finally, she found a role as a leader in the women's club, woman suffrage, and social reform movements and became known as "Federation Gertie" for her dedication to the North Carolina Federation of Women's Clubs.

Gertrude Weil was typical of many northern-educated southern women who found fulfillment in one or more of the many new women's associations and reform interests popular during the Progressive Era. These women—whether or not they married or worked for wages—were activists. At the forefront of social reform, women's clubs, suffrage, education, and other causes, their disproportionate leadership of women's activism in the South demonstrates the influence of education on both the individual and the community. As Anne Scott first argued, women spearheaded the Progressive reform movement in the South.[3] A northern college education provided many of these leaders the motivation to break out of the domestic role elite white southern women had been limited to and undertake new roles within the community. Certainly, some students sought prestigious colleges because they already exhibited leadership abilities, but many learned the skills they needed at school. They gained practical expertise, such as how to organize a meeting or give a speech, as well as self-confidence. They returned home anxious to put their newfound interests and talents to work. Southern women generally organized a decade or two later than their sisters in the North, allowing time for the northern example to influence southern women, who then responded to local conditions.

The correlation between education and activism is evident around the nation. A study of a sampling of prominent women included in the 1914 *Woman's Who's Who of America* found that over 60 percent had some advanced education, and a full 43.8 percent had college degrees, compared to less than 8 percent of the female population as a whole.[4] Like southern graduates of northern colleges, this group of women joined church associations and women's clubs and supported suffrage, with a full 62.4 percent participating in humanitarian work and 54.6 percent in social reform work. Women's clubs were particularly popular, with 77 percent of women reporting membership and 49 percent holding office.[5]

Southern female reformers who came of age before the proliferation of the Seven Sisters, while not attending a northern college, had unusually strong educational opportunities. They also often had exposure to northern teachers or time spent in the North. For example, Caroline E. Merrick, president of the Louisiana WCTU and a leading suffragist, married at age fifteen with little formal education. But the influence of her stepmother, Susan Brewer, a Massachusetts native who raised her, was strong. Caroline recalled that Susan "was instrumental in bringing into Alabama, Mississippi and Louisiana over sixty accomplished teachers, she herself having been at the head of successful schools in New York, Baltimore, Tuscaloosa and Washington. The call of teaching she gave up when she married my father, but the cause of education in the South was greatly promoted by her influence, for which reason she has been compared to Mary Lyon of New England."[6] Belle Kearney, the WCTU leader from Mississippi, had a schoolteacher from Maine who exerted a strong influence on her desire (unfulfilled) to attend a northern women's college, while Elizabeth Fisher Johnson and Lide Smith Meriwether, temperance and suffrage leaders in Tennessee, both attended schools run by Emma Willard or her protégées.[7]

For southern women coming of age between 1875 and 1915, attending a northern college was particularly influential because they were exposed to woman's rights issues to a greater degree than they would have been had they stayed in the South. Agnes Scott College in Atlanta focused on building Christian character; talk of social activism, woman's rights, and suffrage did not invade the campus until 1917. Meanwhile, beginning in the 1870s, Progressive professors at northern colleges introduced students to poverty and social issues on a theoretical level in the classroom as well as showed them what they could do about such problems in settlement houses and other social welfare associations. Exposure to poverty in the North—whether through Jacob Riis's photographs or at a settlement house in the city—opened their eyes to poverty and the needs of many in the South. Southern graduates of northern colleges flocked to volunteer work in women's clubs or suffrage or education reform because they wanted to utilize the skills they honed in school to better their communities without necessarily working for wages. Whether single or married, southern women believed they could still be proper ladies while doing volunteer work, even for liberal causes.

In particular, many alumnae of northern colleges led the suffrage movement in the South. Historian Elna Green argues that the movement emerged from the doldrums after 1910 in part because higher education was well on its way to producing a "New Woman." In particular, she found that a northern college education or other northern influence was often the influential factor in why suffrage leaders took up the cause. Historian Sarah Wilkerson-Freeman discovered the same influence for North Carolina suffragists, claiming that many had "a high level of education [and] exposure to other regions outside the South." Eight of the leaders in the state she profiled were educated either in the North or in the Midwest, although only one, Gertrude Weil, had attended one of the Seven Sisters.[8] Historian Rebecca Montgomery also contended that a northern education, whether formal or informal (contacts with northern women), brought education reformers in Georgia to reconsider gender roles. "Ironically," she writes, "institutional discrimination [the lack of colleges for women in the South] intended to shore up the old social order had, in effect, pushed southern daughters out of their region and into the seedbed of the women's rights and Progressive movements."[9] This chapter explains exactly how that education led to women's public activism generally and the suffragist movement specifically.

Notably, women from throughout both the upper South and the Deep South became activists, and, unlike their antebellum foremothers, such as Angelina and Sarah Grimké, they were not exiled from home because of the radical nature of their views. While some women profiled in this chapter, such as Sophonisba Breckinridge, lived in the North, many returned home to the South to do their work. Northern-educated suffragists can be found from the Deep South state of Alabama to the border state of Kentucky. M. Carey Thomas, a Quaker from Maryland, was capable of ensuring that her own racist views held sway at Bryn Mawr while she presided there, while Alabamian Virginia Foster Durr would eventually work to support the civil rights movement. Why individual women became active when their sisters did not is not attributable to patterns of residence, either before or after college. What is clear is that southern women educated at the Seven Sisters were disproportionately likely to lead women's activism than their sisters who remained home in the South.

Because society placed so much emphasis on women's duty to the home and family, southern women agonized over their decision to leave home and attend college, they felt guilty while they were away at school, and when they returned they struggled to create new roles that would reconcile familial duty with their newfound independence. In 1896 Helen Starrett recognized that many college graduates returned home unsure of how to readjust to life there. Starrett reminded students not to avoid housekeeping lest one appear spoiled; that boys might be afraid of them; and that it was acceptable for those who did not marry right away to work. She encouraged those who did not work to find usefulness in housework, improving their families and their communities. As Jane Addams explained concerning the benefits of Hull House to the settlement workers who lived there, perhaps college students became so active because they understood that working to help others was the best way to help themselves.[10]

Many alumnae who became social activists had parents who encouraged them, especially given the history of parents' support for their education in the North. Others became active despite their parents' disapproval or tried to channel their energies into only the most respectable outlets for women, such as church work or organizations like the Junior League. The appeal of social welfare reform was so strong because students changed greatly while they were at school, especially those who were exposed to the possibilities of women's activism. As we have seen, students became more independent. Independence came from living on their own as well as from intellectual development and was strengthened by extracurricular activities.[11]

Women were joiners, and the Seven Sisters were replete with associations. By the 1890s students had shed many of the restrictions held over from seminary days and created a vibrant student culture.[12] At Vassar two of the most prominent associations included Qui Vive and the Temous et Mores House of Commons, both debating societies. The societies had an open debate with each other once a year before the entire college. Student government associations played substantial roles in regulating student behavior at Vassar, Bryn Mawr, and Wellesley. One of the most important clubs at Bryn Mawr was the Graduate Club, which sponsored monthly talks by professors and addresses by prominent speakers. Bryn Mawr also had debating clubs, a chess club, a glee club, and an athletic association. Smith College's literary societies tapped not only the brightest literary talents but also some of the most popular students. Students wrote and read papers on literature and heard guest speakers.[13]

Because these were women's colleges, women developed and ran the organizations themselves, albeit with the guidance of male and female faculty advisors. In 1908 Lucy Sprague Mitchell, an educator who graduated from Radcliffe, observed that women students who attended single-sex schools had to develop their own social and other activities and therefore came to be more self-possessed than their peers at coeducational institutions.[14] More recently, historian Helen Horowitz has argued, "Exposure threatened to reveal the most carefully guarded secret of the women's colleges, that in a college composed only of women, students did not remain feminine. Through college organizations, they discovered how to wield power and to act collectively; through aggressive sport, to play as a team member and to win; through dramatics, to take male roles."[15] Southern students' experiences at the Seven Sisters echo these observations. Georgian Mary Comer initially showed a definite lack of self-confidence when she hesitated to take on a leadership role as a freshman at Smith College. She explained to her mother that the classes took turns having a student lead the prayer meeting, but Mary told her mother, "I drew the line there. There are so many girls who only want the chance and who go to church regularly and are much more capable than I. Imagine my leading a prayer meeting! Why it would almost be mockery." Perhaps Mary was referring to a crisis of faith, but more likely she was admitting her insecurity at having scarcely arrived at Smith.[16]

Southern students participated in all of the extracurricular activities, including drama, literary and debating societies, Christian organizations, and athletic associations. Mary McBee, a Smith College student, joined Phi Kappa Psi, the German Club, the Southern Club, and the Missionary Society (of which she was president, 1905–6), played basketball and hockey, strummed a guitar in the mandolin club, sang in Chapel Choir, and served in several class offices, although she was unsuccessful in her bid to be class president after she was nominated. A decade later, Nell Battle Lewis was editor of the monthly *Board* and belonged to Phi Beta Kappa, Phi Kappa Psi, the Philosophical Society, the Biology Society, Blue Pencil, Spectator, the Novel Club, the Orangemen, GOD, and White Wings; she also participated in the Senior Dramatics Society production of *Twelfth Night*.[17] Both students and their parents realized how beneficial their activities were for developing responsibility and leadership. "I am so pleased to hear May [Mary] presided at the Art Club for such things help one so much in case of manner and self possession," Mary Elinor Poppenheim wrote her daughters at Vassar in 1886. "I don't think anything so improving to young girls, as to have responsibilities thrown on her."[18]

More specifically, just as in the mid-nineteenth century, women learned how to draft petitions, give speeches, and write tracts for the abolitionist movement, skills they then applied to the suffrage movement. College students learned how to conduct meetings (especially parliamentary procedure), arrange events, and give speeches in their extracurricular activities. When Sophonisba Breckinridge helped her aunt found the Daughters of the American Revolution she claimed that, as president of her class at Wellesley, "some experience in drafting constitutions and administering parliamentary procedure" helped her with the process. Learning correct parliamentary procedure was important because it made women appear more businesslike. Mary Poppenheim learned organizing skills when she planned her senior class supper following commencement exercises. She had to arrange for class speakers, secure a table that would seat thirty-six, purchase favors, decorate the table, plan the seating, and write introductory speeches for the toasts.[19]

Students who were active in drama undoubtedly learned how to project their voices and become more comfortable speaking in public. At Wellesley North Carolinian Sue Hall was a member of the Shakespeare Club, in which she participated in readings, including performing a male role. She parlayed her skills into class government and was elected president of the sophomore class.[20] Louisa Poppenheim also played a man in a Hall Play at Vassar and acted in "Trig Ceremonies," a skit the sophomores wrote and performed for the freshmen as a rite of passage into trigonometry. Louisa participated in school government not only as a class officer but also as president of the Student Association, the most prestigious student position on campus. Other class officers included Mary Poppenheim, Sophonisba Breckinridge, Agnes Raoul, Emma Garrett Boyd Morris, and Helen Keller.[21] Emma's class prophecy even had her running for president of the United States.

Although some parents expressed concern at the voting that took place for class elections, most approved of the responsibility and took pride in their daughter's leadership. When Sophonisba was elected class president, her father told her, "It will also do you good;—character is developed by responsibility and power to do something by having power to exercise." William was particularly proud that Sophonisba was the first southern student to be elected president.[22] Sophonisba's mother, however, was more squeamish when it came to girls voting. She did not approve of putting a girl in the position of an election and once Sophonisba was elected teased her that she would no longer have time to write but would neglect her family.[23] Like Issa Breckinridge, Mary Elinor Poppenheim also cautioned her daughter about voting, admonishing Mary, "If I were you I would be very retiring and ladylike whenever there is any voting to be done." Parents voiced their concerns because they feared students were practicing for presidential elections of a different sort—and thus potentially embracing woman suffrage. Mary Elinor Poppenheim continued her warning, "and avoid having any thing to do with a party that savors of woman's rights." On the other hand, Grace Richmond's mother had few qualms about her daughter's introduction to voting at Vassar. She told Grace that because class officer elections resembled political caucuses, "by the time you finish Vassar you will be capable of entering politics."[24]

Parents were probably taken aback by ballot box stuffing and other controversies surrounding elections on campus. Mary Poppenheim wrote home to tell her mother that she had been elected vice president of the Student Association. "And there is a grand row now in process," she added, "about the illegality of my defeat for the Presidency of Qui Vive[,] the Senior Society. My friends all say that there was not a quorum the night that the election came off." Mary explained that she lost by one vote because she was not present. Instead, she was attending meetings of the Shakespeare and Dickens societies—"our societies which the nicest girls belong to"—with her friends. But, she added, she was not interested in being president of the society because "there is too much work to do." Mary claimed that she had turned down the chance to remain president of the Art Club because the president had to do too much organizational work. She added, "I would rather be a member so I can stay away when I like and make all the motions I want."[25] Squabbles over quorums and an acute understanding of the responsibilities as well as benefits of office served Mary and other students well when they led women's clubs and other organizations that were also rife with competition over leadership.

A short story by a Bryn Mawr student from Birmingham, Alabama, suggests that the author struggled with the idea of woman suffrage—she feared that women were not ready for impersonal politics. In the story "Epoch Making" by Cora Armistead Hardy, the freshman class nominated candidates for president and then voted a week later. The delay was intended to give students time to carefully consider the merits of the candidates but ultimately led to slander and corrupt politicking. While her story did not endorse woman suffrage, it revealed the political education students received at college.[26]

Students also gained political experience through the mock presidential elections held at several colleges. Gertrude Weil claimed that the Smith College victory for William McKinley, while not reflecting her vote, did teach her about presidential elections and "political methods."[27] While a minority as Democrats, southern students did their best to support their candidate. At Vassar Democratic students supporting Grover Cleveland literally threw water on a parade for Blaine, and in 1896 William Jennings Bryan advocates would not allow William McKinley supporters to sing in his support.[28] Nell Battle Lewis led a political rally at Smith nearly twenty years later, with students representing candidates from the political parties. Introducing the candidates, Nell claimed that female students did not vote based on the physical appearance of President Wilson and his adversaries but debated real issues. Sue Hall followed the local elections carefully as citizens voted on temperance measures. Sue told her father that "it would be a good thing if women could vote on this question."[29]

Extracurricular activities that focused directly on social welfare reform prompted southern students to become activists. College settlement clubs inspired many students to take up social work, as did the professors who led these organizations and the courses they taught. The college settlement movement began when Vida Scudder, a Smith graduate and professor at Wellesley, together with other professors and a trustee bought a house on Rivington Street in New York, where students and alumnae lived among those whom they desired to help. Some students agreed to live for the year, while others visited overnight or for several weeks only. They organized clubs and classes to teach English and other skills to women and children in the neighborhood and provided a safe and wholesome setting for relaxation and entertainment for young working women. The group then formed the College Settlement Association in 1890, eventually attracting students and other women to a variety of settlement houses.[30] Settlement homes were particularly popular with college graduates, who represented 60 percent of the College Settlement Association residents in its first five years. Vassar, Smith, and Wellesley students disproportionately dominated, in part due to the network of professors and students they developed. Settlements appealed to students in part because the communal living arrangements echoed college life while providing a socially acceptable alternative to marriage or teaching.[31] Josie Simrall was particularly influenced by Vida Scudder while she was at Wellesley. Because of Scudder's interest in college settlement work, Josie considered starting a settlement in Cincinnati with a friend when she returned home.[32] While on spring vacation, fellow Wellesley student Sue Hall went to see Christendom House, a college settlement in New York supported by the missionary society at Wellesley. Sue, whose sister Jessie eventually became a missionary, described the night she spent there to her mother in terms of the religious influence at the settlement. "This is a 'gospel settlement,'" she explained, "and they go to the root of the evil, holding that intellectual without spiritual will not go far."[33] Her strong Christian orientation dovetailed neatly with Wellesley's character—the college's original president, Henry Durant, tried to convert students to evangelical Christianity.

The Consumers' League was also popular with students. The national organization was founded in 1899 in order to encourage consumers to demand protection and fair conditions for working women. Florence Kelley, the general secretary for over thirty years, helped the league expand across the nation, with campaigns including labeling products made in approved conditions to encourage their consumption and working to increase protective labor legislation.[34] After Gertrude Weil heard Kelley speak at Smith, Gertrude wrote home suggesting that they work to have Consumers' League labels in Goldsboro also.[35]

Courses in sociology, economics, political science, and other social sciences opened many women's eyes to the needs of those around them. Thirty years before the Nineteenth Amendment, Professor J. B. Clark of Smith claimed that women should study political history and economy because women might one day vote, and even if they did not vote themselves, they were influential members of society, especially as social reformers.[36] While students entering college may not have been studying with enfranchisement in mind, their courses certainly steered them to social reform and, for some, to the woman suffrage movement. At Smith, several courses taken by Gertrude Weil and Mary Comer focused on poverty, delinquency, urban conditions, and socialism. Gertrude's class notes for a political economics course indicate that she learned that "Poverty is Preventable." Her teacher pushed students to consider capitalism as a cause of poverty and to seek solutions that included suffrage, eight-hour days, equal pay for equal work, and more equitable distribution of wealth. In particular, her notes focus on the history of women in the labor market, including the rise of industrialization and the resultant family wage system.[37]

Activist professors frequently brought reformers to campus for lectures that directly influenced students. Courses and speakers, including Jane Addams, offered suggestions as to effective methods for enacting change. Speakers were also effective because of their emotional impact. Mrs. Ballington Booth's lecture on prison reform moved Mary Comer. She reported to her mother that despite the woman's shabby appearance, Booth's earnest call for reform captivated Mary.[38]

Wellesley was considered a hotbed of social activism, with a faculty that included Vida Scudder, Katherine Coman, Emily Greene Balch, and others who worked for the Consumers' League and settlement houses. Balch's courses on social economy included discussion of "the dependent, defective, and delinquent classes" as well as problems of housing, sanitation, education, and recreation. Furthermore, students visited institutions and made a study of conditions in the north end of Boston.[39] Wellesley student Virginia Foster Durr, writing a paper on the budget of a steelworker family, discovered what poverty was about. "I began to realize," she recalled, "that people had a hard time living and didn't get paid enough."[40] Upon her return to Alabama, Virginia volunteered first with the Junior League and Red Cross and then with more liberal associations, including the Southern Conference for Human Welfare and United Church Women, finally supporting the civil rights movement.

While at Wellesley Sophonisba Breckinridge was on the board of directors of the Christian Association her senior year and taught workers at the Charles

River Village because Wellesley students were encouraged to uplift factory workers.[41] She also organized a Thanksgiving service for the local asylum for women.[42] Sophonisba was an academic who used her scholarship to better the community. Every winter term for nearly thirty years she lived at Hull House, where she worked closely with Jane Addams and Florence Kelley. There Sophonisba pushed the settlement workers to conduct investigations and collect data to guide their social work. Chicago's chief sanitary inspector asked her and Edith Abbot to help survey city housing, and through the Immigrants Protection League she tried to help new immigrants find work and housing.[43] She was also a factory inspector and worked on the juvenile court, the juvenile protective agency, the Children's Bureau, the NAACP, and the Urban League.[44] Sophonisba lobbied for the Shepherd-Towner Act for infant and mother care funding and for a national anti–child labor law and had a close relationship with Grace Abbot at the federal Children's Bureau.[45] Sophonisba devoted the first part of her book *Women in the Twentieth Century: A Study of Their Political, Social and Economic Activities* to a summary of the activities of women in women's clubs, the WCTU, the Consumers' League, and a myriad of other organizations to which women belonged. She often lamented the lack of interest at the local level in the lofty social reform agenda of leaders in the organizations.[46]

Wellesley also influenced students to a life of service through its motto, "Not to be ministered to but to minister," which North Carolinian Connie Guion remembered staring at in bronze above the Tiffany window in the chapel at Wellesley. Connie became a successful doctor in New York City and emeritus professor of medicine in the medical college of Cornell University, and she had a building named for her at New York Hospital. As a professional, she remembered the commitment to service she learned at Wellesley and worked to improve the hospital's clinics that served the poor. Connie was also inspired by her grandfather and great-uncles, doctors with formal medical degrees, as well as her mother, who, though lacking a formal education, practiced medicine informally, treating sick slaves and family members. Before entering medical school in New York, Connie spent several years teaching at Sweet Briar College in Virginia because she wanted to help prepare students to transfer to northern schools.[47] Connie Guion claimed that she learned much more than chemistry, zoology, and anatomy at Wellesley. Wellesley gave her the opportunity to learn from other women, both students and faculty, and she gained a powerful belief in women fostered by Wellesley's founders, the Durants. She also benefited from friendships with a diverse group of people and grew in self-confidence. Connie credited Wellesley with preparing her "to meet the demands of the life I had chosen. I felt a sense of security, courage, determination. When Miss Hazard handed me that diploma I was thinking, 'Nothing can stop me now, with this diploma in hand.' "[48] Many other graduates also cited the Wellesley motto, including Ruth Toof, who wrote in 1956, "I have always been grateful for the influence of the 'Motto' over the old College Chapel platform," which inspired her throughout her life as a civic leader in Memphis. Edith Simpson, who held offices in the DAR, Daughters of the Republic of Texas, the PTA, and the AAUW, claimed, "I've always followed the Wellesley motto." Martha Cecil, a missionary to China for thirty-six years, credited the impact of the motto on her missionary work. Marguerite Fitzgerald of Maysville, Kentucky, asserted that "Wellesley has meant a great deal—education, dear friends, and a philosophy of life. How often I repeat the Wellesley motto!"[49] The motto's emphasis on service, combined with the example set by Wellesley professors and the intellectual basis for social work learned in political science and economics classes, was a potent source of inspiration for graduates.

At Smith, Gertrude Weil's courses and extracurricular activities and the events she attended moved her to bring some of the activism she encountered at college home to Goldsboro, North Carolina. She quickly became chair of the Publication Committee of the North Carolina Federation of Women's Clubs because Sallie Cotton, a leader in women's clubs and family friend, believed Gertrude would be able to improve the image the public had of women's clubs. Gertrude rose quickly in federation leadership and was nominated for its presidency at the young age of thirty-five. By that time, however, Gertrude had already begun to dedicate more time to the woman suffrage movement. She declined the position, instead becoming president of the North Carolina Equal Suffrage League in 1920. Armed with a degree equal to that from the best men's colleges, she said about woman suffrage, "When I came home I wondered why people made speeches on something so obviously right. Women breathed the same air, got the same education; it was ridiculous, spending so much energy and elocution on something rightfully theirs."[50] Her biographer argued that her education at Smith "taught her to appreciate her own intellectual capacity and ability as well as that of her sex, she learned to use her intellect to question social injustices and seek answers."[51] Thus, at Smith Gertrude honed the intellectual capacity necessary to lead a social movement as well as exposed herself to professors and speakers who were living examples of how to proceed. Gertrude was also secretary of the North Carolina Conference for Social Service and organized and was first president of the North Carolina League of Women Voters.[52]

Vassar too had a reputation for cultivating social reform. Two of the most inspirational professors were Maria Mitchell and Lucy Salmon. Maria Mitchell was an astronomy professor who lived in the observatory rather than a residence hall and rejected restrictive rules for students. She demanded equal salaries for female faculty members at Vassar, and she invited woman's rights activists to speak on campus. Maria "judged everything from the standpoint of 'How is this going to affect women.'" She also pushed Vassar's president to be more broad-minded in his ideas concerning women; specifically, Mitchell wanted women to feel free to choose a career instead of marriage. Lucy Maynard Salmon was a historian who also urged the Vassar administration to end social restrictions on students, wore culottes to bicycle around campus, and encouraged students to take greater responsibility for themselves through student government. In political economy classes Professor Herbert Mills assigned students the task of visiting a factory and answering a series of questions on its capital, profits, and employees. To complete her assignment, Emma Garrett Boyd Morris visited the Exposition Cotton Mills in Atlanta. Emma's Charities and Corrections course exam forced her to consider a social Darwinist argument that the "ill-adapted be left to die" and to answer questions on topics including beggars, dependent children, free medical dispensaries, and state charity boards. Professor Laura J. Wylie also motivated many students to consider the world beyond their own. As a professor of English literature, Wylie transmitted her interest in social welfare—she had worked at the Rivington Street settlement house after her own graduation from Vassar—to her students. She pushed them to consider "the social implications of literature."[53] Vassar's president James Monroe Taylor also inspired several students, including Augusta Choate, who founded a girls' school in Massachusetts where she tried to show the same "warm interest" in her students that Taylor had shown to Vassar students. She believed such attention would push them to achieve more after graduation.[54]

The idea behind settlements—reaching out to the less fortunate and living among them—took a different spin at Vassar, where students had a particular interest in the domestic workers on campus. In 1908 they opened a house on campus for domestic workers called the Maids Club House with ten thousand dollars raised by students. Women who worked in the laundry or dining hall and those who cleaned the dormitories, recitation rooms, and parlors were free to socialize and relax in the house. Students also organized music, cooking, and sewing classes, lectures on travel and other topics, tutoring, and other "improvements" for the maids. The club clearly had selfish aims as well, to improve relations between Vassar graduates as homemakers and their household help by developing relationships between students and help.[55] The Maids Club House highlighted the privileged position of students who expected to hire domestic workers after college.

The reaction of southern women to the Maids Club House would be interesting, given that in the South domestic workers were almost always African American. Many southern women believed that northern solutions to the "problem" of domestic servants did not translate to the South because of this.

Mary Elinor Poppenheim depended on African American servants even as she faulted them for being irresponsible and ineffective without her careful supervision. "Lucy is trying to do right but she is a child and a *negro*, that covers all," she wrote Mary.[56] Mary Poppenheim agreed with her mother. At home in Charleston she told the Century Club that white southern women faced a set of problems with their servants different from that faced by northern women because servants in the South were black. She encouraged club members to train their servants, reminding them that slaves had grown up under the positive influence of their white master, but "social amenities, order and cleanliness . . . are unknown in the negro houses of the modern negro." Clubwomen often debated the "domestic servant problem" and occasionally made more structured attempts to train servants through "Better Servant Schools."[57]

Louisa Poppenheim's work in women's clubs reflected her exposure to women's activism and reform at Vassar. She became president of the South Carolina Federation of Women's Clubs and an officer of the national General Federation of Women's Clubs, and she participated in many other reform associations. Through the Charleston Civic Club Louisa pushed for a playground for African American children and a jail matron for women prisoners.[58] Her older sister Mary Poppenheim was no less active, though more "conservative" in her activism, as president-general of the United Daughters of the Confederacy, an organization dedicated to honoring and preserving the Lost Cause of the Confederacy. But even she associated her leadership skills with the experiences she gained at Vassar. She was directly influenced by Professor Lucy Salmon to pursue history, which she did as one of the first female members of the South Carolina Historical Society and through her work in the UDC. Mary headed the state historical committee within the UDC, which promoted southern history through regulating textbooks, donating books to libraries, sponsoring essay contests, and collecting and publishing recollections of the Civil War. Through the UDC Mary also helped to compile South Carolina women's recollections of the Civil War for publication, and she wrote a history of the national UDC. Lucy Salmon's influence was long-lasting. In the 1920s Mary donated newspapers from the Civil War time period to Vassar at Lucy's request. In 1933 Mary wrote that the Century Club, a predominately literary club that she and her sisters had organized over thirty-five years earlier, had included "Modern Trends in History and Biography" on its program of study. Mary reread a pamphlet on modern history written by Lucy Salmon in order to prepare for the discussion. She wrote a glowing letter to Adelaide Underhill, secretary for alumnae news, describing Lucy Salmon's continued influence on her: "I do not think any one has had a greater influence on my thinking than that wonderful woman and I did and do still feel that her character, as well as her mental outlook, had a powerful influence on me. I wish I could get back to Vassar some day."[59] Mary and Louisa both continued to hold firm ties to Vassar College, writing regularly to Adelaide Underhill, hosting Vassar presidents James Taylor and Henry Mac-Cracken when they visited Charleston, belonging to the Vassar Southeastern Alumnae Association, and returning to Vassar for reunions and to speak to current student association officers.[60]

At Mount Holyoke, by 1910 teachers were taking students to canning factories and assigning Jacob Riis's books in their courses.[61] In addition to drawing attention to community service, Mount Holyoke provided graduates a sense of motivation—they were trained to succeed in life. Mary Cheek, who became president of Rockford College, reminded her classmates, "What a wonderful thing it is to have been and to be a Holyoke 1913er and to feel that Holyoke and 1913 expect something worth while from each of us. We are bound to succeed and what a success it will be!"[62] Decades earlier, students had already been encouraged to use their abilities in service to others, whether as missionaries, teachers, or mothers. Alice McLellan Birney used her educational background to help her consider how to make motherhood more professional. Originally from a cotton plantation outside of Georgia, Alice attended private school in Atlanta and spent one year at Mount Holyoke. Widowed at a young age, she hoped to be a doctor but gave up medical studies in favor of selling advertising in order to support herself. She then married Theodore Birney, a lawyer. Well placed in society, Alice wanted advice for child rearing to make mothering a more scientific than haphazard process. She began reading on the subject but felt that there was little information available to better educate mothers. She decided that a national organization of mothers could provide the opportunity for mothers to meet with each other, study child development, and improve their children's schools. Supported by Phoebe Apperson Hearst and Frances Cleveland, the First Lady, Alice launched her movement in a meeting held at the White House that attracted more than two thousand people. She was made president of the National Congress of Mothers, which eventually became the PTA. Although little is known about her year at Mount Holyoke, her intelligence and higher educational training sent her to the library when she was confronted with the task of child rearing. In addition, her mother provided the emotional and practical support she needed. Harriet McLellan actively participated in the National Congress of Mothers; at the first meeting in 1897 she was in charge of the literature bureau, which displayed the best contemporary books on child rearing. Harriet McLellan also made it possible for Alice to travel and attend meetings by caring for her young children.[63] The energy that southern women brought to their studies at northern colleges is evident in their social service work following graduation. Perceiving a problem in society, they quickly set about studying the problem and designing a solution.

Many southern college graduates, rather than volunteering at urban settlement houses aiding poor immigrants, chose to work with the rural mountain people of Kentucky. Due to the initial work of May Stone, a Wellesley graduate from Louisville, other college students from the Seven Sisters followed friends to the mountains. The Kentucky Federation of Women's Clubs provided the initial opportunity for May Stone to travel with Katherine Pettit of Lexington to Hazard in eastern Kentucky. The Reverend J. T. Mitchell had written to the federation asking for someone to come to the mountains to help mothers build better homes. May was a secretary of the federation, and she heard Katherine's report on a traveling library project to the mountains. May was the only child of a wealthy lawyer. She knew Sophonisba Breckinridge (they had entered Wellesley together), who in turn knew Jane Addams, and a network of women's settlement workers grew from these connections. Initially active in women's clubs and the DAR, May was renowned for her charm and quiet manner and considered the "ladyest" by the mountain people. Her success came from her ability to discern how to push for higher education, aiding individuals she felt were capable with her own funds while never encouraging widespread migration from the mountains.

May Stone and Katherine Pettit volunteered to answer Reverend Mitchell's request for aid to mothers. They set up a six-week camp under a large tent in Hazard, where they taught cooking and sewing classes, new songs and games for children, and simple health practices. The following summers saw longer "Industrials" in Hindman and Sassafras. In 1901 and 1902 May and Katherine traveled east to raise money to build a permanent settlement house in Hindman, which they ran under the auspices of the WCTU. By 1911 the school had two hundred students. May remained in the mountains for forty-five years serving its inhabitants and was remembered for her words, "If you need me, I'll be glad to help." Katherine Pettit eventually left the Hindman school in the care of May Stone and opened a new settlement house in Pine Mountain.[64]

Other notable southern women enticed to the settlement homes by May Stone and Katherine Pettit included Curry Breckinridge, the sister of Sophonisba Breckinridge, Laura Josephine Webster, and Abby Winch "Winnie" Christensen. Laura Webster, a Smith alumna from Orangeburg, South Carolina, taught in Asheville, North Carolina, before serving as assistant principal at Hindman from 1911 to 1914. Like Sophonisba Breckinridge, she ultimately left Kentucky for Chicago, where she worked at United Charities of Chicago while studying at the Chicago School of Civics and Philanthropy (which Breckinridge helped found). Laura credited her history courses at Smith for providing a "combination of breadth of view and training in accuracy" but regretted not taking additional sociology or economics classes, which would have spoken more directly to her reform work.[65] Winnie Christensen's mother, Abby

Holmes Christensen, was a northerner who attended Mount Holyoke before her marriage to South Carolina state senator Neils Christensen. Winnie and Abby were active in local women's clubs. Winnie graduated from Radcliffe in 1910 and taught at Pine Mountain for twenty-five years, which she said was her most satisfying achievement.[66] Later, Melville Otter Briney, who graduated from Vassar in 1921, visited the Pine Mountain School before eventually becoming a columnist for the *Louisville Times*.

The Kentucky mountain settlement work also spurred Kentuckian Zelinda "Linda" Neville to seek treatment for trachoma, a contagious eye disease that caused blindness when not treated. From a prominent family in Lexington, she spent her postcollegiate years caring for her ailing father and tutoring students (including Margaret Preston) in preparation for eastern college entrance examinations. Linda's introduction to women's social reform came when a group of women met to protest a murder committed by a crime family in Lexington. Linda became the secretary and vice president of the Associated Charities and with her sister Mary was active in the Lexington Civic League, the Gleaners of Christ Church, and the WCTU. Her friend Katherine Pettit invited her to visit Hindman thirteen years after her graduation from Bryn Mawr. She spent the rest of her life fighting the disease, both by bringing mountain people to the city for treatment and by taking urban doctors to the mountains to serve at eye clinics. Linda explained how she reconciled her privileged background with the menial labor she did for the blind: "I was a graduate of Bryn Mawr College for whom my father had wished for culture and I was doing things of a menial nature, meeting patients, often myself attending to their personal wants." She claimed that once she saw the circumstances in which the blind lived, she realized how petty her own cultural and social life was. Linda used her own inheritance as well as money raised from private donors and the state to fund her project and was instrumental in the founding of the Kentucky Society for the Prevention of Blindness. She was able to use her background and education to deal with doctors, wealthy donors, and state officials yet still relate to mountain folk without condescension.[67]

Not all women were equally moved by the college settlement and other social reforms they were exposed to during college. Margaret Preston heard a talk on college settlements while at Bryn Mawr and then visited a settlement where her cousin Mary Preston worked. Margaret felt pressure to volunteer at the settlement, reading stories to children, but she admitted, "I really don't see any use in it." She complained further when her money was stolen while she was there. "That shows how little an effect all this work really has on them. Excuse me from ever living in the slums if I can help it. I think it is awful for a lady like Mary Preston to have to do that." Despite her attitude, when Margaret returned home to Lexington she taught at the local industrial school.[68] She also immersed herself in women's clubs, the Civic League, and her church. Margaret remained cynical, however, complaining that her meetings were mostly "talky-talky" and didn't accomplish much. Although she was thrilled to attend a meeting of Sorosis, the New York women's club credited with starting the women's club movement, even there she groused that the program on Dickens was "too long and not read well."[69] Yet despite her cynicism, Margaret actively worked to better her community. For her alumnae surveys from Bryn Mawr, Margaret reported that she worked at her Sunday school, was Woman's Auxiliary president at her church as well as on the diocesan board of the Woman's Auxiliary, chaired the Women in Fayette County organization of the Democratic Party from 1934 on and off, and belonged to the UDC, the DAR, Colonial Dames, and the Woman's Club of Central Kentucky for over forty years. At age seventy-five she gave up trying to report everything, stating that her list of volunteer activities was too big to enumerate![70]

Students at women's colleges became interested not just in social reform but specifically in woman's rights and suffrage. Historian Elna C. Green found that a comparison of suffragists and antisuffragists in the South reveals a higher concentration of college degrees among suffragists. For example, 19 percent of Alabama suffragists attended college, and an additional 10 percent attended a seminary or institute. Given that less than 8 percent of American women attended college at the time, this is a disproportionately high number. Leaders of the Southern Association of College Women were all prosuffrage as well.[71]

While little discussion of suffrage took place on campuses in the early 1880s, Julia Hammond was exposed to women's clubs through the matron of her boardinghouse while at Radcliffe, where she heard speeches on the advancement of women and witnessed women who were willing to argue publicly with men.[72] She explained to her mother that the club was "for the general advancement of women, from reformed clothers to voting." She also recommended that her mother read a book by Frances Power Coffe on the duties of women.

After 1910, as the woman suffrage movement began to gain momentum nationally, it made its way into debates on women's college campuses. At Vassar a 1911 poll still showed that a majority of the women were not in favor of it. In 1909 the administration forced student Inez Milholland to hold a suffrage meeting outside campus buildings in the cemetery, but by 1915 the college president endorsed woman suffrage. Despite this lack of official and student support, feminist influences at Vassar included Professors Lucy Salmon and Maria Mitchell. In comparison to southern college Sophie Newcomb, even this low level of prosuffrage sentiment at Vassar was quite advanced. Newcomb did not offer economics until 1911 and even then explicitly reassured students and parents alike that offering these classes did not mean that students would become suffragists.[73] Wellesley had its share of feminist teachers, including Ellen Amanda Hayes, who took students to the home of Lucy Stone and Henry Blackwell to show them the example of a feminist marriage.[74]

The liberal atmosphere on some campuses toward woman suffrage and, at minimum, toward women's abilities undoubtedly influenced many students. Although Margaret Preston's primary influence was her mother, a suffragist, undoubtedly the change in self-confidence she experienced while away at school strengthened her resolve in the fight for suffrage. She later recalled that she enjoyed working with her mother and other women in the movement. Suffrage activism strengthened the bonds between women, and the parades and meetings were exciting, especially when the women encountered opposition.[75]

With such strong feminist influences at school, the instrumental role that northern-educated southern women played in the suffrage movement is not surprising. They embodied a common southern fear that intellectual, educated, northern-influenced women were at the center of the demand for woman suffrage.[76] Although obviously not all southern suffragists had attended a northern college, they disproportionately led the movement, including leading suffragists from Smith College (Gertrude Weil and Nell Battle Lewis), Bryn Mawr (Flora Gifford, Margaret Preston, and Linda Neville), Wellesley (Sophonisba Breckinridge, Annette Finnigan, Angie Perkins, and Maria Daviess), Mount Holyoke (Loula Adams), and Vassar (Zaida Kirby, Katherine Burch Warner, Elizabeth Roden, Kate Tuttle, and Eleonore Raoul).

Furthermore, although some of these women were from larger cities like Atlanta, many came from small southern cities or rural towns. By 1900 only fourteen southern cities were included in the one hundred most populous cities in the nation, and only one-third of the southerners at the Seven Sisters came from these cities. Historian Jean Friedman argued that the rural nature of the South, along with the influence of kin and evangelical religion, prevented women from evolving female networks of reform as early as northern women did in the nineteenth century. She found that women's church societies, which drew women into the WCTU and eventually woman suffrage, were limited to larger cities. Friedman concluded, "Thus changes in sexual roles evolved slowly in the South because modernization never fully displaced the traditional Southern community" based on church and kin.[77] Thus, the presence of women who had traveled north for their education had the potential to revolutionize small towns by exposing women to networks of reform that they would otherwise have been cut off from. Gertrude Weil was from Goldsboro, North Carolina. However, her influence, along with that of Irene and Eve Stanley, both Mount Holyoke alumnae, meant that the town had an active women's club with progressive ideas regarding education, social reform, and, especially, woman suffrage. That did not mean that suffrage was easily accepted in Goldsboro or any other town in the South; to the contrary. Even Gertrude Weil, president of the state's Equal Suffrage Association, had to defend the femininity and race supremacy of southern suffragists. She claimed, "The Leaders of the suffrage movement, national and State, have been and are women of unimpeachable moral character, upholding the highest standards of society." She also denied that granting women suffrage would endanger white supremacy, as the state could continue to allow only those voters who met qualifications (the method used to disenfranchise black voters).[78]

Annette Finnigan was a philanthropist who moved to Houston in 1874 before graduating from Wellesley in 1894. She was apparently introduced to suffrage issues at Wellesley. After graduation she moved to New York to join her family then living there and became corresponding secretary of the New York Equal Suffrage League. She returned to Houston with her family in 1903 and founded the Houston Equal Suffrage League with her sisters, Katherine and Elizabeth. Although they were unable to procure a woman to the city school board, they were credited with introducing the subject of woman suffrage to a conservative community. As her state suffrage league president, Annette spent years lobbying the legislature in Austin. An astute businesswoman, she also presided over the Hotel Bazos, a prestigious hotel in Houston, before she had to curtail her work due to ill health. That did not stop her involvement in the community, and she made large contributions to the Houston Museum of Fine Arts and the public library and donated land for a park named for her.[79]

Sophonisba Breckinridge was elected national secretary of the National American Woman Suffrage Association, the largest national woman suffrage organization. She supported a federal amendment even when fellow Kentuckian Laura Clay broke with the federal amendment in favor of states' rights. Sophonisba's own mother did not support suffrage, which made a stay in the same boardinghouse with Susan B. Anthony while in Washington, D.C., somewhat awkward. Sophonisba's father, she remembered, was "always for fair play," but Anthony had to discuss sewing with Sophonisba's mother instead! Sophonisba was also surely influenced by other notables and relatives in Kentucky, including Laura Clay and Sallie Preston. Sophonisba drew from her academic studies and research in her support of woman suffrage. In an article published in the *Annals of the American Academy of Political and Social Science* she argued that women's lack of political power was directly related to the low wages that women earned; women were both exploited and excluded.[80]

Atlantan and Vassar graduate Agnes Raoul grew up in a family of suffragists.

Her mother and her sisters Eleonore (a graduate of the University of Chicago), Mary, and Rebecca were all suffragists in Atlanta. Eleonore presided over the Atlanta branch of the Equal Suffrage Party, traveling around the state giving speeches. In 1915, after marching in the largest suffrage parade to date in New York, she returned to Atlanta to lead the first suffrage parade there. She was one of four women riding horseback. Eleonore Raoul also purchased an automobile that had belonged to Anna Howard Shaw, president of NAWSA, and raffled it off to raise money. Eventually, Eleonore led the Atlanta League of Women Voters.[81]

Louisa Jones graduated from Teachers' College, founded the first free kindergarten in Alabama in 1898 for mill children, taught, and was a member of women's clubs. Loula Rhyne Adams was a North Carolina suffragist who attended Mount Holyoke. She taught before her marriage to a doctor and was president of her local UDC chapter, her local women's club, and her church Home Missionary Society. Katherine Burch Warner, born in Tennessee, was a Vassar graduate and women's club leader. As president of the Tennessee Woman Suffrage Association, she addressed a rally of over 2,500 supporters in 1916, although she was against the more militant wing of the woman suffrage movement, led by the National Woman's Party.[82] Wellesley alumna Maria Daviess was a painter and novelist and a founder and vice president of the Nashville Equal Suffrage League. She became interested in women's rights after reading John Stuart Mill and Olive Schreiner. Sarah Norcliffe Cleghorn was a Virginia suffragist who spent one year at Radcliffe. She wrote and spoke in favor of woman suffrage and many other social reform causes, including prison reform and child protection. Linda Neville, while dedicating herself to blindness prevention, also served three years as president of the Fayette County Equal Rights Association. Ann Hero, born in New Orleans and educated at Vassar, taught chemistry at Sophie Newcomb College and presided over the New Orleans College Equal Suffrage League and the New Orleans Southern Association of College Women.[83] Vassar alumna and Savannah native Virginia Nisbet in 1914 declared herself a suffragist but lamented that there was not yet an organization in her city. Meanwhile, she belonged to the Kindergarten Club, the PTA, Associated Charities, and King's Daughters and was president of the Savannah Federation of Women's Organizations. She finally joined the Equal Suffrage Party, which then became the local League of Women Voters, and served as the secretary of the Board of Education in Savannah and assistant superintendent of schools. Patty Semple, a Vassar graduate and sister of Vassar graduate and geographer Ellen Semple, was a suffragist in Louisville. As president of the Louisville Woman's Club, she pushed clubwomen to demand school board suffrage successfully in 1912.[84] Some southern suffragists remained in the North, such as Atlantan C. Mildred Thompson, who was teaching at Vassar, her alma mater. She marched in the second New York suffrage parade with professor Lucy Salmon and spoke on suffrage "wherever anyone would listen."[85] In 1930, on the tenth anniversary of the Susan B. Anthony amendment, Thompson contended that the passage of woman suffrage was important despite arguments that their voting had made a negligible political difference. Thompson wrote that "the achievement of votes for women has banished some of the bugaboos about 'women's place in the home' and 'women always inferior to men.'"[86]

Southern suffragists, despite their dedication to the cause, fought a losing battle in the South, even as the national woman suffrage amendment passed in 1920. Most southern states did not ratify the amendment, although border state Tennessee did cast the deciding vote in favor. Nell Lewis later recalled, "It was quite a sensation to be a young Southern woman just slapped in the face by her state" when the North Carolina senate voted 25–23 to postpone its vote on the amendment until 1921. Woman suffrage was so controversial that most state federations of women's clubs in the South did not endorse it until after 1915, with the North Carolina Federation of Women's Clubs delaying its approval until 1918. Many southern clubwomen were hesitant to associate themselves with this more radical social reform.[87]

Having been educated at the best colleges, challenged to think for themselves, and held to high expectations of intellectual ability, southern alumnae of northern schools believed in women's equality—or at least their capability. Consequently, they not only sought larger roles for themselves in society but also challenged men and women to reconsider gender roles. Inspired by their teachers, they believed that once women achieved the same level of education as men, they would be able to make a contribution to the community, whether through social reform, political participation, or a profession. Most importantly, they began to consider their own desires, whether that meant forgoing marriage, serving the social claim instead of the family claim, or otherwise seeking their own happiness. Clara Conway, founder of the Clara Conway Institute in Memphis, tried to prepare students for Wellesley and Vassar because she wanted them "to take part in the work of the world." She continued, "The stale, worn-out argument that higher education detracts from womanliness has lost its force. . . . Everywhere one sees high bred women in careers. Independence is one of the highest attributes of womanhood."[88] Conway followed her own advice not only as an educator but also as a founding member of the Nineteenth Century Club. The club, which had many college graduates, tackled social reform in Memphis, encouraging greater civic involvement from women. Conway was a notable force for women's activism because she justified greater public roles less because of maternalism—defending women's civic work as municipal housekeeping or an extension of women's natural role as a housekeeper and family caretaker—

and more due to women's independence. Conway argued that a woman's duty to herself was first. "This duty is her highest responsibility, not her duty to her husband," she argued.[89]

Both Gertrude Weil and Sophonisba Breckinridge could directly trace their support of woman suffrage to their studies at college (and graduate school, in Sophonisba's case). As noted at the beginning of this chapter, Gertrude came to her focus on women's and children's economic conditions through her social and political science courses. As a professional, Sophonisba, too, studied conditions for working women, among other issues. Both came to realize that women's actual lived condition, their poverty, and their lower wages were related to their lack of political power. Sophonisba contended that women needed to experience their own satisfaction in life through direct involvement, whether it be voluntary social reform organizations, wage work, or political activism. Furthermore, she pointed out that colleges were the incubators of women's rights: "It is in the college and the university gymnasiums that preparation is being made for full participation by women in the activities requiring continuity and stability. It is in the laboratories and libraries of colleges and universities that scientific bases for emancipation are being assembled," she warned.[90] Thus influenced by their studies, Sophonisba and Gertrude took up the suffrage cause.

C. Mildred Thompson's beliefs about women's rights were shaped by her youth in Georgia, her undergraduate education at Vassar, and her experience teaching there. Mildred believed in the power of a liberal arts education to free the mind and to push individuals to embrace a rational democracy. She thought that women needed a college education to prepare them to contribute to society—and she wanted their contributions to go beyond childcare and housework. While never disparaging women's roles in the home, Mildred told Vassar students—and everyone else who would listen—that women needed to pursue careers and political activism. She always stressed women's abilities and encouraged them to live up to their potential in the home, the workplace, and the community. She also skewered psychoanalysts Ferdinand Lundberg and Maryna Farnham, authors of *Modern Woman: The Lost Sex*, retorting that women were fine, it was men who were the lost sex, frustrated with their loss of dominance over women. Women were equal to men and could be found in the saloon, wearing pants and short hair, as well as in all career fields they desired while not abandoning the home, Mildred claimed. Mildred returned to Georgia after forty years at Vassar, bringing her confidence in women's activism to her new role as an advocate for women's education in the South.[91]

Louisa Poppenheim, who endorsed only "limited suffrage" (i.e., an educational requirement that spoke to race as well as class concerns) and never overtly participated in the suffrage movement, had somewhat different ideals for womanhood in the South. At Vassar, she and her sister Mary began to think differently from their mother about women's rights. While their mother reminded them "not to have anything to do with a party that savors of woman's rights," Mary wrote to Louisa, then still home in Charleston, that she prophesied that she "would be a second Susan B. Anthony coming to W[ashington] to hand a petition for woman's Rights to the Pres[ident]."[92] Louisa and Mary hosted Lila Meade Valentine, a Virginia suffragist, when she spoke on the cause in Charleston. But even after the death of their mother they did not join the suffrage associations, instead dedicating themselves to women's clubs and the UDC. Louisa was influenced by her time at Vassar, which led her to embrace the need for more educational opportunities for women and greater public activism. She, however, was more circumscribed in her language and would not have spoken of women's equality with men for fear that she be accused of ignoring their differences. To her, the modern southern woman meant "modern education and broad philanthropy." Louisa stressed sectional identity—southern women had unique conditions, but, rather than limiting women's abilities, they demanded women's activism. "Wherever a college woman is found in the South," she proclaimed, "she is serving some club faithfully" along the lines of civics, philanthropy, and education.[93] Connecting a college education to women's activism, she published a poem in her monthly journal for southern clubwomen, the *Keystone*, which read in part,

> They say that college women
> All have over-rated minds;
> And are only filled with learning
> By a process known to grinds.
>
> Yet look at all your school boards
> At your pulpits and elsewhere,
> If you don't see a woman,
> You'll find her influence there.

Louisa also reprinted Vassar president Dr. James Taylor's article "What College Does for Girls," which argued that a liberal education was necessary as women entered charity work and the professions. Louisa wanted women to lobby legislatures for libraries, secure matrons for jails, and demand playgrounds for children. She also wanted them to retain womanly qualities as they approached male political powers to achieve their goals—women were to be patient, tender, kind, and so on. But that did not exclude them from public duty. "Let all who can," she exhorted her female readers of the *Keystone*, "without regard to sex, for Truth is sexless, contribute stones to add to the strength of the arch."[94] Louisa Poppenheim understood that women needed appropriate outlets into which they could channel their energy without endangering their femininity or "womanliness." "Woman soul," she proclaimed to women who were distraught over their lack of direction, "you are just about to awaken to the real meaning of life." Such reform work would then allow for women to develop their own potential as well as aid the community. "Life to us all must mean service for others," she continued. "The life you have lived in service to those near and dear to you has really been a service for yourself."[95] Like Jane Addams, Louisa Poppenheim contemplated a life of service not only for its benefits to society, to others, but also for its benefits to herself as a woman.

The activism of college graduates was possible only because their mothers supported them. Many mothers not only approved of their daughters' activism but also set examples of service in women's clubs, church societies, and the suffrage movement. In a study of mother-daughter relationships in the Northeast and Midwest at the turn of the century, historian Linda Rosenzweig argued that despite reports at the time in the popular press calling attention to discord between mothers and daughters, this relationship was actually very strong. As more and more middle- and upper-class women had the opportunity to attend college, pursue a career, and become active in public life, their experiences began to differ dramatically from those of their mothers. Rather than finding that these changes caused conflict or that daughters chose different lifestyles as a means of rebelling against their mothers, Rosenzweig argued that the most activist women had the full support of their mothers. Such support was what enabled daughters to embark on such new ventures. She speculated that changes in family life in the late nineteenth century, including fewer children and more leisure time for women, may have allowed mothers to focus more on their daughters' development.[96]

Many of the southern students studied herein had active mothers. Daughters reveled in their mothers' public roles. North Carolinian Sue Hall told her mother she was thrilled to learn that she had joined Sorosis because it would help her to stay young. Maggie Hall was particularly active in church work, setting a strong example for her daughter Jessie, also a Wellesley graduate, who became a missionary in China. Maggie was president of the women's auxiliary to the Young Men's Christian Association and a long-time supporter of foreign missions through the Presbyterian Church. The first president of the Woman's Foreign Missionary Union, she wrote to women at other Presbyterian churches asking them to organize Foreign Missionary Unions at their churches, raised funds for foreign missionaries, and coordinated annual meetings of the unions throughout the Wilmington Presbytery, where they heard from foreign missionaries and raised funds.[97] Orie Latham Hatcher's mother, Oranie Snead Hatcher, helped establish the Baptist Women's Missionary Union and the Baptist Home for Aged Women in Virginia, along with serving as a trustee for Hartshorn Memorial College.[98] Other mothers were active in less progressive organizations, including Issa Breckinridge. Sophonisba's father proudly wrote to her when the Confederate Ladies Memorial Association made her mother president. He claimed that it kept Issa busy organizing and enabled her to renew friendships with good families they had not seen while living in Washington, D.C., during his congressional term.[99]

Mina Weil was one of the most active mothers. Mina presided at the founding of the Goldsboro Women's Club (along with Eva Stanley, Mount Holyoke class of 1892, and Irene Stanley, Mount Holyoke class of 1894) and was its president in 1903–4. That day she (jokingly?) wrote Gertrude, "Very much love is all I have time to send to-day. I have just joined a Woman's Club, so I am too busy to write letters to my children, or go and tend to dinner." This club came about in the aftermath of a visit to Goldsboro by feminist Charlotte Perkins Gilman. After a speech by Gilman, Mina wrote Gertrude that she did not agree with everything Gilman advocated but did enjoy hearing her speak. The new club was then dedicated to Gilman and prompted a nervous reaction from men in town. Mina claimed that a group of men outside the building derided the club: "They'll be wanting the vote next and that will be too dreadful." She also chaired the Ladies' Benevolent Society Relief Committee, was a trustee of the graded schools, and worked for child labor legislation.[100] Gertrude was interested in her mother's club work, proud of her accomplishments, and eager to work with her upon her return home from college. At Smith, Gertrude became involved in the Home Culture Club, established by the author George Washington Cable. The idea of the club was to bring together people of different classes. Gertrude shared her vision for founding a similar club at home with her mother. "I had already thought on the possibilities of instituting a Home Culture Club in Goldsboro. It would be a splendid thing once it got to going—if the people knew what it means," Gertrude wrote. Gertrude also taught the working class through the Home Culture Club, greatly influenced by its secretary, Adeline Moffat from Tennessee, on whom she had a crush.[101] Meanwhile, Mina Weil described her club's purpose and its meetings to Gertrude, hoping they would have a positive influence on the community. Gertrude was imagining the discussion of parliamentary law. "Poor Janet," she mused about her younger sister, "growing up in that fearfully intellectual atmosphere of clubs."[102] Through her club work, Mina Weil became acquainted with some of the leading women in North Carolina, including Sallie Cotton, the state federation president. After a visit from Cotton, Gertrude teased her mother that she would be "stuck up" and no longer talk to ordinary people.[103] Letters between mother and daughter show Gertrude's admiration for her mother's club work, intellect, and social skills. Gertrude and her mother fed off each other, her mother influenced by the Chautauqua course and women like Cotton at home in North Carolina and Gertrude influenced by Miss Moffat and the social work she did while at Smith.

Gertrude Weil also was influenced by her aunt Sarah, a native of Boston who had suggested that Gertrude attend Smith College. Sarah Weil founded the Ladies' Benevolent Society and was active in the Goldsboro Women's Club, through which she helped enact the North Carolina Library Commission, on which she served. Despite their activism, neither Sarah nor Mina joined the Goldsboro Equal Suffrage League, which Gertrude organized in 1914. Her biographer suggests that when Gertrude surpassed her mother and aunt in her liberal espousal of women's rights, she looked instead to her friends, especially Sallie Simms Kirby, for support. Thus, both family and friends sustained Gertrude.[104] Gertrude also worked for suffrage with Laura Weil Cone, a friend of her sister. Laura attended Dana Hall, the preparatory school associated with Wellesley, but when her father suddenly died she returned to North Carolina along with her family and finished her education at North Carolina Woman's Normal College.

Margaret Preston's mother was also busy with club work. She told Margaret that she too was tired, in part because her club was "very active, almost too much so, but I do not attend all the meetings."[105] Many letters back and forth between mother and daughter mention club meetings attended, revealing both Sarah Preston's reluctant leadership and Margaret's admiration for her prominent role in clubs. "I have to preside at a Club Meeting," Sarah wrote. "Now that is something I hate but I am gathering up all my resources and after all how a thing is managed it passes so soon."[106] She complained enough that Margaret wrote her, "I am sorry you are president against your will." Sarah believed club leadership was too much work, but Margaret reassured her, "I think it is an honour and I am very pleased you were chosen so unanimously. I like to have you prominent in everything, but I realize how you hate the trouble."[107]

Although Mary Elinor Poppenheim supported her daughters' club work after graduation, attending conventions and hosting social events for their clubs, she sent mixed messages to her daughters about her own activity. She explained that during the Civil War, as founder and president with her sister of the local Soldier's Aid Society, she had given a report to an audience of men and women and did not follow the then common convention of turning her back to the audience when speaking. Yet despite this example of courage, once married and the mother of four, she no longer seemed to envision a role for herself in women's organizations. Appointed to the refreshment committee of the Carolina Art Society bazaar, she first complained that her assignment was too large, then concluded, "I am sick of the refreshment department already, and will drop it as soon as I can; it don't suit me to work outside of home."[108] She implied that it was difficult for mothers to work in public even on a voluntary basis. Perhaps this was why her daughters, who were the most active in women's organizations, remained unmarried. After her mother died, Louisa wrote to a fellow clubwoman, "My dear Mother was so vital a part of my life: she was the center of our home, the inspiration in all my sister and I ever did, our closest friend and companion."[109]

Although it was Lilian Wyckoff Johnson's father who sent her to Wellesley, her mother, Elizabeth Fisher Johnson, was well known in Memphis for her social work. Elizabeth was well educated: she attended a boarding school in Macon that was run by teachers trained at Emma Willard's schools. Willard's influence seems evident from Elizabeth Johnson's pioneering social work in Memphis. In 1875 she started the Woman's Christian Association and presided over it until her death nine years later, working to improve the lives of women and children in her city. Elizabeth's language was not radical (she emphasized women's natural and Christian duty to aid other women and children), but her work was in the 1870s. The Woman's Christian Association opened a home for prostitutes under the guidance and financial support of Elizabeth, who reminded women, "Don't forget the Son of Man came to seek and save that which was lost."[110] Elizabeth Johnson was also exposed to another Willard, Frances Willard, the well-known temperance leader and suffragist. Elizabeth attended the national organizing convention of the Women's Christian Temperance Union in 1874 and eventually became the first president of the state union. She heard Annie Wittenmyer, the first WCTU president, speak in Memphis in 1876 and then entertained Willard on her first trip South in 1881. Elizabeth told the National WCTU that southern women had to be convinced that Paul's letter forbidding women from preaching did not apply to temperance work and, more generally, to public service. She echoed Willard's call not only to "Do Everything" but also to start by doing something, whether it be praying for temperance or lobbying the legislature. She suggested that Memphis women should "do something, if it is only to gather young girls off the streets to teach them dressmaking, fine mending, cooking, household economy."[111] Lilian Johnson's work in education and rural reform and eventually civil rights echoed her mother's call for women's public activism.

Margaret Mitchell remembered her mother's dedication to woman suffrage. May Belle Mitchell was among the earliest suffragists in Georgia, apparently because she objected to paying taxes on land she inherited without having a voice in politics. Margaret recalled being taken as a young child, with a "Votes for Women" banner tied around her waist, to a suffragists' rally, featuring nationally known suffragists, where her mother spoke. May Belle resisted the long domination in Georgia of suffragists Rebecca Latimer Felton and her sister Mary Latimer McLendon, whom May Belle considered too racist, reflecting the populist backcountry. She and Frances Smith Whiteside therefore broke with the Georgia Woman Suffrage Association to form the Georgia Equal Suffrage League, which eventually became the League of Women Voters.[112] These mothers were all unusually well educated themselves and supported their daughters' education and activism.

Once students returned home to the South, in addition to activist mothers, the Southern Association of College Women (SACW) also incubated social reformers. The SACW recognized the unique role that college-educated women could play in social reform in the South, a theme that dominated the 1909 and 1910 annual meetings. Annie May Dimmick of Montgomery, Alabama, speaking at the SACW meeting in 1910, argued that conditions in the South compelled college women to community service. Annie May was a Wellesley graduate who taught at Montgomery Girls' High School in Alabama to 1911. She was highly active in women's clubs, a charter member and president of the Montgomery branch of the SACW, president of the city Federation of Women's Clubs, president of the Alabama Federation of Women's Clubs, active in the YWCA and her Episcopal church, a trustee of the Alabama College for Women, and a director of the local Carnegie Library.[113] "Surely no section of the country gives more a call of our services than our own beloved south," she said, "where we combine our old traditions of learning and refinement with an actual pioneer condition—a service that the organization by its mere existence is the upholding of an ideal of genuineness in education." Annie May proposed that college women were particularly able to "investigate conditions, compile facts, and present the results in such a concrete way as to lead to action."[114]

Annie May's colleague Emma Garrett Boyd Morris, a Vassar graduate from Atlanta, contended that college women had to use their talents to serve their community. The eldest of three sisters, Emma was influenced by her deep religious faith, "corralling" friends and family to go to Sunday school, and a strong sense of responsibility. While at Vassar, Emma was president of the Southern Club and the Student Government Association and studied charities, corrections, and political economy, including factory conditions, under Herbert Mills. When she returned home, through the Atlanta chapter of the SACW and the Atlanta Women's Club, Emma led many of Atlanta's social betterment reforms, lobbying for legislation limiting child labor and in favor of compulsory education, school physical examinations, parks and playgrounds, and juvenile courts. She led a procession of SACW members carrying a 205-foot-long petition with over five thousand signatures demanding compulsory education, and she helped establish social settlements and day nurseries. At the same time, she nurtured college graduates returning home to Atlanta and began to lecture on drama and literature.[115] Emma worked through the SACW and other organizations to address child labor, compulsory education, and other legislative reforms centered on children and educational issues. Addressing the SACW in 1910, she reminded her colleagues, "Those of us who have been given a college education consider it a trust and an impetus for serving those less fortunate. I hope that you may carry from this meeting some inspiration for service."[116]

Emma claimed that Vassar graduates in Atlanta were loyal to Vassar and inspired to take up social reform in order to demonstrate their loyalty to the school and "to make the Vassar influence felt in our community." She described the half-dozen graduates of Vassar living in Atlanta, members of the newly formed Vassar Club there, who wanted to make a difference in their community. The Vassar Club was originally founded by Atlantan newcomer Frances Liggett Wey, a Vassar alumna who had struggled to pay her tuition as the daughter of missionaries in the American West. Frances founded the club to help young women prepare for entrance examinations and to enable them to find the financial aid they needed to attend Vassar or other colleges. Like Emma Boyd, she believed "college education was a precious privilege and carried with it a special responsibility," and the club sought to perform meaningful community service. One member suggested aiding the working boys and men at a city night school. The students often had no supper until 10:00 p.m., after classes ended. The Vassar Club decided that assisting those who were so eager to be educated was a worthy endeavor, and they obtained a room for the students to use as a heated, safe club room where supper was served nightly for a minimal expense. Emma Boyd claimed that the availability of supper helped the students to attend school more regularly and that the boys appreciated the attention given to them by the Vassarites and the community. "This is only a little enterprise, and but one of hundreds which are being carried on everywhere by Vassar women," she wrote, "in their loyalty to the college and its ideals—the beauty of thought, and the sympathy, the helpfulness and comradeship which comes from increased knowledge."[117] Education, then, served to inspire helpfulness and sympathy.

Women at the turn of the century flocked to many all-female social reform organizations, from women's clubs to the WCTU. Such an atmosphere of activist women would have felt familiar to those graduating from women's colleges. While at school they saw examples of women professors, women guest speakers, not to mention fellow students, and naturally sought power and meaning in women's clubs and other women's groups when at home. Gertrude Weil especially "developed a need to be part of an activist sisterhood" because women supported each other and made her feel a sense of accomplishment, pride, and purpose.[118]

Across the South, women's clubs owe a debt to northern colleges. The first president of the Alabama Federation of Women's Clubs, Mary LaFayette Robbins of Selma, graduated from Greensboro College for Women and studied at Vassar.[119] The South Carolina state federation had more than one northern graduate as its president: Louisa Poppenheim was one of the founding members and second president, and Minnie Melton Burney, a Wellesley alumna, presided over the federation from 1908 to 1910. In North Carolina Gertrude Weil gave up her leadership of the North Carolina federation to dedicate herself to the suffrage movement. Northern college alumnae filled the rosters of Tennessee women's clubs, including the Nineteenth Century Club of Memphis, which included Lillian Wyckoff Johnson (Wellesley), charter member Grace Carlisle Smith (Wellesley), 1902 club president Mattie Jones (Vassar), and 1905 club president Augusta Lamar Heiskell (Wellesley). When Vassar president Dr. James Taylor addressed the club in 1905, his audience included eleven Vassar alumnae. In Knoxville Mary Boyd Temple, first president of the Ossoli Circle, founded in 1885 and known as the first southern women's club, represented the club at the initial meeting of the General Federation of Women's Clubs in New York. These women's clubs were not just literary but also led the social welfare branch of the Progressive reform movement in the South, focusing on education, health, sanitation, child labor, and other important issues. The Ossoli Circle sponsored a traveling library and initiated the movement for the state Vocational School for Girls, while Grace Smith led the Department of Philanthropy of the Nineteenth Century Club, cooperating with the city's board of health to sponsor a female sanitary inspector who would examine working conditions for women. Mary Temple was a local and national officer in the Daughters of the American Revolution in addition to her work in women's clubs. She wrote a book on Margaret Fuller and was especially concerned with the uplift of rural and mountain whites in Tennessee.[120] While southern colleges also furnished many clubwomen, the northern influence was disproportionately high.

The alumnae files of graduates from the Seven Sisters read like a who's who of women's organizations. At a minimum, the vast majority of graduates were active in church-related activities and women's clubs. The interest in suffrage led many to membership in the League of Women Voters. Most importantly, these women did not simply list clubs on their résumé; rather, they founded clubs, they presided over them, they lobbied the legislature for their causes, they raised money, they were activist women who took on leadership roles. Stretching herself too thin, Katherine Carson of Smith complained that her church and club work was too much. "I live to do it, but it is hard not to do *too much*," she wrote in her alumnae survey.[121] Equally overwhelmed, Sophie Marks quipped that she joined the "Society for the Abolition of All Clubs, Societies, and Associations."[122] Vassar alumna Mary Lancaster, although busy taking care of her son, "remembers that a college woman must be interested in the community." She visited a factory weekly and was to lead a class on industrial democracy at her YWCA, among other signs of her interest in the community.[123]

Social activism was the perfect outlet for these women's skills and desires to do something with their lives. While many women remained single, making a career in paid employment more viable, married women and a substantial number of single women sought instead to find fulfillment of the social claim through volunteer social reform work. Many, like Linda Neville, had the security of financial independence because they came from wealthy families and did not need to work for wages. Others combined wage work with reform, including Sophonisba Breckinridge.

For southern women educated at northern colleges, intellectual stimulation, professors who served as role models, and participation in extracurricular associations all fostered independence and self-sufficiency. The rigor of academics they experienced, combined with less control over their social lives and greater independence born of living so far from home, made their northern sojourn potentially more liberating than attending college in the South would have. Furthermore, students were exposed to college settlements, progressive professors, and women's clubs to a greater extent than they would have been in the South. Many of the mothers who allowed their daughters to travel so far from home tended often to be active themselves and supported their daughters' work. Mary Poppenheim quite explicitly associated her Vassar education with her leadership in women's organizations. After she became national president-general of the UDC, Mary modestly claimed that "it was my association with '88, which has done so much to enable me to accomplish the little I have for the U.D.C."[124] Eva Stanley, Mount Holyoke class of 1892, a women's club founder, an officer in her church women's auxiliary, and a social worker, claimed, "All I am doing today Mount Holyoke is responsible for."[125] Despite its entrenched racial and gender hierarchies, the South, indeed, was a better place because of these college women. They did what they could to improve their communities, struggled against the status quo, and succeeded often enough to make a difference.

By the 1920s southern women's colleges had begun to improve in academic standards, in large part due to the work of the Southern Association of College Women. Fittingly, that organization merged with the Association of Collegiate Alumnae to become the national American Association of University Women. Southern women were more easily able to attend accredited colleges closer to home. The twentieth century brought dramatic changes to higher education. The Ivy League colleges became coeducational, while some of the Seven Sisters have retained their identity as women's colleges. As the number of college students has grown dramatically, so has the interregional movement of students— universities like Duke University now attract students from across the country. But in the late nineteenth and early twentieth centuries a select group of southern women took advantage of a special opportunity to gain an education and make a difference in their communities by disseminating the progressive values they learned in the North.

NOTES

Introduction

1. Margaret Preston to Sarah Preston, October 17, November 15, 1904, n.d. (ca. November 1904), Preston-Johnston Papers.

2. Margaret Preston to Sarah Preston, January 20, January 27, 1905, February 16, March 16, 1906, Preston-Johnston Papers. Margaret's aunt was Jessie Preston Draper of Hopefale, Massachusetts. Margaret's cousins, Zelinda Neville, class of 1895, and Mary Neville, class of 1894, were Bryn Mawr graduates, and her cousins Margaret Wickliffe Brown and Mary Brown Waite attended Bryn Mawr but did not graduate.

3. Philip Johnston to Margaret Preston, September 17, 1910, Preston-Johnston Papers.

4. Margaret Preston to Philip Johnston, September 26, 1916, January 31, 1917, Preston-Johnston Papers.

5. Kelley, *Learning to Stand*, 1–2; Gordon, *Gender and Higher Education*, 31.

6. Chafe, *Women and Equality*, 27–29; Wilkerson-Freeman, "Emerging Political Consciousness," ii.

7. Solomon, *In the Company*, 64.

8. Campbell, *The "Liberated" Woman*, 39.

9. On southern women and higher education in the South during the antebellum period see Farnham, *The Education of the Southern Belle*; for the postwar period see McCandless, *The Past in the Present*. For a classic study of southern women's gender roles see Scott, *The Southern Lady*. For higher education of women at the turn of the century see Solomon, *In the Company*; Palmieri, *In Adamless Eden*; Gordon, *Gender and Higher Education*; Horowitz, *Alma Mater*; and Antler, "After College, What?" For the SACW, see Proceedings of the Fourteenth Annual Meeting, 1917, 78–108.

10. McCandless, *The Past in the Present*, 1.

11. Montgomery, *The Politics of Education*, 38.

12. Solomon, *In the Company*, xx. In the late eighteenth and early nineteenth centuries, academies and seminaries also cultivated reasoning, intellectual curiosity, and independent thinking, which drew women into more public roles; see Kelley, *Learning to Stand*, 48.

13. Solomon, *In the Company*, xix–xxi.

14. Scott, "The Ever Widening Circle," 8.

15. Ibid., 15.

16. Friedman, "Orie Latham Hatcher," 200.

17. For white southern women's role in the Progressive Era South see Turner, *Women, Culture, and Community*; Scott, *The Southern Lady* and *Natural Allies*; Sims, *The Power of Femininity*; and Johnson, *Southern Ladies, New Women*.

18. Caroline Merrick's stepmother was a Massachusetts-born teacher who, Merrick claimed, was called the "Mary Lyon of the South"; Elizabeth Johnson and Lide Meri-

wether attended schools run by Emma Willard or by her protégées; and Belle Kearney was influenced by a schoolteacher from Maine. See Merrick, *Old Times*, 6–8; Wedell, *Elite Women*, 25–26, 40–41; and Kearney, *A Slaveholder's Daughter*, 31.

19. Approximately 50 percent of Vassar students, 60 percent of Mount Holyoke and Bryn Mawr students, and 70 percent of Wellesley students returned South. *Bryn Mawr College Calendar*; *Alumnae Register*; *Vassar College Alumnae Register*; and *Mount Holyoke College Biographical Directory*. While a great number returned to their hometowns and never left, others moved to larger cities in their state or other southern states. Some students returned to the South for a number of years before settling in the North, or vice versa. I based my classifications on where a student appeared to have spent most of her life postgraduation.

20. Shadron et al. calls for investigation of these women and their influence ("The Historical Perspective," 162).

21. Hobson, *Tell about the South*, 6–12. The phrase "tell about the South" comes from William Faulkner's *Absalom, Absalom!*

22. This study is limited to white women because so few African American women from the South attended these schools at this time, making comparison difficult. For an excellent study of the experiences of African American women at the Seven Sister colleges see Perkins, "The African American Female Elite." For examples of women whose experiences influenced their decision to fight for civil rights see Durr, *Outside the Magic Circle*, 101, 116–20, 244–45, 255–60, 279, and Jacoway, "Down from the Pedestal," 345–52, on Adolphine Terry, a Vassar graduate who worked to desegregate schools in Little Rock, Arkansas.

23. Solomon, *In the Company*, 21.

24. Franklin, *A Southern Odyssey*, 274–78; and Ezell, "A Southern Education," 303–27.

25. *Smith College Official Circular*, 1875–1915; *Wellesley College Calendar*; *Catalogue of Mount Holyoke College*; *Vassar College Catalogue*; and *Bryn Mawr College Program*. Percentages at Smith were .7 percent of their class in the 1880s, 1.3 percent in the 1890s, 4.4 percent from 1900 to 1909, and 12.8 percent between 1910 and 1915. At Vassar the percentage of southern students rose from 2.6 percent in the 1880s to 14.2 percent after 1910, while the percentage rose from 5 to 11 percent in the same years at Wellesley. See also Jordan, "Smith College," 217.

26. From archives throughout the South as well as college archives I located more than a dozen extensive collections as well as several smaller collections of letters between students and parents, siblings, or other relatives. The vast majority of these letters are from 1880 to 1915, although a few collections extend back to 1875 or forward through 1920.

27. Using college catalogs that listed students and their hometowns (with the exception of Wellesley, where I used the 1891 and 1922 student and alumnae registers), I created a database of southern students. I then used college alumnae directories to trace the students, collecting data on marriage, number of children, wage work, volunteer work, and primary place of residence. The database currently includes 1,016 names. Of these students, 555 graduated. A small number of students, usually schoolteachers themselves, were considered "specials" or nondegree students. This practice was common

in the 1870s and 1880s. The students were primarily drawn from the classes of 1875 to 1915, though access to information for each school varied slightly. Exact numbers are as follows: 319 students from Wellesley, classes of 1875–1915; 141 from Bryn Mawr, 1886–1910 (Bryn Mawr did not open until 1885); 357 from Vassar, 1875–1915; 67 from Mount Holyoke, 1875–1915; and 132 from Smith, 1875–1915. See *Smith College Official Circular*; *Wellesley College Calendar*; *Catalogue of Mount Holyoke College*; *Vassar College Catalogue*; and *Bryn Mawr College Program*. Because of these slightly different dates I analyzed the data by decade.

28. For periodization of the first generations of college students and changes in the 1920s see Solomon, *In the Company*, 95, chap. 9; Palmieri, *In Adamless Eden*, 199–200; Gordon, *Gender and Higher Education*, 4–5. For the influence of faculty during the Progressive Era see Palmieri, *In Adamless Eden*, 149–54. Oates and Williamson, "Women's Colleges," 795–806; Tidball, "Women's Colleges," 504–17.

29. Some of the most notable southern women at northern universities included Laura Clay, a suffragist from Kentucky who attended the University of Michigan; Celeste Parrish, a Georgian education reformer who attended Cornell; M. Carey Thomas, the president of Bryn Mawr who attended Cornell; and Julia Thomas Irvine, a Cornell alumna who became the fourth president of Wellesley. There are not enough primary sources for a full study of southern women's experiences at these schools, however. Weil quoted in Wilkerson-Freeman, "Women and the Transformation," 220. See McGuigan, *A Dangerous Experiment*, for women at Michigan, and Conable, *Women at Cornell*, on women at Cornell; and Gordon, *Gender and Higher Education*, 52–120, on women at the University of California and the University of Chicago. Gordon argues that between 1860 and 1890 women students were not made welcome on most coeducational campuses but were ridiculed or ignored (*Gender and Higher Education*, 25). On Elizabeth Messick see Talbot, *More Than Lore*, 8; and Elizabeth Messick Houk File. Houk later was elected county superintendent of schools in Shelby County, Tennessee.

30. Allen, "Economic Relation," 353. Lynn Gordon found that most southern college students were the daughters of New South professionals rather than the daughters of farmers (*Gender and Higher Education*, 48–49).

31. College Registers, 1875–1910. I examined entries for all students prior to 1910. Registers for classes after this date are restricted.

32. Sicherman, "Colleges and Careers," 136.

33. Solomon, *In the Company*, 64.

34. This study considers students from the states of the former Confederacy plus slave-holding states Maryland and Kentucky (Maryland, Virginia, North Carolina, South Carolina, Georgia, Alabama, Florida, Mississippi, Louisiana, Texas, Tennessee, and Kentucky). I judged Maryland and Kentucky to have the strongest identification with slavery of the slave states that did not secede.

35. Information compiled from *Bryn Mawr College Calendar*; *Alumnae Register*; *Vassar College Alumnae Register*; and *Mount Holyoke College Biographical Directory*.

36. Only fourteen southern cities made it into the top one hundred most populated American cities, according to the U.S. census from 1900. I found that 327 of the 1,019 students, or 32 percent, were from these cities. The cities were Baltimore, New Orleans,

Louisville, Atlanta, Richmond, Charleston, Savannah, San Antonio, Norfolk City, Houston, Covington, Augusta, Mobile, and Birmingham.

37. Talbot and Rosenberry, *The History*, 56.

38. McCandless, *The Past in the Present*, 1, 157–58.

One. "In the Wonderland of the Mind": The Benefits of a Liberal Arts Education

1. Pyron, *Southern Daughter*, 30–31, 45–46, 62, quotation on 45–46.

2. Farr, *Margaret Mitchell*, 31–33.

3. Solomon with Nolan, "Education, Work," 139–55, quotation on 142.

4. Solomon, *In the Company*, 1–7, 14–16, 20–21.

5. Ibid., 24; Farnham, *The Education of the Southern Belle*, 2–3.

6. Farnham, *The Education of the Southern Belle*, 3.

7. Clinton, "Equally Their Due," 39–60, quotation on 42; Kelley, *Learning to Stand*, 21–22.

8. Farnham, *The Education of the Southern Belle*, 120, 127, 139–40, quotation on 139.

9. Clinton, "Equally Their Due," 59–60.

10. Solomon, *In the Company*, 22.

11. On Vassar see Herman, "College and After"; Gordon, *Gender and Higher Education*, 121–63; Crawford, *College Girl of America*, 59–76, esp. 65–68; Rogers, *Vassar Women*; Taylor, *Before Vassar Opened*.

12. On Bryn Mawr see Crawford, *College Girl of America*, 118–35; and Frankfurt, *Collegiate Women*; on Smith see Hilliard, "Smith College"; on Wellesley see Converse, *Wellesley College*, 16–46.

13. On Radcliffe see Robinson, "Curriculum," 33–40; on Mount Holyoke see Cole, *A Hundred Years*, 102, 183–98.

14. On southern colleges see McCandless, *The Past in the Present*, and "Progressivism," 302–25; Farnham, *The Education of the Southern Belle*; and Dean, "Covert Curriculum."

15. *Nation*, May 7, 1908, 412. John Hope Franklin found a similar notion of superior northern schools and a more serious attitude toward learning in general in the region in the antebellum era (*A Southern Odyssey*, 195).

16. Gordon, *Gender and Higher Education*, quotation on 51; McCandless, *The Past in the Present*, chap. 4. Gordon refers specifically to Agnes Scott and Sophie Newcomb, but I think that her observation would be true for the other southern colleges more generally.

17. For the opposing view that virtues are not inherently masculine or feminine see Hanscomb, "The Ethical Purpose," 307–12.

18. Goucher, "The Advisable Differences," 577–99, quotations on 580.

19. In response to McBryde, Alice Palmer argued that teaching them to be fine women would automatically make them better wives and mothers but also queried as to why men's colleges were not teaching boys to be better fathers ("The New England Association," 594).

20. Johnson, "The Education," 88–97.

21. Gordon, *Gender and Higher Education*, 39.

22. McBryde, "Womanly Education," 471–72.

23. McCandless, *The Past in the Present*, 57.

24. Crawford, *College Girl of America*, 150–52.

25. Crane, "A Diplomatic Crusade," 259–96, quotation on 267–68.

26. Gordon, *Gender and Higher Education*, 145, 171–75.

27. Corley, "Higher Education," 462.

28. First quotation in Gordon, *Gender and Higher Education*, 171 (catalog of Agnes Scott Institute, 1903–4); second quotation in McCandless, *The Past in the Present*, 13.

29. Lewis quoted in McCandless, *The Past in the Present*, 53.

30. Quoted in ibid., 138.

31. Montgomery, *The Politics of Education*, 47.

32. Of course, it had strict social rules and emphasized the homelike nature of the dorms. Although it had single female teachers, the dean made every attempt to ensure that the teachers were attractive and had good manners: "We do not want cranky old maids," he said (Birnbaum, "Making Southern Belles," 218–46, 236).

33. McCandless, *The Past in the Present*, 23–27.

34. Ibid., 33–35.

35. Gordon, *Gender and Higher Education*, 165–77.

36. Crawford, *College Girl of America*, 154, 235–39.

37. Felter, "The Education of Women," 351–63; Worthington, "Higher Education," 405–14.

38. Josephine Simrall to Charles Simrall, September 27, 1891, Simrall Papers.

39. Margaret Preston to Sarah Preston, October 10, November 5, 1904, February 18, November 18, 1905, Preston-Johnston Papers.

40. Clarke, *Sex in Education*.

41. Zschoche, "Dr. Clarke Revisited," 545–69; *Health Statistics*, 5–17, 21.

42. Margaret Preston to Sarah Preston, November 5, 1904, Preston-Johnston Papers.

43. Issa Breckinridge to Sophonisba Breckinridge, December 2, 1884, Breckinridge Family Papers.

44. Julia Hammond to Mrs. Hammond, May 11, 1881, Bryant Cumming Hammond Papers.

45. Isabella Simrall to Josephine Simrall, September 11, 1890, Simrall Papers. See also Mary Elinor Poppenheim to Mary and Louisa Poppenheim, March 3, 1885, in Johnson, *Southern Women at Vassar*, 65–66.

46. Isabella Simrall to Josephine Simrall, September 17, 1892, Simrall Papers.

47. Issa Breckinridge to Sophonisba Breckinridge, December 2, 1884, Breckinridge Family Papers. Fathers seemed to be less concerned about health, although even Sophonisba's father also told her that it was better to be healthy than to have too hard a schedule. William Breckinridge to Sophonisba Breckinridge, March 22, 1885, Breckinridge Family Papers.

48. Quoted in Gianakos, "Southern Women at Mount Holyoke," 23–24.

49. Dr. J. A. Bayard Kane to Sarah Preston, October 1905; see also letters from Aunt Jessie urging her to stay home if she was not strong enough. Jessie Draper to Sarah Preston, October 9, October 15, 1904, Preston-Johnston Papers.

50. Jordan, "Smith College," 218.

51. Farnham, *The Education of the Southern Belle*, 20–23, 72–86.

52. This argument is also articulated by Beecher, *Educational Reminiscences*, 4–5, 184–89.

53. Mitchell, "Address," quotation on 19.

54. Gertrude Weil to Mina Weil, December 2, 1900, Gertrude Weil Papers.

55. Thomas, "Should the Higher Education of Women Differ," 9–10; Talbot, *The Education of Women*; and Robinson, "Curriculum," 25.

56. Allen, "Economic Relation," 354–55.

57. Thwing, "Should Woman's Education Differ," 728–36. See also Markle, "Sex in Education," 206–14, which argues that maternity is a physical function and therefore the purpose of education is not to prepare for it.

58. Thompson, "Vassar—Its Tradition," 4; and clipping, folder 3, C. Mildred Thompson File.

59. Hope Chamberlain, *This Was Home*, 93, quoted in Scott, *The Southern Lady*, 73.

60. Quoted in Butler, *Education for Equality*, 24–25; see also McCandless, *The Past in the Present*, 318.

61. Parrish, "Shall the Higher Education," 383–96. See also Rickert, "Where the College Has Failed," 15–16. Although educated at Vassar, Lilian W. Johnson wanted women to learn domestic science and to have their schools be specifically for women ("Annual Address," 69–70). Southern educators differed in their ideas about the utilitarian benefits of a college education for women. Emilie McVea, president of Sweet Briar College, had the opposite opinion. In 1922 she said women's colleges did not think "with reference to professional requirements. . . . In a day when utility has too often been the test of a college course, the devotion to culture as such is commendable." She also said that the women's colleges were "calmly unaware of industrial, rural, or educational problems at their very doors" (McCandless, *The Past in the Present*, 59–60, 76).

62. For examples of this kind of article see "The Education of Women."

63. Knupfer, "The Urban and Rural Reform Activities," 4, 11. Furthermore, Johnson eventually decided to work for a normal school rather than a college, conceding that teachers were so desperately needed (ibid., 14).

64. "Addresses at the Inauguration," 4, 11–12, 25–31, quotations on 4, 26, 27.

65. Excerpt from Sophia Smith's last will and testament (Seelye, *Early History*, 224–25).

66. Isabella Simrall to Josie Simrall, January 21, 1891, and Josie Simrall to Isabella Simrall, n.d. (ca. spring 1892), Simrall Papers.

67. Mary Elinor Poppenheim to Mary Poppenheim, February 11, 1883, in Johnson, *Southern Women at Vassar*, 26.

68. Durr, *Outside the Magic Circle*, 50.

69. Solomon argues that students had to passionately want to go and have their families support them (*In the Company*, 63). Of course, some of the southern women did not want to go, but their parents wanted them to, so they went. Palmieri found that both parents were strong influences on the Wellesley faculty (*In Adamless Eden*, 62–70).

70. Gianakos, "Southern Women at Mount Holyoke," 13; Lilian Wyckoff Johnson to Emily Dutton, May 30, 1929, SACW files, American Association of University Women

Archives; quotation in "Annals of the Class of 1885," Alumnae Biographical Files, Wellesley.

71. "Short Biographical Sketches of the Members of the Class of Eighteen Hundred and Eighty-nine," in Class of 1888 (green binder), Class Files.

72. Hope Summerall Chamberlain, unpublished manuscript, quoted in Scott, *The Southern Lady*, 72–73, 160, 215–16.

73. Allen's survey found ten college mothers in 1902, so they could have graduated in the 1870s or 1880 ("Economic Relation," 353).

74. Isabella Simrall to Josie Simrall, February 6, 1890, Simrall Papers.

75. Isabella Simrall to Josie Simrall, March 1, 1892, Simrall Papers.

76. Wilkerson-Freeman, "Emerging Political Consciousness," 3, 9, 16, 22, 28; Rountree, *Strangers in the Land*, 18, 119. Mina had wanted to study medicine but did not because she was too busy with children.

77. Issa Breckinridge to Sophonisba Breckinridge, September 20, October 15, 1884, Breckinridge Family Papers; Fitzpatrick, *Endless Crusade*, 5. Her father likely chose Wellesley because he knew Henry Fowle Durant and he approved the reputation of the school.

78. Issa Breckinridge to Sophonisba Breckinridge, April 6, 1885, December 2, 1884, Breckinridge Family Papers; William Breckinridge to Sophonisba Breckinridge, November 16, 1902, quoted in Christopher Lasch, "Sophonisba Preston Breckinridge," in James, *Notable American Women*, 1:233.

79. Friedman, "Orie Latham Hatcher," 39–40, 44.

80. Cornett, "Angel for the Blind," 17.

81. Daviess, *Seven Times Seven*, 49.

82. Mary Comer to Lillia Hall Comer, November 26, 1901, Mary Comer Correspondence.

83. Pyron, *Southern Daughter*, 81.

84. Agnes Raoul to Mary Raoul, September 17, 1899, Raoul Family Papers.

85. Apple, *Cautious Rebel*, 72–74; Kearney, *A Slaveholder's Daughter*, 31–45.

86. Sarah Wadley Diary, October 18, 1860, and Sarah Cornwall Shewmake Journal, May 1, 1857, both cited in Scott, *The Southern Lady*, 73–74.

87. Grace Richmond to Mrs. Richmond, February 5, 1882, Theodore Richmond Papers.

88. Klotter, "Family Influences," 24–25.

89. Keller, *The Story of My Life*, 83.

90. Margaret Preston to Sarah Preston, January 20, January 27, 1905, Preston-Johnston Papers.

91. Margaret Preston to Mrs. Preston, January 5, 1905, and passim, Preston-Johnston Papers.

92. Margaret Preston to Sarah Preston, February 16, 1905, Preston-Johnston Papers.

93. Sue Hall to Maggie Hall, November 2, 1896, Hall Family Papers; Charles Simrall to Isabella Simrall, September 7, 1889, Simrall Papers.

94. Sue Hall and Martha Cecil, Alumnae Biographical Files, Wellesley; O. S. Sumner to Sophonisba Breckinridge, September 29, 1884, quoted in Barr, "A Profession," 43.

95. Vassar College Centenary Class of 1913, 50th Bulletin, 1963, 49, Class Files.

96. Vassar Class of 1898 50th Anniversary Bulletin, 1949, 10–11, Class Files.

97. Grace Richmond to Theodore Richmond, November 20, 1881, Theodore Richmond Papers.

98. Julia Tutwiler to Ida Tutwiler, n.d. (1872), Ida Tutwiler Papers.

99. Mary Poppenheim to Mary Elinor Poppenheim, May 8, 1887, in Johnson, *Southern Women at Vassar*, 165.

100. Mary Poppenheim to Mary Elinor Poppenheim, October 12, 1887, in Johnson, *Southern Women at Vassar*, 178.

101. Kelley, *Learning to Stand*, 154–90; Sicherman, "Reading and Ambition," 74.

102. Sicherman, "Reading and Ambition," 75–77, 80–84. See also Radway, *Reading the Romance*.

103. Mary Comer to Mrs. Lillia Hall Comer, February 10, March 2, March 16, March 5, March 9, March 16, 1903, Mary Comer Correspondence; Mary Poppenheim to Mary Elinor Poppenheim, May 23, 1885, in Joan Marie Johnson, *Southern Women at Vassar*, 74.

104. *Keller, The Story of My Life*, see esp. chaps. 18, 21, quotation on 96.

105. Florence Harrison to Thomas Harrison, October 26, 1919, Thomas Perrin Harrison Papers.

Two. "We Do Want More Southern Girls to Come": Entrance Requirements, Preparatory Departments and Schools, and Alumnae Networks

1. Campion and Stanton, *Look to This Day!* 6–7, 109, 110–20, 147, 157.

2. Quoted in Friedman, "Orie Latham Hatcher," 45.

3. Shadron et al., "The Historical Perspective," 162.

4. Heath, "A Tribute."

5. Friedman, "Orie Latham Hatcher," 50–66.

6. Johnson, "Standing up for High Standards"; "Southern Association of College Women," 96; and DeMoss, "Fearless Stand," 249–60.

7. Robinson, "Curriculum," 15, 22, 51.

8. College Registers.

9. Pamphlet, Walnut Hill School, box 20, folder 7, 9–10, Headmistress Association of the East Papers.

10. Scott, "The Ever Widening Circle," 10–11.

11. Farnham, *The Education of the Southern Belle*, 112.

12. Scott, "The Ever Widening Circle," 12–13.

13. Wedell, *Elite Women*, 25–26. Lide Meriwether was born in Virginia in 1830 and attended Emma Willard Seminary in Washington, Pennsylvania. She then traveled to the "west" to Arkansas and then Memphis to teach to repay the debt owed for her and her sister's education.

14. Pressly, "Educating the Daughters," 246–75.

15. Howes, *American Women*; Emelyn Hartridge, Alumnae Biographical Files, Alum-

nae/i Association of Vassar College (AAVC); and Pressly, "Educating the Daughters," 250–51.

16. Pressly, "Educating the Daughters," 252, 271–75.

17. Alumnae Biographical Files, Wellesley.

18. Connie Guion, Alumnae Biographical Files, Wellesley.

19. Moffett, "Wellesley North and South."

20. Jordan, *Women of Guilford County,* 73–78, 128.

21. Mary Petty, Alumnae Biographical Files, Wellesley; and Virginia Terrell Lathrop, "The Petty Sisters," *Alumnae News,* February 1952, 10–12, in Alumnae Biographical Files, Wellesley.

22. Helen Jenkins, Alumnae Biographical Files, Mount Holyoke.

23. Margaret Booth, Alumnae Biographical Files, Mount Holyoke.

24. Clippings, Class of 1906 Individuals, Mary McBee, box 1689, Alumnae Biographical Files, Smith; Strauch, *Ashley Hall,* 7, 13. McBee purchased the property inexpensively from Otto Witte, a man with six daughters who wanted it to become a girls' school.

25. Mary Galbraith, Alumnae Biographical Files, Wellesley.

26. Mayer, "A Higher Education," 100–111.

27. Pokempner, "Unusual Qualifications," 78.

28. Ibid., 79. In 1890 female faculty members had studied at Harvard Annex, Bryn Mawr, Boston University, Cornell, MIT, Wellesley, and Vassar in the United States as well as Oxford, Cambridge, and other colleges in Europe (Beirne, *Let's Pick the Daisies,* 10–11).

29. Pokempner, "Unusual Qualifications," 84.

30. College Registers.

31. Folder 18, and Harriet Poynter, "A Biography of a School," bound volume, Science Hill Female Academy Papers. Also see Hahn, "A History of Science Hill Female Academy," 43.

32. Charles A. Logan to Mrs. Poynter, March 20, 1915, folder 9, and Poynter, "Biography of a School," Science Hill Female Academy Papers.

33. Daviess, *Seven Times Seven,* 57.

34. Ibid., 81–82, 89.

35. Leonard, *Woman's Who's Who;* and James, *Notable American Women.*

36. Cornett, "Angel for the Blind," 26. Mary was class of 1894, Zelinda class of 1895.

37. Pressly, "Educating the Daughters," 251, 270, quote from their catalog, on 270.

38. Pyron, *Southern Daughter,* 62–64.

39. Agnes Raoul to Mary Raoul, October 12, 1899, Raoul Family Papers.

40. Pressly, "Educating the Daughters," 270.

41. Wedell, *Elite Women,* 15–22.

42. Wilkerson-Freeman, "Emerging Political Consciousness," 5–8.

43. Ibid., 11–12.

44. Durr, *Outside the Magic Circle,* 36–52.

45. Breckinridge, "Autobiography," Sophonisba Breckinridge Papers.

46. Bashaw, *Stalwart Women,* 116.

47. Colton, "The Various Types of Southern Colleges."

48. A.Y., "Entrance Requirements," and letters in reply.

49. Emelyn Hartridge, Alumnae Biographical Files, Vassar.

50. Mary Poppenheim to Mary Elinor Poppenheim, October 12, 1887, and Mary Elinor to Mary Poppenheim, February 9, 1888, in Johnson, *Southern Women at Vassar*, 176, 188, 191–92.

51. Mary to Louisa Poppenheim, May 29, 1891, in Johnson, *Southern Women at Vassar*, 213.

52. Mary Poppenheim to Louisa Poppenheim, June 14, 1891, and Mary Elinor Poppenheim to Louisa Poppenheim, June 14, 1891, in Johnson, *Southern Women at Vassar*, 214–15.

53. Agnes Raoul to Mary Raoul, June 4, 1899, Raoul Family Papers.

54. Sue Hall to Maggie Hall, March 2, March 13, 1899, Hall Family Papers.

55. Peacock, *Margaret Mitchell*, 47.

56. "Radio Speech, January 25, 1938, Vassar Opera Scholarship Benefit," typescript, folder 3, C. Mildred Thompson File.

57. Talbot and Rosenberry, *The History*, 50.

58. May Lansfield Keller was born in Baltimore in 1877 to Jennie Simonton and Wilmer Lansfield Keller. Wilmer was a native Baltimorean, while her mother came from New England. May attended the Little Dames' School, run by Miss Alice Davis, a relative of Gen. Robert E. Lee, and then Girls' Latin School from 1888 to 1894 before attending Goucher (Woman's College of Baltimore), graduating in 1898. She visited the University of Chicago but decided to pursue her doctorate in Germanic philology in Germany after a professor at Chicago asked her why she should continue her studies if she did not have to earn a living on her own. She then taught German at Wells College in Aurora, New York (near Cornell), before returning home to teach English at the Woman's College of Baltimore. At Goucher, Keller remained active in Pi Beta Phi, the national sorority she had joined as an undergraduate, in particular traveling to Gatlinburg, Tennessee, to organize a settlement school sponsored by the sorority. In 1914 she was asked to be dean of a new school, Westhampton College in Richmond, a position she retained for thirty-two years (and she lived there eighteen years more). See Turnbull, *May Lansfield Keller*, 3–27, 42, quotation on 25.

59. *Nashville Banner*, February 28, 1932.

60. Montgomery, *The Politics of Education*, 40.

61. 1887 class letters (written 1897), 24, quoted in Gianakos, "Southern Women at Mount Holyoke," 36.

62. William Breckinridge to Sophonisba Breckinridge, October 26, 1891, Breckinridge Papers.

63. William Breckinridge to Sophonisba Breckinridge, September 22, 1884, Breckinridge Papers.

64. Quotation from Sarah's obituary, *Lexington Herald*, February 28, 1923, clipping in Preston-Johnston Papers.

65. Mary Neville wrote to Margaret Preston, December 4, 1904, and Sarah Preston to Margaret, December 2, 1904, Preston-Johnston Papers.

66. Her grandmother Margaret W. Preston (1819–98) went to Lafayette Female Academy, Shelby Female Academy, and Edward Barry's Select Institute for Young Ladies and then to Madame Sigoigne's School for Young Ladies in Philadelphia (where she had to take remedial classes to catch up). She and her sisters were close enough to visit their brothers, who were attending Yale, Harvard, and Princeton. Her husband, William, went to Yale and Harvard and was a representative in Congress and ambassador to Spain. Margaret's children were also highly educated. Her daughters went to a convent school in Manhattanville, New York, while her son, Robert Wickliffe Preston (Wick), went to Exeter, Washington and Lee, the University of Virginia, Yale, and Harvard Law School. He finally rebelled against formal training after encountering a black student in his Harvard class in 1872. See Hollingsworth, "She Used Her Power Lightly," viii, 46, 179–80.

67. Heath, "A Tribute."

68. Pyron, *Southern Daughter*, 81.

69. Gianakos, "Southern Women at Mount Holyoke," 36.

70. Ninth annual bulletin, 1908, and tenth annual bulletin, 1909, class of 1899, box 1, Class Files.

71. For the purpose of this book, I defined possible sibling sets as students sharing the same last name from the same town. While it is possible that some of these common names were a coincidence or, more likely, those of cousins, alumnae directories and other sources show that the majority were sisters.

72. Gianakos, "Southern Women at Mount Holyoke," 21; Emma Grant, 1895, Alumnae Biographical Files, Mount Holyoke.

73. Mary Poppenheim to Louisa Poppenheim, March 10, 1884, in Johnson, *Southern Women at Vassar*, 41.

74. Allen, "Economic Relation," 351–62. This survey of thirty questions received answers from one hundred women: Mount Holyoke, twenty-eight, Vassar, twelve, Smith, twenty-three, Wellesley, sixteen, and the remaining twenty-one from Radcliff, Bryn Mawr, and thirteen other colleges and universities. Although the survey includes 20 percent who did not attend the Seven Sisters, these respondents made up the vast majority and therefore offer a basis of comparison to the southern women studied here.

75. Mary Haskell diary, January 27, 1894, vol. 32, fol. 221, Jacob Florance Minis Papers.

76. Mary Comer to Lillia Comer, November 9, 1900, Mary Comer Correspondence.

77. Mary Comer to Lillia Comer, n.d. (ca. November 1900), Mary Comer Correspondence.

78. Julia Hammond to Katharine Hammond, April 7, 1881, Bryant Cumming Hammond Papers.

79. Eloise Whitaker to Mamma, January 5, 1896, and Eloise Whitaker to Liz, January 5, 1896, Eloise Whitaker Papers.

80. See McCracken, "The Women of America," 466, for a comparison of Bryn Mawr and Smith.

81. Bennett, "Seven Colleges," 13, 64.

82. Crawford, *College Girl of America*, 26–27, 65, 68, 77, 87–88, 120.

83. Butchart, "Mission Matters," 1–17. The number may be much greater, as this number was drawn from only the one-fifth of the teachers whose education was known.

84. *Historical Sketch*, 22–23.

85. Robinson, "Curriculum," 25; Cole, *A Hundred Years*; *Prospectus*, 16–18; see also Hooker, "Mount Holyoke College," 545–63.

86. *Historical Sketch*, 9.

87. Lyon, "Mount Holyoke Female Seminary," 1–2.

88. Gordon, *Gender and Higher Education*, 122, quotation from Raymond, *Vassar College*, 18.

89. Hanscom and Greene, *Sophia Smith*, 43–78. Thomas W. Higginson wrote "Should Women Learn the Alphabet," published in *Women and the Alphabet*, 1–36. Hilliard, "Smith College," 18; Seelye, *Early History*, 12–13.

90. Doty, "Life at a Girls' College," 865–72, quotations on 865–67.

91. Fallows, "Undergraduate Life," 37–58.

92. Hackett, *Wellesley*, 31.

93. Converse, *Wellesley College*, 78.

94. Hackett, *Wellesley*, 42–45.

95. Meigs, *What Makes a College?* 17–18, 38, 65–68.

96. *An Acre for Education*; and Smith, "The Harvard Annex," 568–74.

Three. From Homesick Southerners to Independent Yankees: The Campus Experience

1. Mary Elinor Poppenheim to Mary Poppenheim, February 22, 1883, and Mary Poppenheim to Mary Elinor Poppenheim, March 8, 1886, in Johnson, *Southern Women at Vassar*, 27, 94.

2. Mary Poppenheim to Mary Elinor Poppenheim, February 2, March 1, 1885, in Johnson, *Southern Women at Vassar*, 63.

3. Sutherland, *Confederate Carpetbaggers*, 70.

4. Agnes Raoul to Mary Raoul, January 8, 1900, Raoul Family Papers.

5. The graduation rate between 1875 and 1915 for all students at Vassar was 72.3 percent and for southern students 74 percent; at Smith 68.4 percent for all students and 67.7 percent for southern students; at Mount Holyoke 55.9 percent for all students and 46.3 percent for southern students; at Bryn Mawr it was 59.4 percent (through 1915) and 62.4 percent for southern students; and at Wellesley 57.6 percent for all students (using a sample of students every five years) and 52.2 percent for southern students. Information compiled from *Bryn Mawr College Calendar*; *Alumnae Register*; *Vassar College Alumnae Register*; and *Mount Holyoke College Biographical Directory*.

6. Mary Comer to Lillia Hall Comer, April 14, April 20, April 24, May 14, 1902, Mary Comer Correspondence.

7. Anne Elizabeth Lee Papers.

8. Aida Seifert, Alumnae Biographical Files, Wellesley. Tiziana Rota found that at Mount Holyoke, of the students who left early between 1881 and 1884, 24 percent left

to work, 21 percent transferred to another school, 11 percent left for health reasons, and 7 percent left at their families' request ("Between 'True Women,'" 237).

9. Barbara Tunnell, Alumnae Biographical Files, Smith.

10. Hall, "Coming of Age," 20–21.

11. Margaret Preston to Sarah Preston, November 10, November 30, 1904, Preston-Johnston Papers. In an undated letter from November 1904 she also lamented that when she was having difficulty with her menstrual period, there was nobody there to ask for help. Keckie was Cecile, the niece of Elise, the Preston's Alsatian housekeeper. "Autobiography," manuscript, Preston-Johnston Papers.

12. William Breckinridge to Sophonisba Breckinridge, September 20, 1884, and Issa Breckinridge to Sophonisba Breckinridge, September 20, 1884, Breckinridge Family Papers.

13. Issa Breckinridge to Sophonisba Breckinridge, September 20, 1884, Breckinridge Family Papers.

14. Mary Desha to Sophonisba Breckinridge, (fall) 1884, Breckinridge Family Papers.

15. Mary Elinor Poppenheim to Mary and Louisa Poppenheim, January 8, 1887, in Johnson, *Southern Women at Vassar*, 146.

16. See, for example, Mary Elinor Poppenheim to Mary Poppenheim, February 11, 1883: "I think the money is what keeps Mrs. C. from sending Jessie [to Vassar] altho' she dresses very richly. I am reconciled to your being away when I see the advantages and know how many want to go who can't. When you come home we will realize the benefit to all." In Johnson, *Southern Women at Vassar*, 26.

17. Mary Poppenheim to Mary Elinor Poppenheim, February 20, 1883, in Johnson, *Southern Women at Vassar*, 26–27.

18. Julia Hammond to Katherine Hammond, March 11, 1881, and to Mrs. Hammond, April 10, 1881; see also Julia Hammond to Katherine Hammond, n.d. (ca. April or May 1881), Bryant Cumming Hammond Papers.

19. Julia Hammond to Katherine Hammond, March 24, 1881, Bryant Cumming Hammond Papers.

20. Julia Hammond to Katherine Hammond, n.d. (ca. April or May 1881), Bryant Cumming Hammond Papers.

21. Julia Hammond to Mrs. Hammond, April 22, June 8, April 10, 1881, Bryant Cumming Hammond Papers.

22. Margaret Preston to Sarah Preston, November, October 4, October 31, November 17, 1904, and n.d. (ca. October 1904), and Sarah Preston to Margaret Preston, October 10, October 14, 1904, Preston-Johnston Papers.

23. Sarah Preston to Margaret Preston, November 7, 1904, January 5, 1905, Preston-Johnston Papers.

24. Margaret Preston to Sarah Preston, March 5, June 7, November 12, 1905, March 16, 1906, March 7, 1907, Preston-Johnston Papers.

25. The examination was dated December 14, 1880, but it is unknown when she sent it home. Box V, folder 134, Bryant Cumming Hammond Papers.

26. Julia Hammond to Emily Hammond, March 6, 1881, Bryant Cumming Hammond Papers.

27. Julia Hammond to Emily Hammond, March 6, March 11, 1881, Bryant Cumming Hammond Papers.

28. Julia Hammond to Emily Hammond, March 2, 1881, Bryant Cumming Hammond Papers.

29. Sue Hall to Maggie Hall, May 31, 1897, Hall Family Papers.

30. Agnes Raoul to William Raoul, November 5, 1899, Raoul Family Papers.

31. Mary Comer to Mrs. Lillia Hall Comer, n.d. (ca. November 1900), January 24, 1901, Mary Comer Correspondence.

32. Mary Comer to Lillia Hall Comer, February 8, October 21, 1901, Mary Comer Correspondence.

33. Mary Comer to Lillia Hall Comer, December 7, 1902, Mary Comer Correspondence.

34. Gertrude Weil to Mina Weil, October 7, 1897, Gertrude Weil Papers.

35. Durr, *Outside the Magic Circle*, 52, 63.

36. Sophonisba Breckinridge to William Breckinridge, January 22, 1886, Breckinridge Family Papers.

37. Margaret Mitchell to Steve Munnerlyn, March 17, 1918, quoted in Farr, *Margaret Mitchell*, 46.

38. Peacock, *Margaret Mitchell*, 121–23; Pyron, *Southern Daughter*, 86–88. Pyron blamed Margaret's unhappiness on her inability to step outside the traditional southern lady role without reprisal.

39. Pyron, *Southern Daughter*, 85–86; Peacock, *Margaret Mitchell*, 21–22.

40. Pyron, *Southern Daughter*, 99.

41. Louisa Poppenheim to Mary Elinor Poppenheim, March 18, 1888, in Johnson, *Southern Women at Vassar*, 197. See also Solomon, *In the Company*, 98.

42. Gianakos, "Southern Women at Mount Holyoke," 50; Lucy Walker, Class Letters, Mount Holyoke.

43. Margaret Preston to Sarah Preston, October 10, 1904, Preston-Johnston Papers.

44. Cornett, "Angel for the Blind," 25.

45. Mary Poppenheim to Kitty Poppenheim, May 29, 1887, in Joan Marie Johnson, *Southern Women at Vassar*, 170–71; Gordon, *Gender and Higher Education*, 53–55; Horowitz, *Campus Life*, 12, 42–44. These authors discuss male students and violence but do not, however, note any violence of the type that Mary describes on the part of female students.

46. Margaret Preston to Sarah Preston, November 1904, March 26, 1906, Preston-Johnston Papers.

47. Margaret Preston to Sarah Preston, November 5, 1904, Preston-Johnston Papers.

48. Margaret Preston to Sarah Preston, April 20, 1906, Preston-Johnston Papers.

49. Louisa Poppenheim to Mary Elinor Poppenheim, September 17, 1885, in Johnson, *Southern Women at Vassar*, 76.

50. Mary Elinor Poppenheim to Mary Poppenheim, February 11, May 23, 1883, in Johnson, *Southern Women at Vassar*, 25, 30.

51. Mary Elinor Poppenheim to Mary Poppenheim, March 18, 1886; Louisa Poppenheim to Mary Elinor Poppenheim, October 14, 1886; and Mary Elinor Poppenheim to

Mary and Louisa Poppenheim, October 19, 1886, in Johnson, *Southern Women at Vassar,* 102–3, 133–35.

52. Mary Poppenheim to Mary Elinor Poppenheim, October 9, 1887, in Johnson, *Southern Women at Vassar,* 175–76.

53. Mary Elinor Poppenheim to Mary Poppenheim, March 18, 1886, in Johnson, *Southern Women at Vassar,* 103.

54. William Breckinridge to Sophonisba Breckinridge, October 22, 1884, March 7, 1885, Breckinridge Family Papers.

55. B. Frank Hall to Jessie Hall, October 3, 1901, Hall Family Papers.

56. Agnes Raoul to Mary Raoul, September 24, 1899, Raoul Family Papers.

57. Margaret Mitchell to Eugene Mitchell, March 18, in Farr, *Margaret Mitchell,* 47.

58. Gertrude Weil to Mina Weil, March 6, 1898; Mina Weil to Gertrude Weil, November 2, 1898; and Gertrude Weil to Mina Weil, January 16, 1899, in Gertrude Weil Papers.

59. Margaret Mitchell to Harvey Smith, 1927, quoted in Pyron, *Southern Daughter,* 74.

60. Pyron, *Southern Daughter,* 54.

61. Quoted in Hobson, *Tell about the South,* 174.

62. Gordon, *Gender and Higher Education,* 165–75.

63. Mary Comer to Lillia Hall Comer, November 9, 1900, Mary Comer Correspondence.

64. Bessie Josephine Joyner entered Vassar as a freshman from Kelly, Mississippi.

65. Julia Hammond to Mrs. Hammond, May 5, 1881, Bryant Cumming Hammond Papers.

66. Agnes Raoul to Mary Raoul, September 26, 1899, Raoul Family Papers.

67. Gratz (?) Dent to Mary Comer, March 8, 1902, Mary Comer Correspondence.

68. Initially awed by the smart girls in her physics class, Julia Hammond was glad to report when she knew the qualities of ether and they did not. Julia Hammond to Mr. Hammond, March 21, 1881, Bryant Cumming Hammond Papers.

Four. A Southerner in Yankeeland: Southern Clubs, Yankee Ways, and African American Classmates

1. Annie Elizabeth Lee to Cazenove Lee, October 28, 1877, Anne Elizabeth Lee Papers.

2. Annie Lee to Cazenove Lee, January 5, 1879, November 7, 1878, Anne Elizabeth Lee Papers.

3. Annie Lee to Cazenove Lee, January 9, 1878, Anne Elizabeth Lee Papers.

4. "Civil War, Bethlehem Linked to Wellesley College History," clipping, *Bethlehem Globe-Times,* October 16, 1947, Anne Poe Harrison, Alumnae Biographical Files, Wellesley.

5. Moffett, "Wellesley North and South," 5, 9.

6. Julia Hammond to Emily Hammond, March 6, March 11, 1881, Bryant Cumming Hammond Papers.

7. Franklin, *A Southern Odyssey,* 4–5, 53–80, quotation on 5.

8. Sutherland, *Confederate Carpetbaggers,* 2, 14–19, 43–45, quotation on 44.

9. Ibid., 61.

10. Sutherland, "Southern Fraternal Organizations," 588–89.

11. Golia, "Southern Daughters," 4.

12. On women's loyalty to the Confederacy see Faust, *Mothers of Invention*; Edwards, *Scarlett Doesn't Live Here Anymore*; Rubin, *A Shattered Nation*, 208–9, 230–39; Campbell, *When Sherman Marched North*, 74, 102. On the northern image of the southern rebel girl see Silber, *Romance of Reunion*.

13. Sutherland, *Confederate Carpetbaggers*, 152–54, 169.

14. Julie Golia argues that while southern men interacted with Yankees at work, southern women turned to each other for their social lives. It is particularly striking how much southern students still turned to each other despite forming strong bonds with northern students. See Golia, "Southern Daughters," 7–8.

15. Hobson, *Tell about the South*, 6–12, 87–88. Hobson, however, argues that many postbellum southerners wrote about the South for themselves rather than for northerners to reassure southerners after defeat. While southern students spoke to each other about their southern identity, especially in the context of Southern Clubs, given their location they also had to address northern classmates.

16. Margaret Preston to Sarah Preston, May 30, April 2, 1905, Preston-Johnston Papers.

17. Margaret Preston to Philip Johnston, February 22, 1914, Preston-Johnston Papers.

18. Margaret Preston to Sarah Preston, May 30, 1905, Preston-Johnston Papers. See also Margaret Preston to Sarah Preston, April 2, May 21, 1905, Preston-Johnston Papers.

19. John Hope Franklin found the same kind of comparisons in the antebellum period. He cites a Virginian who praised Virginia lightning and thunder as being superior to the northern variety, a comparison Franklin labeled absurd (*A Southern Odyssey*, 168).

20. Ibid., 204; Sutherland, *Confederate Carpetbaggers*, 78.

21. Annie Elizabeth Lee to Cazenove Lee, January 14, 1878, Anne Elizabeth Lee Papers.

22. On the United Daughters of the Confederacy see Cox, *Dixie's Daughters*; on southern women's clubs see Johnson, *Southern Ladies, New Women*, esp. chap. 2.

23. Gianakos, "Southern Women at Mount Holyoke."

24. Campion and Stanton, *Look to This Day!* 12, 66.

25. Ibid., 167, 179–80.

26. Virginia Morris Nixon, unpublished typescript, 2–3, (1939), filed under Morris in Margaret Mitchell Marsh Papers, University of Georgia, Athens, quoted in Harwell, "A Striking Resemblance," 40–41.

27. Julia Hammond's father, Harry, was a Confederate veteran, her great-uncle was Wade Hampton, and her grandfather was James Henry Hammond, the senator and well-known defender of slavery; Connie Guion's father was a veteran; Charles Simrall was from Cincinnati but was a Confederate sympathizer; B. Frank Hall was a Confederate sergeant; Christopher Poppenheim was a Confederate sergeant, and all of Mary Elinor Poppenheim's brothers served; Annie Lee's father, Cassius, was a Confederate who was captured and jailed and who then escaped to Canada; Emelyn Hartridge's father was a Confederate colonel; William Breckinridge was a Confederate colonel; while Gertrude Weil's father was too young, both her uncles were Confederate veterans; Margaret Preston's grandfather William Preston was a major general; Helen Keller's father, Arthur,

was a captain, and her grandfather was a brigadier general; William Raoul was a Confederate captain. See Bleser, *Hammonds of Redcliffe*, 9–16; Campion and Stanton, *Look to This Day!* 12; Johnson, *Southern Women at Vassar*; Cornett, "Angel for the Blind," 14; Barr, "A Profession," 3; Heath, "A Tribute"; Wilkerson-Freeman, "Emerging Political Consciousness," 2, 4–5; Reiman, "Helen Keller," 12:472; and the guides to the Theodore Richmond Papers, the Simrall Papers, the Hall Family Papers, the Anne Elizabeth Lee Papers, and the Preston-Johnston Papers.

28. *South Carolina State* (Columbia), July 13, 1902, 1; see also Sutherland, *Confederate Carpetbaggers*, 81, for examples of southerners feeling ridiculed in the North.

29. Hatcher, "The Virginia Man," 650–52, quotation on 651.

30. William Breckinridge to Sophonisba Breckinridge, December 17, 1884, Breckinridge Family Papers.

31. B. Frank Hall to Jessie Hall, March 1, 1902, Hall Family Papers.

32. Katharine Hammond to Harry Hammond, August 16, 1893, Bryant Cumming Hammond Papers.

33. Julia Hammond to Mrs. Hammond, May 5, 1881, Bryant Cumming Hammond Papers; "Autobiography," Sophonisba Breckinridge Papers.

34. Sue Hall to Maggie Hall, October 13, 1897, Hall Family Papers. See also Sutherland, *Confederate Carpetbaggers*, 80, for examples of fear of becoming like a northerner.

35. Mary Haskell diary, February 9, 1892, vol. 32, fol. 221, Jacob Florance Minis Papers. Haskell, the niece of Minis's first wife, Louisa Gilmer, married him in 1926. Stephanie J. Shaw makes a similar argument for African American women in *What a Woman Ought to Be*.

36. Their sense of southern nationalism lasted long after the demise of the Confederate nation. See Rubin, *A Shattered Nation*.

37. Sophonisba's father loved Kentucky, but he realized that his children might not stay there. See William Breckinridge to Sophonisba Breckinridge, April 19, 1885, Breckinridge Family Papers.

38. Mary Elinor Poppenheim to Mary and Louisa Poppenheim, April 30, May 4, 1886, in Johnson, *Southern Women at Vassar*, 115–16.

39. Mary Elinor Poppenheim to Mary and Louisa Poppenheim, February 28, 1888, in Johnson, *Southern Women at Vassar*, 196.

40. DeSaussure, *Old Plantation Days*, 17–26, 42, 116. The book is discussed in Gardner, *Blood and Irony*, 175–76.

41. Mary Poppenheim to Mary Elinor Poppenheim, September 28, 1884, and Mary Poppenheim to Mary Elinor Poppenheim, October 9, 1887, in Johnson, *Southern Women at Vassar*, 57–58, 176.

42. Class day book, Vassar College class of 1888, 34, in Orie Latham Hatcher Scrapbook, Class Files.

43. Mary Elinor Poppenheim to Mary and Louisa Poppenheim, March 18, 1886, in Johnson, *Southern Women at Vassar*, 103.

44. Quoted in Golia, "Southern Daughters," 1.

45. Clippings, Hall Family Papers.

46. Gianakos, "Southern Women at Mount Holyoke," 27–28, 32–33.

47. Issa Breckinridge to Sophonisba Breckinridge, November 6, 1884, Breckinridge Family Papers.

48. Quoted in Gianakos, "Southern Women at Mount Holyoke," 20. The other student from the South in the class of 1888 was Loula Rhyne of Charlotte, North Carolina.

49. Agnes Caldwell, Alumnae Biographical Files, Wellesley.

50. Sue Hall to Maggie Hall, March 27, 1898, Hall Family Papers.

51. Annie Lee to Cazenove Lee, January 1, 1878, Anne Elizabeth Lee Papers.

52. Sue Hall to Maggie Hall, May 2, November 21, 1897, Hall Family Papers.

53. William Breckinridge to Sophonisba Breckinridge, November 1, 1886, October 8, 1884, Breckinridge Family Papers.

54. Quoted in Thompson, *Education for Ladies*, 68.

55. Agnes Raoul to Mary Raoul, September 23, September 28, 1899, Raoul Family Papers. Agnes referred to Mary Waire of Savannah.

56. Agnes Raoul to Mary Raoul, October 29, 1899, Raoul Family Papers.

57. Sutherland, "Southern Fraternal Organizations," 590.

58. Knupfer, "The Urban and Rural Reform Activities"; and "The Southern Association of College Women," typescript, n.d. (ca. June 1903), American Association of University Women Archives; *Vassarian* (yearbook), 1895, Vassar.

59. Sue Hall to Maggie Hall, February 2, March 4, and April 4, 1900, Hall Papers; *Mortarboard* (yearbook), 1897, 52–53, Barnard.

60. Sue Hall to Maggie Hall, February 4, March 4, April 4, May 1, 1900, Hall Family Papers.

61. Sue Hall to Jessie Hall, October 24, 1901, Hall Family Papers.

62. Sue Hall to Maggie Hall, January 27, 1901, Hall Family Papers.

63. Campion and Stanton, *Look to This Day!* 167.

64. Lucy Salmon to Emma Garrett, November 22, 1897, in Emma Garrett Morris Scrapbook, Alumnae Biographical Files, Vassar.

65. Box 30, Gertrude Weil Papers.

66. *Class Book, Smith College*, 92.

67. *Smith College Weekly*, May 3, 1916, 4. My appreciation to Nanci Young, archivist, Smith College Archives, for bringing this article to my attention.

68. *Smith College Weekly*, March 6, 1935. My appreciation to Nanci Young, archivist, Smith College Archives, for bringing this article to my attention.

69. "Looking Backwards," in Emma Garret Morris Scrapbook, Alumnae Biographical Files, Vassar.

70. *Social Science Review* 23 (March 1949): 93; Barr, "A Profession," 158; and Fitzpatrick, *Endless Crusade*, 192.

71. Gianakos, "Southern Women at Mount Holyoke," 60–61.

72. Nielsen, "The Southern Ties."

73. On southern writers of the Lost Cause see Sutherland, *Confederate Carpetbaggers*, chaps. 7, 8; Gardner, *Blood and Irony*.

74. Class day book, Vassar College Class of 1889, 48, in Helen Tunnicliff Catterall, Alumnae Biographical Files, Vassar.

75. "Short biographical sketches of the class of eighteen hundred and eighty-nine," Class Files.

76. Barbara Tunnell, Alumnae Biographical Files, Smith; Frances Jewell McVey, Alumnae Biographical Files, Alumnae/i Association of Vassar College (AAVC); Maglin, "Vida to Florence," 14.

77. Howes, *American Women.*

78. Caroline Ware, "C. Mildred Thompson, Activist," folder 11, C. Mildred Thompson File.

79. Grace Richmond to Theodore and Harriet Richmond, September 16, 1881, Theodore Richmond Papers.

80. Grace Richmond to Harriet Richmond, November 18, October 23, 1881, and Harriet Richmond to Grace Richmond, October 23, 1881, Theodore Richmond Papers.

81. Horowitz, *The Power and Passion*, 20.

82. On antebellum southerners defending slavery in the North see Franklin, *A Southern Odyssey*, 217–53.

83. McLaurin, "Rituals of Initiation," 5–24.

84. Anne Lee to Cazenove Lee, January 14, 1878, Anne Elizabeth Lee Papers.

85. Anne Lee to Cazenove Lee, March 23, 1878, Anne Elizabeth Lee Papers.

86. Daviess, *Seven Times Seven*, 86.

87. Randolph, "Another Day," 14–17.

88. Sue Hall to Maggie Hall, November 27, December 4, 1898, Hall Family Papers.

89. Sue Hall to Maggie Hall, April 12, 1899, Hall Family Papers.

90. Josephine Simrall to Isabella Simrall, October 26, 1891, Simrall Papers. Mary Haskell also wrote a paper entitled "Why Northern people in the South do not find colored servants satisfactory" while at Wellesley. Mary Haskell diary, February 9, 1894, Jacob Florance Minis Papers.

91. Gertrude Weil to Mina Weil, November 15, November 9, October 13, 1897, Gertrude Weil Papers. Gertrude lived in George Washington Cable's sister's boardinghouse. The play was *White Aprons*, a play about Sir Berkeley, governor of Virginia. See Gertrude Weil to Mina Weil, January 17, March 2, March 21, 1901. At Smith Mary Comer also played an "Old Mammy on the Southern Plantation" at the entertainment for her junior class party. Mary Comer to Lillia Hall Comer, March 9, 1903, Mary Comer Correspondence.

92. Gertrude Weil to Mina Weil, January 15, 1901, Gertrude Weil Papers; Wilkerson-Freeman, "Women and the Transformation," 28.

93. Founded in 1881 as Atlanta Baptist Female Seminary, Spelman Seminary was renamed in 1884 after Laura Spelman Rockefeller. The school became Spelman College in 1924.

94. "Non-Discrimination at Vassar," typescript, folder 10, C. Mildred Thompson File; Perkins, "The African American Female Elite," 718–56.

95. For the segregation policies of Vassar and Mount Holyoke see Gordon, *Gender and Higher Education*, 46, and Solomon, *In the Company*, 76.

96. Perkins, "The African American Female Elite," 718–56; Horowitz, *The Power and Passion*, 226–27, 341–43, 381–83.

97. Sim, "My Secret History," 70–76.

98. For African American women and higher education see Perkins, "The African American Female Elite"; and Gordon, "Race, Class," 7–32.

99. Stewart, *Portia*, 18–33.

100. Quotation in ibid., 42. See also Hill, *Booker T.'s Child*, 36.

101. Portia Washington to Booker T. Washington, September 4, 1901, in Harlan, *The Booker T. Washington Papers*, 6:200.

102. For reports based on the interview see *Birmingham Age-Herald*, November 23, 1901, reprinted in Harlan, *The Booker T. Washington Papers*, 6:322–27. There were also articles in the *Boston Globe*, October 20, 1901, and the *New York Sun*, November 3, 1901. Quotes following, unless otherwise indicated, come from this interview.

103. *Boston Transcript*, November 10, 1902, 8; Booker T. Washington to Julian La Rose Harris, October 16, 1902, in Harlan, *The Booker T. Washington Papers*, 6:549–50; *New York Age*, November 13, 1902.

104. *Indianapolis Freeman*, December 28, 1901, reprinted in Harlan, *The Booker T. Washington Papers*, 6:360–63.

105. Gertrude Weil to Mina Weil, January 21, 1900, Gertrude Weil Papers.

106. Clipping, Gertrude Weil, Alumnae Biographical File, Smith.

107. Sue Hall to Maggie Hall, September 23, 1898, Hall Family Papers.

108. Mary Comer simply told her mother, with no comment, that there were two black girls in the incoming class. Mary Comer to Lillia Hall Comer, October 11, 1902, Mary Comer Correspondence.

109. Issa Breckinridge to Sophonisba Breckinridge, September 19, September 26, 1884, Breckinridge Family Papers.

110. William Breckinridge to Sophonisba Breckinridge, October 3, 1884, Breckinridge Family Papers.

111. Breckinridge, "Autobiography," Sophonisba Breckinridge Family Papers; and Fitzpatrick, *Endless Crusade*, 182.

112. Breckinridge, *Women in the Twentieth Century*, 24.

113. Pyron, *Southern Daughter*, 84–85.

114. Durr, *Outside the Magic Circle*, 57–58.

115. Ibid., 101, 116–20, 244–45, 255–60, 279.

116. Jacoway, "Down from the Pedestal," 345–52. Her colleague in the fight was Vivion Lenon Brewer, born in Iowa but raised in Little Rock and a graduate of Smith College.

117. Langston, "The Women of Highlander," 146; Knupfer, "The Urban and Rural Reform Activities," 24–27, 30–31.

118. Friedman, "Orie Latham Hatcher," 40–41, 115.

119. Quoted in Wharton, "Reconstruction," 302. See also Elizabeth Studley Nathans, "C. Mildred Thompson, Scholar," folder 11, C. Mildred Thompson File.

120. Margaret Josephine Holley, Alumnae Biographical Files, Wellesley.

121. My appreciation to the anonymous reader of this manuscript for pointing out the possible significance of religion. See Knotts, *Fellowship of Love*; and Johnson, "The Shape of the Movement," 201–23.

Five. After College: The Marriage and Career Dilemma

1. Sophonisba Breckinridge to William Breckinridge, March 9, 1887, Breckinridge Family Papers.

2. Sophonisba Breckinridge to William Breckinridge, June 10, 1887, Breckinridge Family Papers; Sophonisba Breckinridge, "Autobiography," manuscript, Sophonisba Breckinridge Family Papers; Barr, "A Profession," 108–9; Fitzpatrick, *Endless Crusade*, 9–12. During this time, Sophonisba's depression may have also been the result of her guilt over being at Wellesley rather than with her mother, given her mother's death in 1892 and the scandalous affair her father had. See Breckinridge, "Autobiography"; and Barr, "A Profession," 45–47, 103, 112–14.

3. Fitzpatrick, *Endless Crusade*, 81, 176–77.

4. Breckinridge, *Women in the Twentieth Century*, 108, 187.

5. Glazer and Slater, *Unequal Colleagues*, chap. 1.

6. Chambers-Schiller, *Liberty*; and Franzen, *Spinsters and Lesbians*, chaps. 1, 3.

7. On marriage rates see Solomon, *In the Company*, 120; Frankfurt, *Collegiate Women*, 54–55, 73–75; and Dean, "Covert Curriculum," 248. On the percentages of American women who never married see Palmieri, *In Adamless Eden*, 147; and Smith, "Family Limitation," 121, table 1. Women at coeducational universities probably married at similar rates. For example, a survey of the first 990 female students at Sage College (the women's college of Cornell) between 1875 and 1895 found that 50 percent had married. See Conable, *Women at Cornell*, 87.

8. *Vassar College Alumnae Register*; *Mount Holyoke College Biographical Directory*; and *Smith College Alumnae Biographical Register*. I chose to compare Mount Holyoke, Smith, and Vassar because they provide a range, including one of the most popular northern destinations (Vassar), one of the least popular and most career oriented (Mount Holyoke), and one in the middle (Smith). I was unable to compare Wellesley students because career information is not accurately reported in the alumnae directories. I used directories that were published more than twenty years after graduation, so that one can assume that the vast majority of all graduates who married at some time in their lives (and reported it to their school) were captured in these directories. I limit these numbers to students who graduated because college data on nongraduating class members varied so widely from school to school and class to class.

9. Dean, "Covert Curriculum," 248; Brett, "A Different Kind of Being," 13–22.

10. Gordon, *Gender and Higher Education*, 173–74.

11. Solomon, *In the Company*, 119–22. At least 22 of 138 (15.9 percent) southern Wellesley graduates, 15 of 128 (12.5 percent) Vassar graduates, and 5 of 44 (11.4 percent) Mount Holyoke graduates married more than ten years after graduation. See *Alumnae Register*; *Vassar College Alumnae Register*; and *Mount Holyoke College Biographical Directory*. I have been unable to determine the ages of the husbands.

12. Barbara Sicherman found that Radcliffe students were on average age twenty-nine in the 1890s ("Colleges and Careers," 140–41).

13. Goodsell, *The Education of Women*, 42.

14. Cited in Palmieri, *In Adamless Eden*, 219–20; and Seelye, "The Influence of Education," 624–25. See also Jordan, "The College Graduate"; Shinn, "The Marriage Rate"; Gardner, "College Women and Matrimony." For articles condemning the lower marriage rates see, for example, Peck, "For Maids and Mothers," and Smith, "Higher Education of Women."

15. Allen, "The Economic Relation," 356–59.

16. "Mount Holyoke after the Fire," manuscript, n.d., Mary K. Hoffmeier, Alumnae Biographical Files, Mount Holyoke.

17. Palmieri, *In Adamless Eden*, 222–31. For the notion that college stripped women of beauty see "The New England Association of Colleges and Preparatory Schools," 595–96.

18. Herman, "College and After," 310–15, 327–33.

19. Frankfurt, *Collegiate Women*, 28–35.

20. Solomon, *In the Company*, 95; Gordon, *Gender and Higher Education*, 5; and Perun and Giele, "Life after College," 375–98.

21. Grace Richmond to Theodore Richmond, January 3, January 15, 1882, Theodore Richmond Papers.

22. Josie Simrall to Isabella Simrall, February 28, 1892, Simrall Papers.

23. Durr, *Outside the Magic Circle*, 59–60.

24. On faculty influence see Palmieri, *In Adamless Eden*, 189–91.

25. Wedell, *Elite Women*, 18.

26. Agnes Raoul to Mary Raoul, July 28, 1899, Raoul Family Papers.

27. King, "Free among the Dead," 139–59.

28. Montgomery, "Southern Gender Reform," 9.

29. Parrish, "The Womanly Woman," 778.

30. Helen Catterall, class of 1889 scrapbook, Alumnae Biographical Files, Vassar.

31. *Keystone*, September 1899, 14.

32. Cornett, "Angel for the Blind," 199–200.

33. Elizabeth Veach, 1918, Class Letters, Mount Holyoke; Campion and Stanton, *Look to This Day!* 188, 240 (quotation).

34. Dorothy Burdick, February 17, 1944, Class Letters, Mount Holyoke.

35. Durr, *Outside the Magic Circle*, 66.

36. Sophonisba Breckinridge to William Breckinridge, June 6, 1887, Breckinridge Family Papers.

37. Issa Breckinridge to Sophonisba Breckinridge, September 17, 1884, Breckinridge Family Papers.

38. Issa Breckinridge to Sophonisba Breckinridge, October 14, October 7, 1884, Breckinridge Family Papers.

39. Issa Breckinridge to Sophonisba Breckinridge, December 2, 1884, Breckinridge Family Papers; Barr, "A Profession," 25.

40. Bashaw, *Stalwart Women*, 37; clippings, Frances Jewell McVey, Alumnae Biographical Files, Alumnae/i Association of Vassar College (AAVC).

41. Margaret Preston to Sarah Preston, March 5, March 16, 1905, Preston-Johnston Papers.

42. Margaret Preston to Philip Johnston, August 20, 1910, Preston-Johnston Papers.

43. Margaret Preston to Philip Johnston, September 26, 1916, January 31, 1917, Preston-Johnston Papers.

44. Hollingsworth, "She Used Her Power Lightly," 131–35, 198, 217 n. 115.

45. Aphra Phelps, class of 1909, 1950 questionnaire, Alumnae Biographical Files, Wellesley.

46. Mary Poppenheim to Mary Elinor Poppenheim, March 5, 1889, and n.d., Poppenheim Family Papers.

47. Mary Elinor Poppenheim to Mary Poppenheim, October 28, 1886, in Johnson, *Southern Women at Vassar*, 135.

48. Silber, *Romance of Reunion*, 40, 63–64, 90, 186, 192–93.

49. Dawson, "The Natural History of Woman," *Charleston News and Courier*, September 20, 1873, quoted in Roberts, "Sarah Morgan Dawson," and Hamilton, *A Vision for Girls*, 23.

50. Smith, "Statistics of College," 18–19; Herman, "College and After," 289.

51. Gordon, *Gender and Higher Education*, 153.

52. Worthington, "Higher Education," 405–14, quotation on 412. Worthington did get married and lived in San Diego, where she operated a private school and was a social worker and the author of articles on social work. Daisy Worthington, Alumnae Biographical Files, Alumnae/i Association of Vassar College (AAVC).

53. Mary Poppenheim to Mary Elinor Poppenheim, October 12, 1887, in Johnson, *Southern Women at Vassar*, 177.

54. My appreciation to Joan Cashin for pointing out the significance of these phrases.

55. Julia Hammond to Harry Hammond, March 14, March 27, May 29, 1881, Bryant Cumming Hammond Papers.

56. Katherine Hammond to Harry Hammond, August 16, 1893, Bryant Cumming Hammond Papers.

57. Bleser, *Hammonds of Redcliffe*, 141–42.

58. Chambers-Schiller, *Liberty*, 130.

59. Cashin, "Decidedly Opposed"; Glover, *All Our Relations*.

60. Strauch, *Ashley Hall*, 78; Cornett, "Angel for the Blind," 26, 170.

61. Connie Guion and Florence Converse, Alumnae Biographical Files, Wellesley; Abby Winch Christensen, Alumnae Biographical Files, Radcliffe; Maglin, "Vida to Florence," 13–20.

62. Stowe, "The Thing Not Its Vision," 113–30.

63. Carroll Smith-Rosenberg coined the phrase in her influential article "The Female World of Love and Ritual."

64. Sahli, "Smashing," 17–27, for Mitchell's concerns see 22.

65. See, for example, Grace Richmond to Theodore Richmond, October 17, 1881, Theodore Richmond Papers; and Margaret Preston to Sarah Preston, March 23, 1906, Preston-Johnston Papers.

66. Sahli, "Smashing," 24–25; Rupp, "Imagine My Surprise," 395–410. Rupp argues that it is not appropriate to call lesbian those women in relationships with other women

who did not identify themselves that way; at the same time, their commitment to other women should be recognized and not denied.

67. Sarah Bruce to Morelle Bruce, April 27, May 6, July 4, 1889, Bruce Family Papers. My appreciation to Jane Turner Censer for drawing my attention to these letters.

68. As with marriage rates, these statistics are based on graduates. At Mount Holyoke, between 1880 and 1915 (there were no southern graduates between 1875 and 1880) 89 percent of all graduates worked and 84 percent of southern graduates; at Smith between 1880 and 1915 (there were no southern graduates between 1875 and 1880) 69 percent of all graduates worked and 65 percent of southern graduates. The difference between southern students and the rest of the population was widening in the early 1910s. At Mount Holyoke, between 1910 and 1915, 92 percent of total graduates worked and 87 percent of southern graduates. At Smith, between 1910 and 1915, 73 percent of total graduates worked and 63 percent of southern graduates. Information from *Vassar College Alumnae Register*; *Mount Holyoke College Biographical Directory*; and *Smith College Alumnae Biographical Register*. The Association of Collegiate Alumnae Survey of 1915, which surveyed almost 17,000 alumnae from the Seven Sisters, Wells College, and Cornell, found that nearly 70 percent were employed. See Van Kleeck, "A Census," 560.

69. Robinson, "Curriculum," 16, 19; Herman, "College and After," 251.

70. Smith, "Statistics of College," 17–18.

71. Campbell, *The "Liberated" Woman*, 54.

72. Quoted in Friedman, "Orie Latham Hatcher," 152; Kilman, "Southern Collegiate Women," 22–26; Palmieri, *In Adamless Eden*, 32.

73. McCandless, "From Pedestal to Mortarboard," 353–55.

74. Scott, *The Southern Lady*, 111; Kearney, *A Slaveholder's Daughter*, 40–41.

75. Palmieri, "Patterns of Achievement," 64.

76. Durr, *Outside the Magic Circle*, 65.

77. Solomon, *In the Company*, 117.

78. Glazer and Slater, *Unequal Colleagues*, 105; Kearney, *A Slaveholder's Daughter*, 40–41.

79. Mary Elinor Poppenheim to Mary Poppenheim, February 9, 1888, in Johnson, *Southern Women at Vassar*, 193; Louisa Poppenheim, "A Message from the Second President of the Federation and one who also served faithfully as its publicity chairman," *South Carolina Federation Bulletin*, April 1926, 1.

80. Cornett, "Angel for the Blind," 24.

81. Hatcher, "The Virginia Man," first quotation 650, second quotation 652.

82. Eleanor Belknap, ninth annual bulletin, 1907, and tenth annual bulletin, 1908, class of 1898, box 2, Class Files.

83. Addams, "The Subjective Necessity," 92. See also Talbot, "The College," 349–58.

84. Addams, "Filial Relations," 36, 40–41, 44–46.

85. See, for example, Issa Breckinridge to Sophonisba Breckinridge, January 22, March 29, 1885, Breckinridge Family Papers; Barr, "A Profession," 34.

86. Sophonisba Breckinridge to William Breckinridge, March 9, 1887, n.d. (1885), Breckinridge Family Papers.

87. William Breckinridge to Sophonisba Breckinridge, March 30, 1885, October 8, 1884, Breckinridge Family Papers.

88. Sophonisba Breckinridge to William Breckinridge, June 10, 1887, Breckinridge Family Papers.

89. Higham, *Writing American History*, 77–83. Frances Willard, president of the Women's Christian Temperance Union, was known for her love for bicycling. See Bordin, *Frances Willard*, 208.

90. Barr, "A Profession," 108–9.

91. "Sophonisba Preston Breckinridge," *Wellesley Magazine*, October 1948, 35.

92. Breckinridge entered the University of Chicago in 1894–95 and then returned home to Kentucky briefly in 1896–97 before returning to Chicago permanently. She got her doctorate in monetary policy in 1901, then her JD, and then a teaching position in 1904 (Barr, "A Profession," 167–84).

93. Fitzpatrick, *Endless Crusade*, 50.

94. Ibid., 81–87.

95. Klotter, "Family Influences," 128–29, quotation on 129.

96. Breckinridge, *Women in the Twentieth Century*, vii.

97. Ibid., 105–14, first quotation on 107, second quotation on 114.

98. Bronson, "Ellen Semple," 5–6, 81–110; Ellen Semple, Alumnae Biographical Files, Alumnae/i Association of Vassar College (AAVC).

99. Pyron, *Southern Daughter*, 91.

100. Peacock, *Margaret Mitchell*, 21.

101. Ibid., 33, 37, 42, 49, 71, 104.

102. Pyron, *Southern Daughter*, 141–45, 176–77, quotation on 143.

103. Ibid., 39, 58–59, 70, 74, 143.

104. Mary Chase to Mrs. Kavanagh, October 19, 1938, Alumnae Biographical Files, Wellesley.

105. Josie Simrall to Charles Simrall, April 17, 1892, folder 33, clippings, Simrall Papers; and Josie Simrall, Alumnae Biographical Files, Wellesley.

106. Sue Hall to Maggie Hall, May 10, 1901, Hall Family Papers.

107. Antler, "After College, What?" 409–35.

108. Wedell, *Elite Women*, 99.

109. Margaret Preston to Sarah Preston, February 2, 1905, Preston-Johnston Papers.

110. Julia Hammond to Catherine Hammond, March 3, April 9, 1881, Bryant Cumming Hammond Papers.

111. I found that 71 percent at Bryn Mawr, 74 percent at Mount Holyoke, and 78 percent at Vassar of the southern graduates who worked for wages taught at some point. Information from *Vassar College Alumnae Register*; *Mount Holyoke College Biographical Directory*; and *Bryn Mawr College Calendar*. Sicherman found that 80 percent of those working were teaching, and 60 percent of all graduates were teaching, using a 1915 survey from nine colleges ("Colleges and Careers," 147–48).

112. Mary Galbraith, class of 1898, Alumnae Biographical Files, Wellesley.

113. Loula Rhyne in Leonard, *Woman's Who's Who*.

114. Sparks, May 31, 1890, Class Letters, Mount Holyoke; Gianakos, "Southern Women at Mount Holyoke," 44–45.

115. "First Class Letter of the Class of 1911," 1912, Class Letters, Mount Holyoke.

116. Quotations in Friedman, "Orie Latham Hatcher," 39, 91, 100–101, see also 86–87, 99–105, 124–28, 145, 190–200; Sarah McCulloh Lemmon, "Orie Latham Hatcher," in James, *Notable American Women*, 2:152–53; "Scope and Content Note," Alliance for Guidance of Rural Youth Papers.

117. Pruitt, "The Education of Julia Tutwiler," 199–226; Schafer, "Julia Strudwick Tutwiler"; and Dorothea E. Wyatt, "Julia Tutwiler," in James, *Notable American Women*, 3:488–90.

118. Thompson, "Vassar—Its Tradition"; clippings, April 27, 1947, and spring 1940, folder 5, C. Mildred Thompson File; and Caroline Ware, "C. Mildred Thompson, Activist," folder 11, Alumnae Biographical Files, Vassar.

119. Wethey, "An American Pioneer," 33–35.

120. Barbara Solomon cited a study of 3,500 graduates from 1869 to 1898 that showed 72 percent taught at some point but that women made up only 1 percent of lawyers and 6 percent of doctors in 1910 (*In the Company*, 127). Smith alumnae through 1905 produced 3,000 graduates: 800 taught, 800 married, 900 had no occupation; Radcliffe's 800 graduates had 350 teachers, 180 married, and 150 unemployed. Of the employed beyond teachers, the two schools produced only 33 doctors, 7 lawyers, 2 ministers, 21 nurses, 85 librarians, 50 writers/journalists, 5 actresses, 2 architects, and 100 in philanthropy or social work. See Fitz, "The College Woman Graduate," 1.

121. Bancroft, "Occupations and Professions," 486–95.

122. Jessie Hall, Cornelia McGhilvary, Nellie Ferger, and Martha Cecil, Alumnae Biographical Files, Wellesley.

123. Guion, "Nothing Can Stop Me Now," 223.

124. North Carolina Students' File.

125. Leonard, *Woman's Who's Who*.

126. Aiken, *Fire in the Cradle*, 89–94, 124–27; Donaldson, "Songs with a Difference," 180–81, quotation on 181; and Rubin, Introduction, 3–28, quotation on 9; Pinckney, "Bulwarks against Change," 40–51, quotation on 51; Bellows, *A Talent for Living*, 1–11, 27–28, 33, 45–47, 132–35, 178.

127. McRae, "To Save a Home," 264.

128. Ibid.

129. Pyron, "Nell Battle Lewis," 63–85, quotations on 69–70; and Green, "Nell Battle Lewis." Lewis quotation is from May 3, 1925.

130. Mina Weil to Gertrude Weil, April 23, 1901, Gertrude Weil Papers.

131. Gertrude Weil to Mina Weil, April 28, 1901, Gertrude Weil Papers.

132. Mina Weil to Gertrude Weil, May 7, 1901, Gertrude Weil Papers.

133. Gertrude Weil to Mina Weil, May 13, 1901, Gertrude Weil Papers.

134. Gertrude Weil to Mina Weil, March 23, 1902, Gertrude Weil Papers.

Six. After College: The Activist

1. Gertrude Weil to Mina Weil, September 27, 1900, Gertrude Weil Papers; Mary Comer to Lillia Comer, February 15, 1903, Mary Comer Correspondence. See Smith College catalogs, 1896–1905, for course titles, including Socialism and Social Reformers, Charities and Corrections: Causes of Degeneracy, Treatment of Dependents and Delinquents, and Practical Sociology: Urban, Social and Economic Conditions.

2. Wilkerson-Freeman, "Emerging Political Consciousness," 29–32.

3. Scott, "The 'New Woman,' " 217–21.

4. Campbell, *The "Liberated" Woman*, 39. The percentage of all women age eighteen to twenty-one who attended college in 1910 was 3.8; it had grown to 7.6 percent by 1920 (Gordon, *Gender and Higher Education*, 2).

5. Notably, women born in the South and still living there were more likely (43.6 percent) to be active in church work, in comparison to 30.4 percent of the group as a whole. See Campbell, *The "Liberated" Woman*, 110, 116, 123–24, 157.

6. Merrick, *Old Times*, 6–8.

7. Kearney, *A Slaveholder's Daughter*, 31; Wedell, *Elite Women*, 25–26, 40–41.

8. Green, "Those Opposed," 20, 163–68; and Wilkerson-Freeman, "Women and the Transformation," 252.

9. Montgomery, *The Politics of Education*, 31, 37–38, quotation on 38.

10. Starrett, *After College, What?* 5–25.

11. Gordon agrees that college "expanded many students' social consciousness and desire for change" (*Gender and Higher Education*, 10, also 27–28).

12. Ibid., 3–4.

13. Welch, "Club Life," 436–38.

14. Antler, "The Educational Biography," 51. Gordon also argues that students coming from a center of women's culture such as a women's college (or a coeducational institution unfriendly enough to women to cause women to band together) strengthened their sense that women had a particular role to play in social reform (*Gender and Higher Education*, 4).

15. Horowitz, *Alma Mater*, 163.

16. Mary Comer to Lillia Hall Comer, October 28, 1900, Mary Comer Correspondence.

17. Notes, class of 1906 individuals, McBee, and class book, 1917, Alumnae Biographical Files, Smith.

18. Mary Elinor Poppenheim to Mary and Louisa Poppenheim, April 19, 1886, in Johnson, *Southern Women at Vassar*, 113.

19. Mary Poppenheim to Mary Elinor Poppenheim, April 25, 1888, in Johnson, *Southern Women at Vassar*, 198; "Autobiography," Sophonisba Breckinridge Papers.

20. Sue Hall to B. Frank Hall, October 23, 1898, Hall Family Papers.

21. Agnes Raoul was elected class president and elected to Theta, an honor society (Agnes Raoul to Mary Raoul, January 27, 1900, Raoul Family Papers). Helen Keller was elected vice president of her freshman class (*The Story of My Life*, 274). Emma was pres-

ident of the Student Association of Vassar (Heath, "A Tribute"; "Looking Backwards," Emma Garrett Morris Scrapbook, Alumnae Biographical Files, Vassar).

22. William Breckinridge to Sophonisba Breckinridge, December 17, 1884, February 11, 1885, Breckinridge Family Papers.

23. Issa Breckinridge to Sophonisba Breckinridge, February 20, February 18, 1885, Breckinridge Family Papers. Sophonisba was elected class president in her first, second, and senior years.

24. Mary Elinor Poppenheim to Mary Poppenheim, February 6, 1884, in Johnson, *Southern Women at Vassar*, 38; Harriett Richmond to Grace Richmond, October 13, 1881, Theodore Richmond Papers.

25. Mary Poppenheim to Kitty Poppenheim, May 29, 1887, in Johnson, *Southern Women at Vassar*, 170–71. Louise T. Wooster, class of 1888, was from Seymour, Connecticut.

26. Harris, "Epoch Making," 169–93.

27. Gertrude Weil to Mina Weil, November 4, 1900, Gertrude Weil Papers.

28. Mary Chase Donahue Baker Scrapbook and class day book, class of 1897, Vassar College, Emma Garrett Morris Scrapbook, Alumnae Biographical Files, Vassar.

29. "Hughes Elected at Smith College," clipping, n.d. (ca. 1916), Nell Battle Lewis, class of 1917, box 1900, Alumnae Biographical Files, Smith; Sue Hall to B. Frank Hall, March 14, 1897, Hall Family Papers.

30. Rousmaniere, "Cultural Hybrid," 45–66; Barus, "What Our College Women Are Doing," 65–68.

31. Rousmaniere, "Cultural Hybrid," 45–66.

32. Solomon, *In the Company*, 110–11; Palmieri, *In Adamless Eden*, 130; Josie Simrall to Isabella Simrall, n.d. (ca. spring 1892), Simrall Papers.

33. Sue Hall to Maggie Hall, April 5, April 12, 1899, Hall Family Papers. She also heard a missionary from China speak on March 17, 1901.

34. Breckinridge, *Women in the Twentieth Century*, 65–66.

35. Gertrude Weil to Mina Weil, May 13, 1901, Gertrude Weil Papers.

36. Clark, "Preparation for Citizenship," 403–6.

37. Wilkerson-Freeman, "Emerging Political Consciousness," 30–31. Jane Addams spoke at Vassar in February 1893. See Nettie Brand de Witt, to her mother, February 16, 1893, in Class Letters, Vassar.

38. Mary to Lillia Hall Comer, November 19, 1900, Mary Comer Correspondence. Weil also heard Booth (Wilkerson-Freeman, "Emerging Political Consciousness," 33–34).

39. Wellesley college calendar, 1908–9, 61. At Vassar, students in Prof. Herbert Mills's course on social science also visited charitable and correctional institutions. Vassar catalog, 1892–93, 54–55.

40. Durr, *Outside the Magic Circle*, 63.

41. Barr, "A Profession," 26.

42. Sophonisba Breckinridge to Issa Breckinridge, November 27, 1887, Breckinridge Family Papers.

43. Fitzpatrick, *Endless Crusade*, 81, 176–77, 191.

44. Barr, "A Profession," 220–21.

45. Fitzpatrick, *Endless Crusade*, 210.

46. Breckinridge, *Women in the Twentieth Century*, pt. 1, esp. 22.

47. Campion and Stanton, *Look to This Day!* 176; Stohlman, "Connie M. Guion," 16–18; Ruth Smith, "Doctor Connie Guion," *Wellesley Alumnae Magazine*, January 1958, Alumnae Biographical Files, Wellesley.

48. Guion, "Nothing Can Stop Me Now," 222–24, 253, quotation on 223.

49. Ruth Toof to Margaret Clapp, September 27, 1956, and Edith Simpson, Martha Cecil, and Marguerite Fitzgerald, Alumnae Biographical Files, Wellesley.

50. Rountree, *Strangers in the Land*, 133.

51. Wilkerson-Freeman, "Emerging Political Consciousness," quotation on 69, see also 56–67.

52. Rountree, *Strangers in the Land*, 129–30.

53. Gordon, *Gender and Higher Education*, 123–24, 129–33; Emma Garrett Morris Scrapbook, Alumnae Biographical Files, Vassar.

54. Twenty-third annual bulletin, 1926, class of 1899, box 2, Class Files.

55. Gordon, *Gender and Higher Education*, 148. The Vassar chapters of the College Settlement Association opened in 1891, the Consumers' League in 1900, the Christian Association predating these from 1863. Paine, "The Maids' Club," 809–11.

56. Mary Elinor Poppenheim to Mary Poppenheim, March 11, 1886, in Johnson, *Southern Women at Vassar*, 100.

57. Mary Poppenheim, "Domestic Service in South Carolina," *Keystone*, May 1905, 12–13.

58. Johnson, *Southern Ladies, New Women*.

59. Mary Poppenheim to Adelaide Underhill, July 26, 1924, July 3, 1933, class of 1888 correspondence, Class Files.

60. Johnson, "This Wonderful Dream Nation!" 40 n. 50.

61. Charlotte King Shea argues that the faculty at Mount Holyoke pushed students to become activists, whether in paid or volunteer work ("Mount Holyoke College").

62. Class letters, class of 1913, College Archives, Class Letters, Mount Holyoke.

63. *Golden Jubilee History*, 13–31; *American National Biography*; James, *Notable American Women*.

64. "Pettit, Katherine," in James, *Notable American Women*, 3:56–58; Stoddart, *The Quare Women's Journals*, 31–43; "Hindman Settlement School," June 1946, pamphlet, Alumnae Biographical Files, Wellesley. Stone apparently immediately endorsed the settlement idea but was not the original choice to go with Pettit; when another woman could not go, Stone went in her place. Ann Cobb, another Wellesley graduate, was a long-standing teacher at the school.

65. "Webster, L. Josephine," class of 1905, 103, box 1677, Alumnae Biographical Files, Smith.

66. Abby Winch (Winnie) Christensen, Alumnae Biographical Files, Radcliffe.

67. Smith, "Linda Neville," 360–76; Cornett, "Angel for the Blind," 32–35.

68. Margaret Preston to Sarah Preston, November 24, 1905, February 11, March 2, 1906, February 11, 1917, Preston-Johnston Papers.

69. Margaret Preston to Sarah Preston, July 26, 1909, February 5, 1912, February 1912 (n.d.), Preston-Johnston Papers.

70. Alumnae Surveys, Alumnae Association of Bryn Mawr College. Margaret's letters from the late teens mention all her teas, parties, and visits as well as clubs, church, civic league, and welfare commission work.

71. Green, "Those Opposed," 62, 163–66.

72. Julia Hammond to Emily Hammond, March 14, 1881, Bryant Cumming Hammond Papers.

73. Solomon, *In the Company*, 111; Gordon, *Gender and Higher Education*, 178, on Newcomb.

74. Palmieri, *In Adamless Eden*, 38–39.

75. "Autobiography," manuscript, Preston-Johnston Papers. See also Margaret's later letters concerning her support for suffrage and encouraging her mother to read Olive Shriner (Margaret Preston to Sarah Preston, March 20, 1914, January 13, 1917, Preston-Johnston Papers). Margaret's only mention of woman suffrage in her college letters was in a letter to her mother in which she reported that her cousin told about the lecture Anna Shaw gave on suffrage and how she made many suffragists that day (December 4, 1904).

76. Woodward, "Woman's Education," 468.

77. Friedman, *The Enclosed Garden*, 6–9, 19–20, 110–11, quotation on 127.

78. Sims, *The Power of Femininity*, 180.

79. Clipping, "Houston Heritage," *Houston Business Journal*, October 18, 1993, Alumnae Biographical Files, Wellesley.

80. Barr, "A Profession," 246–48, 103, 387; Fitzpatrick, *Endless Crusade*, 194.

81. Gidlund, "Southern Suffrage," 30–43.

82. Green, "Those Opposed," appendix; and Taylor, *The Woman Suffrage Movement*, 33, 45, 53, 57, 60.

83. Daviess, *Seven Times Seven*, 250; Leonard, *Woman's Who's Who*. Obviously, not all suffragist leaders were educated at the Seven Sisters. An interesting example of a southern suffragist educated at Cornell University was Dr. Delia Dixon-Carroll, one of the foremost suffragists in North Carolina. The sister of racist novelist Thomas Dixon, she attended Cornell in the 1890s before gaining her medical degree. She remained in the North for her studies "against her parents' wishes" (Wilkerson-Freeman, "Women and the Transformation," 243).

84. Class bulletins, 1914, 1917, 1920, 1928, 1936, class of 1901, Class Files.

85. Clipping, spring 1940, folder 5, and September 28, 1939, folder 3, C. Mildred Thompson File; Ellen Semple, Alumnae Biographical Files, Vassar.

86. Clipping, *New York Times*, October 3, 1930, C. Mildred Thompson File.

87. Smith and Wilson, *North Carolina Women*, 217–18.

88. Wedell, *Elite Women*, 17.

89. Ibid., 21–22.

90. Breckinridge, *Women in the Twentieth Century*, 345.

91. Clippings, February 18, February 19, 1948, folder 5, and clipping, May 20, 1933, folder 3, C. Mildred Thompson File.

92. Mary Elinor Poppenheim to Mary Poppenheim, February 6, 1884, and Mary Poppenheim to Louisa Poppenheim, March 10, 1884, in Johnson, *Southern Women at Vassar*, 38, 42.

93. Louisa Poppenheim, "The Southern Woman in Club Life," address to Louisiana Federation of Women's Clubs, March 1909, box 19, folder 65, South Carolina Federation of Women's Clubs Papers.

94. Quotations in *Keystone*, August 1899, 6, September 1899, 3. Taylor's article was reprinted in September 1902, 5.

95. *Keystone*, June 1899, 1, 3.

96. Rosenzweig, *The Anchor of My Life*, 1–16, 82, 96–97, 112.

97. Sue Hall to Maggie Hall, December 12, 1897; and see various letters and typescripts in the Hall Family Papers, especially "Sketch of Woman's Foreign Missionary Union of the Wilmington Presbytery" (ca. 1911), typescript.

98. Friedman, "Orie Latham Hatcher," 40.

99. William Breckinridge to Sophonisba Breckinridge, June 1, 1891, Breckinridge Family Papers.

100. Rountree, *Strangers in the Land*, 115–17; first quotation from Sims, *The Power of Femininity*, 80; second, Mina Weil to Gertrude Weil, n.d. (May 20, 1898?), Gertrude Weil Papers; third quotation, *Goldsboro Argus*, March 23, 1898.

101. Gertrude Weil to Mina Weil, November 20, November 21, 1898, Gertrude Weil Papers; and Wilkerson-Freeman, "Emerging Political Consciousness," 34–35.

102. Gertrude Weil to Mina Weil, April 18, 1899, Gertrude Weil Papers; Sims, *The Power of Femininity*, 82.

103. Mina Weil to Gertrude Weil, April 23, 1900, and Gertrude Weil to Mina Weil, April 29, 1900, Gertrude Weil Papers.

104. Wilkerson-Freeman, "Emerging Political Consciousness," 58–66; Rountree, *Strangers in the Land*, 123.

105. Sarah Preston to Margaret Preston, November 10, 1904, Preston-Johnston Papers.

106. Sarah Preston to Margaret Preston, January 17, 1905, Preston-Johnston Papers. Sarah Preston told Margaret that in two days she had four club meetings, including the UDC, the Church Auxiliary, the Guild, and the German Club (Sarah Preston to Margaret Preston, November 9, 1905, Preston-Johnston Papers).

107. Margaret Preston to Sarah Preston, March 2, March 7, 1906, Preston-Johnston Papers.

108. Mary Elinor Poppenheim to Mary Poppenheim, February 11, February 22, 1883, in Johnson, *Southern Women at Vassar*, 25–27.

109. Louisa Poppenheim to Emma Fox, April 12, 1916, Emma A. Fox Collection.

110. Wedell, *Elite Women*, 40–41.

111. Ibid., 31–34, 56–55.

112. Pyron, *Southern Daughter*, 22–23, 40–44.

113. Dimmick, Alumnae Biographical Files, Wellesley.

114. Southern Association of College Women, *Proceedings*, 11–14 (n.p.), reel 1:6, quotation on 13.

115. Heath, "A Tribute."

116. Southern Association of College Women, *Proceedings*, 11–14 (n.p.), reel 1:6, quotation Boyd, 11, American Association of University Women Archives. On Boyd see Heath, "A Tribute."

117. [Boyd], "A Vassar Enterprise," 434–35; and Montgomery, *The Politics of Education*, 39–40.

118. Wilkerson-Freeman, "Emerging Political Consciousness," 69.

119. Atkins, *Nineteenth Century Club*, 6.

120. Wedell, *Elite Women*, 160 n. 7, 162 n. 31, 94–95, 99–100, 104; and Leonard, *Woman's Who's Who*.

121. Katherine Carson, 1903, 1928 alumnae questionnaire, Alumnae Biographical Files, Smith.

122. Sophie Marks, 1914, 1931 alumnae questionnaire, Alumnae Biographical Files, Smith.

123. Fifth bulletin, class of 1913, box 2, Class Files.

124. Mary Poppenheim to Miss Underhill, March 19, 1918, class of 1888 correspondence, box 2, Class Files.

125. Eva Stanley, typescript, June 1927, Class Letters, Mount Holyoke.

BIBLIOGRAPHY

Archives

Alliance for Guidance of Rural Youth Papers. Special Collections, Duke University, Durham, North Carolina.

Alumnae Biographical Files. Alumnae/i Association of Vassar College (AAVC), Vassar College Libraries, Poughkeepsie, New York.

Alumnae Biographical Files. Archives and Special Collections, Mount Holyoke College, South Hadley, Massachusetts.

Alumnae Biographical Files. Class Files Special Collections, Vassar College Libraries, Poughkeepsie, New York.

Alumnae Biographical Files. College Archives, Smith College, Northampton, Massachusetts.

Alumnae Biographical Files. Radcliffe College Archives, Schlesinger Library, Radcliffe Institute for Advanced Study, Harvard University, Cambridge, Massachusetts.

Alumnae Biographical Files. Wellesley College Archives, Margaret Clapp Library, Wellesley College, Wellesley, Massachusetts.

Alumnae Surveys. Alumnae Association of Bryn Mawr College, Bryn Mawr, Pa.

American Association of University Women Archives. Washington, D.C. (microfilm).

Breckinridge Family Papers. Manuscript Division, Library of Congress, Washington, D.C.

Breckinridge, Sophonisba, Papers. Special Collections, University of Chicago.

Bruce Family Papers. Virginia Historical Society, Richmond.

Class Files. Class Files Special Collections, Vassar College Libraries, Poughkeepsie, New York.

Class Letters. Archives and Special Collections, Mount Holyoke College, South Hadley, Massachusetts.

Class Letters. Class Files Special Collections, Vassar College Libraries, Poughkeepsie, New York.

College Registers. College Archives, Smith College, Northampton, Massachusetts.

Comer, Mary, Correspondence. Class of 1904, Box 1660, College Archives, Smith College, Northampton, Massachusetts.

Fox, Emma A., Collection. Burton Historical Collection, Detroit Public Library, Detroit, Michigan.

Hall Family Papers. Correspondence, 1881–1901. Special Collections, Perkins Library, Duke University, Durham, North Carolina.

Hammond, Bryant Cumming, Papers. South Caroliniana Library, University of South Carolina, Columbia.

Harrison, Thomas Perrin, Papers. Southern Historical Collection, Wilson Library, University of North Carolina, Chapel Hill.

Headmistress Association of the East Papers. College Archives, Smith College, Northampton, Massachusetts.

Houk, Elizabeth Messick, File. Special Collections, University of Chicago.

Lee, Anne Elizabeth, Papers. Alumnae Biographical Files, Wellesley College Archives, Margaret Clapp Library, Wellesley College, Wellesley, Massachusetts.

Minis, Jacob Florance, Papers. Southern Historical Collection, Wilson Library, University of North Carolina, Chapel Hill.

North Carolina Students' File. Mount Holyoke College, South Hadley, Massachusetts.

Poppenheim Family Papers. South Caroliniana Library, University of South Carolina, Columbia.

Poppenheim, Mary B. and Louisa B., Papers. Special Collections, Perkins Library, Duke University, Durham, North Carolina.

Preston-Johnston Papers. Special Collections, University of Kentucky Library, Lexington.

Raoul Family Papers. Special Collections, Robert W. Woodruff Library, Emory University, Atlanta, Georgia.

Richmond, Theodore, Papers. Southern Historical Collection, Wilson Library, University of North Carolina, Chapel Hill.

Science Hill Female Academy Papers. Filson Club, Louisville, Kentucky.

Simrall Papers. Southern Historical Collection, Wilson Library, University of North Carolina, Chapel Hill.

South Carolina Federation of Women's Clubs Papers. Special Collections, Dacus Library, Winthrop University, Rock Hill, South Carolina.

Thompson, C. Mildred, File. Vassar College Libraries, Poughkeepsie, New York.

Tutwiler, Julia, Papers. Southern Historical Collection, Wilson Library, University of North Carolina, Chapel Hill.

Weil, Gertrude, Papers. North Carolina State Archives, Raleigh, North Carolina.

Whitaker, Eloise, Papers. Southern Historical Collection, Wilson Library, University of North Carolina, Chapel Hill.

Published Primary Sources

A.Y. "Entrance Requirements in Women's Colleges." *Nation*, March 29, 1888, 256–57; and letters in reply, April 12, 1888, 298–99, and April 19, 1888, 320–22.

Addams, Jane. *Democracy and Social Ethics.* New York: Macmillan, 1907. Reprint, Urbana: University of Illinois Press, 2002.

————. *Twenty Years at Hull House.* New York: Macmillan, 1910. Reprint with autobiographical notes, ed. Victoria Bissell Brown. Boston: Bedford/St. Martin's, 1999.

Addresses at the Inauguration of Rev. L. Clark Seelye, as President of Smith College, and at the Dedication of Its Academic Building, July 14, 1875. Springfield, Mass.: Clark W. Bryan and Company, 1875.

Allen, Annie T. "The Economic Relation of the College Woman to Society." *Education* 22 (February 1902): 351–62.

Alumnae Register, 1942 Record Number of the Wellesley College Bulletin. Wellesley College, 1942.

Bancroft, Jane M. "Occupations and Professions for College-Bred Women." *Education* 5 (May 1885): 486–95.

Barus, Mrs. Carl. "What Our College Women Are Doing." *Chautauquan* 11, no. 1 (1890): 65–68.

Beecher, Catharine E. *Educational Reminiscences and Suggestions.* New York: J. B. Ford and Company, 1874.

Bennett, Helen M. "Seven Colleges—Seven Types." *Woman's Home Companion* 47 (November 1920): 13, 64.

[Boyd], Emma L. Garrett. "A Vassar Enterprise in Atlanta's Schools." *Southern Educational Journal* 13 (1900): 434–35.

Breckinridge, Sophonisba. *Women in the Twentieth Century: A Study of Their Political, Social and Economic Activities.* New York: McGraw-Hill Book Company, 1933.

Bryn Mawr College Calendar. Philadelphia: John C. Winston, 1915.

Bryn Mawr College Program. Philadelphia: Sherman and Company, 1885–1910.

Catalogue of Mount Holyoke College. South Hadley, Mass.: Mount Holyoke College, 1875–1915.

Clark, J. B. "Preparation for Citizenship at Smith College." *Education* 9 (February 1889): 403–6.

Clarke, Edward H. *Sex in Education; or, A Fair Chance for the Girls.* Boston: James R. Osgood and Company, 1873.

Class Book, Smith College, 1907. Buffalo, N.Y.: Haursauer-Jones, n.d.

Colton, Elizabeth Avery. "The Various Types of Southern Colleges for Women." Bulletin 2 of 1916 Publications of the Southern Association of College Women (n.p.), 1–23.

Crane, Edith Campbell. "A Diplomatic Crusade." In Morris and Congdon, *A Book of Bryn Mawr Stories,* 259–96.

Crawford, Mary Caroline. *The College Girl of America and the Institutions Which Make Her What She Is.* Boston: L. C. Page, 1905.

Daviess, Maria. *Seven Times Seven: An Autobiography.* New York: Dodd, Mead and Company, 1924.

DeSaussure, Nancy Bostick. *Old Plantation Days: Being Recollections of Southern Life before the Civil War.* New York: Duffield and Company, 1909.

Doty, Douglas Z. "Life at a Girls' College." *Munsey's Magazine* 17, no. 6 (1897): 865–72.

"The Education of Women." *Harper's New Monthly Magazine* 67, no. 398 (1883): 292–96.

Fallows, Alice Katherine. "Undergraduate Life at Smith College." *Scribner's* 24, no. 1 (1898): 37–58.

Felter, William L. "The Education of Women." *Educational Review* 31 (April 1906): 351–63.

Fitz, Rachel Kent. "The College Woman Graduate." *Education.* Reprinted in Research Publications, Inc., *A History of Women,* microfilm reel 946, #8770, 1–11.

Gardner, George E. "College Women and Matrimony." *Education* 20 (January 1900): 285–91.

Golden Jubilee History, 1897–1947. Chicago: National Congress of Parents and Teachers, 1947.

Goodsell, Willystine. *The Education of Women: Its Social Background and Its Problems*. New York: Macmillan Company, 1923.

Goucher, John Franklin. "The Advisable Differences between the Education of Young Women and That of Young Men." *School Review* 7, no. 10 (1899): 577–92.

Guion, Connie. "Nothing Can Stop Me Now . . ." *Wellesley Alumnae Magazine*, May 1965, 222–24, 253.

Hall, Deborah. "Coming of Age." In *The Progressive Era: The Role of Southern Women's Higher Education before 1900 and 1917*, ed. Deborah Hall, 20–21. Lexington: University of Kentucky Press, 1991.

Hanscomb, Elizabeth Deering. "The Ethical Purpose of a Woman's College." *Educational Review* 22 (October 1901): 307–12.

Hanscomb, Elizabeth Deering, and Helen French Greene. *Sophia Smith and the Beginning of Smith College*. Northampton, Mass.: Smith College, 1926.

Harlan, Louis Harlan, ed. *The Booker T. Washington Papers*. Urbana: University of Illinois Press, 1972–89.

Harris, Cora Armistead. "Epoch Making." In Morris and Congdon, *A Book of Bryn Mawr Stories*, 169–93.

Hatcher, Orie Latham. "The Virginia Man and the New Era for Women." *Nation*, June 1, 1918, 650–52.

Health Statistics of Women College Graduates: Report of a Special Committee of the Association of Collegiate Alumnae. Boston: Wright and Potter, 1885.

Higginson, Thomas W. "Should Women Learn the Alphabet?" In *Women and the Alphabet: A Series of Essays*, 1–36. 1859. Reprint, New York: Arno Press, 1972.

Hilliard, Caroline E. "Smith College—An Historical Sketch." *Education* 8 (September 1887): 12–18.

Historical Sketch of Mount Holyoke Seminary. Springfield, Mass.: Clark W. Bryant and Company, 1878.

Hooker, Henrietta Edgecomb. "Mount Holyoke College." *New England Magazine* 15 (January 1897): 545–63.

Howes, Durward, ed. *American Women: The Standard Biographical Dictionary of Notable Women*. Los Angeles: American Publications, 1939. Reprint, Zephyrus Press, 1974.

Johnson, D. B. "The Education of the Southern Girl." *Journal of Proceedings of the Southern Educational Association* (1911): 88–97.

Johnson, Joan Marie. *Southern Women at Vassar: The Poppenheim Family Letters*. Columbia: University of South Carolina Press, 2002.

Johnson, Lilian W. "Annual Address." In *Southern Educational Association*, 65–70. Asheville, N.C.: Hackney and Moale Company Press, 1906.

Jordan, Mary Augusta. "The College Graduate and the Bachelor Maid." *Independent*, July 20, 1899, 1937–40.

———. "Smith College." *New England Magazine* 5, no. 3 (1887): 207–20.

Kearney, Belle. *A Slaveholder's Daughter*. New York: Abbey Press, 1900.

Keller, Helen. *The Story of My Life*. Boston: Houghton Mifflin, 1905. Reprint, New York: Modern Library, 2003.

King, Georgiana Goddard. "Free among the Dead." In Morris and Congdon, *A Book of Bryn Mawr Stories*, 139–59.

Leonard, John W. *Woman's Who's Who of America: A Biographical Dictionary of Contemporary Women of the United States and Canada, 1914–1915*. New York: American Commonwealth Company, 1914.

Lyon, Mary. "Mount Holyoke Female Seminary." 1835. Reprinted in Old South Leaflets, vol. 6, no. 145, pp. 1–11. New York: Burt Franklin, n.d.

Markle, A. L. "Sex in Education." *Arena* 24, no. 2 (1900): 206–14.

McBryde, John M., Jr. "Womanly Education for Woman." *Sewanee Review* 15 (October 1907): 467–84.

McCracken, Elizabeth. "The Women of America: Sixth Paper—The Woman from the College." *Outlook*, February 20, 1904, 461–68.

Merrick, Caroline E. *Old Times in Dixie Land: A Southern Matron's Memories*. New York: Grafton Press, 1901.

Mitchell, S. Weir. "Address to the Students of Radcliffe College." January 17, 1895. Reprint, Cambridge, 1896.

Morris, Margaretta, and Louise Buffum Congdon, eds. *A Book of Bryn Mawr Stories*. Philadelphia: George W Jacobs and Company, 1901.

Mortarboard (Barnard Yearbook). 1897.

"The New England Association of Colleges and Preparatory Schools." *School Review* 7, no. 10 (1899): 577–99.

One Hundred Year Biographical Directory. Mount Holyoke College, South Hadley, Mass., 1837–1937.

Page, Walter Hines. *The Southerner: Being the Autobiography of Nicholas Worth*. New York: Doubleday, Page and Company, 1909.

Paine, Grace Elizabeth. "The Maids' Club at Vassar College." *Good Housekeeping* 56 (June 1913): 809–11.

Palmer, Alice. "The New England Association of Colleges and Preparatory Schools." *School Review* 7, no. 10 (1899): 594.

Parrish, Celeste. "Shall the Higher Education of Women Be the Same as That of Men?" *Educational Review* 22 (November 1901): 383–96.

———. "The Womanly Woman." *Independent*, April 4, 1901, 775–78.

Peck, Harry Thurston. "For Maids and Mothers." *Cosmopolitan Magazine* 26 (January 1899): 329–36.

Pinckney, Josephine. "Bulwarks against Change." In *Culture in the South*, ed. W. T. Couch, 40–51. Chapel Hill: University of North Carolina Press, 1935.

Poppenheim, Louisa. "A Message from the Second President of the Federation and One Who Also Served Faithfully as Its Publicity Chairman." *South Carolina Federation Bulletin*, April 1926, 1.

————. "The Southern Woman in Club Life." Address to Louisiana Federation of Women's Clubs, March 1909. Box 19, folder 65, South Carolina Federation of Women's Clubs Papers, Special Collections, Winthrop University, Rock Hill.

Prospectus of the Vassar Female College. Poughkeepsie, N.Y.: C. A. Alvord, 1865.

Raymond, John H. *Vassar College, a College for Women in Poughkeepsie, New York: A Sketch.* New York: S. W. Green, 1873.

Rickert, Edith. "Where the College Has Failed with Girls." *Ladies' Home Journal* 29 (March 1912): 15–16.

Robinson, Mabel Louise. *The Curriculum of the Woman's College.* Department of the Interior Bureau of Education Bulletin 1918, no. 6. Washington, D.C.: GPO, 1918.

Seelye, L. Clark. *The Early History of Smith College, 1871–1910.* Boston: Houghton Mifflin, 1923.

————. "The Influence of Education on Marriage and Maternity." *Independent,* March 15, 1906, 624–25.

Shinn, Milicent Washburn. "The Marriage Rate of College Women." *Century Magazine,* n.s., 28 (October 1895): 946–48.

Smith College Alumnae Biographical Register. Northampton, Mass.: N.p., 1935.

Smith College Official Circular. Northampton, Mass., 1875–1915.

Smith, A. Lapthorn. "Higher Education of Women and Race Suicide." *Popular Science Monthly* 66 (March 1905): 466–73.

Smith, Mary Roberts. "Statistics of College and Non-College Women." *American Statistical Association* 7 (March–June 1900): 1–26.

Smith, Minna Caroline. "The Harvard Annex." *Education* 6 (May 1886): 568–74.

"Southern Association of College Women." *Chautauquan* 59 (June 1910): 96–98.

Southern Association of College Women. *Proceedings of the Seventh Meeting.* 1910.

————. *Proceedings of the Fourteenth Meeting,* 1917.

Starrett, Helen Ekin. *After College, What? For Girls.* New York: Thomas Y. Crowell and Company, 1896.

Talbot, Marion. "The College, the Girl and the Parent." *North American Review* 192 (September 1910): 349–58.

————. *The Education of Women.* Chicago: University of Chicago Press, 1910.

————. *More Than Lore: Reminiscences of Marion Talbot.* Chicago: University of Chicago Press, 1936.

Talbot, Marion, and Lois Kimball Rosenberry. *The History of the American Association of University Women, 1881–1931.* Boston: Houghton Mifflin, 1931.

Taylor, James Monroe. *Before Vassar Opened: A Contribution to the History of the Higher Education of Women in America.* Boston: Houghton Mifflin, 1914.

Thomas, M. Carey. "Should the Higher Education of Women Differ from That of Men?" *Educational Review* 21 (January 1901): 1–10.

Thompson, C. Mildred. "Vassar—Its Tradition and Its Future." *Vassar Alumnae Magazine* 46 (October 1960): 2–7.

Thwing, Charles F. "Should Woman's Education Differ from Man's." *Forum* 30 (February 1901): 728–36.

Van Kleeck, Mary. "A Census of College Women." *Journal of the Association of Collegiate Alumnae* 11 (May 1918): 560.

Vassar College Alumnae Register. Poughkeepsie, N.Y.: Vassar College, 1939.

Vassar College Catalogue. Poughkeepsie, N.Y.: Vassar College, 1875–1915.

Welch, Margaret Hamilton. "Club Life in Women's Colleges." *Harper's Bazaar*, June 16, 1900, 436–38.

Wellesley College Calendar. Wellesley, Mass.: Wellesley College, 1875–1915.

Woodward, Mary V. "Woman's Education in the South." *Educational Review* 7 (May 1894): 466–78.

Worthington, Daisy Lee. "Higher Education for Women." *Educational Review* 32 (November 1906): 405–14.

Published and Unpublished Secondary Sources

An Acre for Education: Being Notes on the History of Radcliffe College. Cambridge: Crimson Printing Company, 1958.

Aiken, David. *Fire in the Cradle: Charleston's Literary Heritage.* Charleston: Charleston Press, 1999.

Antler, Joyce. " 'After College, What?': New Graduates and the Family Claim." *American Quarterly* 32 (Fall 1980): 409–35.

———. "The Educational Biography of Lucy Sprague Mitchell: A Case Study in the History of Women's Higher Education." In *Women and Higher Education in American History: Essays from the Mount Holyoke College Sesquicentennial Symposia*, ed. John Mack Faragher, 43–63. New York: W. W. Norton, 1988.

Apple, Lindsey. *Cautious Rebel: A Biography of Susan Clay Sawitzky.* Kent, Ohio: Kent State University Press, 1997.

Atkins, Leah Rawls. *Nineteenth Century Club: Celebrating 100 Years of "Mutual Mental Improvement" (1895–1995).* Birmingham, Ala., 1995.

Bank, Stephen P. *The Sibling Bond.* 2nd ed. New York: Basic Books, 1997.

Barr, Nancy Ellen. "A Profession for Women: Education, Social Service Administration, and Feminism in the Life of Sophonisba Preston Breckinridge, 1886–1948." PhD diss., Emory University, 1993.

Bashaw, Carolyn. *"Stalwart Women": A Historical Analysis of Deans of Women in the South.* New York: Teachers College Press, 1999.

Beirne, Rosamond Randall. *Let's Pick the Daisies: The History of the Bryn Mawr School, 1885–1967.* Baltimore: Bryn Mawr School, 1970.

Bellows, Barbara L. *A Talent for Living: Josephine Pinckney and the Charleston Literary Tradition.* Baton Rouge: Louisiana State University Press, 2006.

Birnbaum, Shira. "Making Southern Belles in Progressive Era Florida: Gender in the Formal and Hidden Curriculum of the Florida Female College." *Frontiers* 16 (1996): 218–46.

Bleser, Carol, ed. *The Hammonds of Redcliffe*. New York: Oxford University Press, 1981.

Bordin, Ruth. *Frances Willard: A Biography*. Chapel Hill: University of North Carolina Press, 1986.

Brett, Sally. "A Different Kind of Being." In *Stepping off the Pedestal*, ed. Patricia A. Stringer and Irene Thompson, 13–22. New York: Modern Language Association, 1982.

Bronson, Judith Conoyer. "Ellen Semple: Contributions to the History of American Geography." PhD diss., St. Louis University, 1973.

Butchart, Ronald E. "Mission Matters: Mount Holyoke, Oberlin, and the Schooling of Southern Blacks, 1861–1917." *History of Education Quarterly* 42 (Spring 2002): 1–17.

Butler, Patricia Smith. *Education for Equality: Women's Rights Periodicals and Women's Higher Education, 1849–1920*. New York: Greenwood Press, 1989.

Campbell, Barbara Kuhn. *The "Liberated" Woman of 1914: Prominent Women in the Progressive Era*. Ann Arbor, Mich.: UMI Research Press, 1979.

Campbell, Jacqueline Glass. *When Sherman Marched North from the Sea: Resistance on the Confederate Home Front*. Chapel Hill: University of North Carolina Press, 2003.

Campion, Nardi Reeder, and Rosamond Wilfley Stanton. *Look to This Day! The Lively Education of a Great Woman Doctor: Connie Guion, M.D.* Boston: Little, Brown, 1965.

Cashin, Joan E. " 'Decidedly Opposed to the Union': Women's Culture, Marriage, and Politics in Antebellum South Carolina." *Georgia Historical Quarterly* 78 (Winter 1994): 735–59.

Chafe, William. *Women and Equality: Changing Patterns in American Culture*. New York: Oxford University Press, 1977.

Chambers-Schiller, Virginia Lee. *Liberty, a Better Husband: Single Women in America: The Generations of 1780–1840*. New Haven, Conn.: Yale University Press, 1984.

Clinton, Catherine. "Equally Their Due: The Education of the Planter Daughter in the Early Republic." *Journal of the Early Republic* 2 (April 1982): 39–60.

Cole, Arthur C. *A Hundred Years of Mount Holyoke College: The Evolution of an Educational Ideal*. New Haven, Conn.: Yale University Press, 1940.

Conable, Charlotte Williams. *Women at Cornell: The Myth of Equal Education*. Ithaca: Cornell University Press, 1977.

Converse, Florence. *Wellesley College: A Chronicle of the Years, 1875–1938*. Wellesley, Mass.: Hathaway House Bookshop, 1939.

Corley, Florence Fleming. "Higher Education for Women: Four Church-Related Women's Colleges in Georgia, Agnes Scott, Shorter, Spelman, and Wesleyan, 1900–1920." PhD diss., Georgia State University, 1985.

Cornett, Judy Gail. "Angel for the Blind: The Public Triumphs and Private Tragedies of Linda Neville." PhD diss., University of Kentucky, 1993.

Cox, Karen L. *Dixie's Daughters: The United Daughters of the Confederacy and the Preservation of Confederate Culture*. Gainesville: University Press of Florida, 2003.

Dean, Pamela. "Covert Curriculum: Class, Gender, and Student Culture at a New South Woman's College, 1892–1910." PhD diss., University of North Carolina, 1994.

DeMoss, Dorothy D. "A 'Fearless Stand': The Southern Association of College Women, 1903–1921." *Southern Studies* 26 (Winter 1987): 249–60.

Donaldson, Susan V. "Songs with a Difference: Beatrice Ravenel and the Detritus of Southern History." In *The Female Tradition in Southern Literature*, ed. Carol S. Manning, 176–92. Urbana: University of Illinois Press, 1993.

Durr, Virginia Foster. *Outside the Magic Circle: The Autobiography of Virginia Foster Durr*. Tuscaloosa: University of Alabama Press, 1985.

Edwards, Laura Edwards. *Scarlett Doesn't Live Here Anymore: Southern Women in the Civil War Era*. Urbana: University of Illinois Press, 2000.

Ezell, John S. "A Southern Education for Southrons." *Journal of Southern History* 17 (August 1951): 303–27.

Farnham, Christie Anne. *The Education of the Southern Belle: Higher Education and Student Socialization in the Antebellum South*. New York: New York University Press, 1994.

Farr, Finis. *Margaret Mitchell of Atlanta*. New York: Avon, 1974.

Faust, Drew. *Mothers of Invention: Women of the Slaveholding South in the American Civil War*. Chapel Hill: University of North Carolina Press, 1996.

Fitzpatrick, Ellen. *Endless Crusade: Women Social Scientists and Progressive Reform*. New York: Oxford University Press, 1990.

Frankfurt, Roberta. *Collegiate Women: Domesticity and Career in Turn-of-the-Century America*. New York: New York University Press, 1977.

Franklin, John Hope. *A Southern Odyssey: Southerners in the Antebellum North*. Baton Rouge: Louisiana State University Press, 1976.

Franzen, Trisha. *Spinsters and Lesbians: Independent Womanhood in the United States*. New York: New York University Press, 1996.

Friedman, Belinda Bundy. "Orie Latham Hatcher and the Southern Woman's Educational Alliance." PhD diss., Duke University, 1981.

Friedman, Jean E. *The Enclosed Garden: Women and Community in the Evangelical South, 1830–1900*. Chapel Hill: University of North Carolina Press, 1985.

Fuller, Paul. *Laura Clay and the Women's Rights Movement*. Lexington: University of Kentucky Press, 1975.

Gardner, Sarah E. *Blood and Irony: Southern White Women's Narratives of the Civil War, 1861–1937*. Chapel Hill: University of North Carolina Press, 2004.

Gianakos, Cynthia. "Southern Women at Mount Holyoke: An Inquiry into Distinction." Honor paper, BA, Mount Holyoke, 1979, unpublished, in Mount Holyoke Archives and Special Collections.

Gidlund, Leonora A. "Southern Suffrage and Beyond: Eleonore Raoul and the Atlanta League of Women Voters, 1920–1935." *Atlanta History* 40 (Fall–Winter 1996–97): 30–43.

Glazer, Penina Migdal, and Miriam Slater. *Unequal Colleagues: The Entrance of Women into the Professions, 1890–1940*. New Brunswick, N.J.: Rutgers University Press, 1987.

Glover, Lorri. *All Our Relations: Blood Ties and Emotional Bonds among the Early South Carolina Gentry*. Baltimore: Johns Hopkins University Press, 2000.

Golia, Julie. "Southern Daughters, up North: The New York Division of the United Daughters of the Confederacy." Paper presented at the Southern Historical Association Meeting, 2005.

Gordon, Lynn D. *Gender and Higher Education in the Progressive Era, 1890–1920.* New Haven, Conn.: Yale University Press, 1990.

———. "Race, Class, and the Bonds of Womanhood at Spelman Seminary, 1881–1923." *History of Higher Education Annual* 9 (1989): 7–32.

Green, Elna C. "Those Opposed: Southern Anti-Suffragism, 1890–1920." PhD diss., Tulane University, 1992.

Green, Linda Con. "Nell Battle Lewis: Crusading Columnist, 1921–38." Master's thesis, Eastern Carolina University, 1969.

Hackett, Alice Payne Hackett. *Wellesley: Part of the American Story.* New York: E. P. Dutton and Company, 1949.

Hahn, Lulu Sutherland. "A History of Science Hill Female Academy." PhD diss., University of Kentucky, 1944.

Hamilton, Andrea. *A Vision for Girls: Gender, Education, and the Bryn Mawr School.* Baltimore: Johns Hopkins University Press, 2004.

Harwell, Richard. " 'A Striking Resemblance to a Masterpiece': *Gone with the Wind* in 1936." In *Recasting: Gone with the Wind in American Culture*, ed. Darden Asbury Pyron, 39–55. Miami: University Presses of Florida, 1983.

Heath, Virginia Shropshire. "A Tribute to Emma Louise Garrett Boyd Morris." Pamphlet, 1953, reel I:11, Georgia Division of the American Association of University Women, 1953. American Association of University Women Archives. Washington, D.C.

Herman, Debra. "College and After: The Vassar Experiment in Women's Education, 1861–1924." PhD diss., Stanford University, 1979.

Higham, John. *Writing American History: Essays on Modern Scholarship.* Bloomington: Indiana University Press, 1970.

Hill, Roy L. *Booker T.'s Child: The Life and Times of Portia Marshall Washington Pittman.* Washington, D.C.: Three Continents Press, 1993.

Hobson, Fred. *Tell about the South: The Southern Rage to Explain.* Baton Rouge: Louisiana State University Press, 1983.

Hollingsworth, Randolph. "She Used Her Power Lightly: A Political History of Margaret Wickliffe Preston of Kentucky." PhD diss., University of Kentucky, 1999.

Horowitz, Helen L. *Alma Mater: Design and Experience in the Women's Colleges from Their Nineteenth Century Beginnings to the 1930s.* New York: Alfred A. Knopf, 1984.

———. *Campus Life: Undergraduate Cultures from the End of the Eighteenth Century to the Present.* New York: Alfred A. Knopf, 1987.

———. *The Power and Passion of M. Carey Thomas.* New York: Alfred A. Knopf, 1994.

Jacoway, Elizabeth. "Down from the Pedestal: Gender and Regional Culture in a Ladylike Assault on the Southern Way of Life." *Arkansas Historical Quarterly* 56 (Autumn 1997): 345–52.

James, Edward T., ed. *Notable American Women, 1607–1950: A Biographical Dictionary.* Cambridge, Mass.: Belknap Press of Harvard University Press, 1971.

Johnson, Joan Marie. "The Shape of the Movement to Come: Women, Religion, and the Interracial Movement in 1920s South Carolina." In *"Warm Ashes": Issues in Southern History at the Dawn of the Twenty-First Century,* 201–23. Columbia: University of South Carolina Press, 2003.

———. *Southern Ladies, New Women: Race, Region and Clubwomen in South Carolina, 1890–1930.* Gainesville: University Press of Florida, 2004.

———. "Standing up for High Standards: The Southern Association of College Women." In *The Educational Work of Women's Associations,* ed. Anne Meis Knupfer and Christine Woyshner. New York: Palgrave Macmillan, forthcoming.

———. " 'This Wonderful Dream Nation!': Black and White South Carolina Women and the Creation of the New South, 1898–1930." PhD diss., University of California, Los Angeles, 1997.

Jordan, Paula Stahls. *Women of Guilford County, North Carolina: A Study of Women's Contributions, 1740–1979.* Guilford: Women of Guilford, 1979.

Kelley, Mary. *Learning to Stand and Speak: Women, Education, and Public Life in America's Republic.* Chapel Hill: University of North Carolina Press, 2006.

Kilman, Gail Apperson. "Southern Collegiate Women: Higher Education at Wesleyan Female College and Randolph-Macon Woman's College, 1893–1907." PhD diss., University of Delaware, 1984.

Klotter, James C. "Family Influences on a Progressive: The Early Years of Sophonisba P. Breckinridge." In *Kentucky Profiles: Biographical Essays in Honor of Holman Hamilton,* ed. James C. Klotter and Peter J. Sehlinger, 121–54. Frankfurt: Kentucky Historical Society, 1982.

Knotts, Alice J. *Fellowship of Love: Methodist Women Changing American Racial Attitudes, 1920–1968.* Nashville, Tenn.: Kingswood Books, 1996.

Knupfer, Anne Meis. "The Urban and Rural Reform Activities of Lilian Wyckoff Johnson." In *The Educational Work of Women's Associations,* ed. Anne Meis Knupfer and Christine Woyshner. New York: Palgrave Macmillan, forthcoming.

Langston, Donna. "The Women of Highlander." In *Women in the Civil Rights Movement: Trailblazers and Torchbearers, 1941–1965,* ed. Vicki L. Crawford, Jacqueline Anne Rouse, and Barbara Woods, 145–67. Brooklyn, N.Y.: Carlson Publishing Company, 1990.

Maglin, Nan Bauer. "Vida to Florence: 'Comrade and Companion.' " *Frontiers* 4 (1979): 13–20.

Mayer, Donna Dashell. " 'A Higher Education': The Norfolk College for Young Ladies, 1879–1899." *Virginia Cavalcade* 43 (1994): 100–111.

McCandless, Amy Thompson. "From Pedestal to Mortarboard: Higher Education for Women in South Carolina from 1920–1940." *Southern Studies* 23 (Winter 1984): 348–62.

———. *The Past in the Present: Women's Higher Education in the Twentieth-Century American South.* Tuscaloosa: University of Alabama Press, 1999.

―――――. "Progressivism and the Higher Education of Southern Women." *North Carolina Historical Review* 70 (July 1993): 302–25.

McGuigan, Dorothy G. *A Dangerous Experiment: One Hundred Years at the University of Michigan.* Ann Arbor: University of Michigan Press, 1980.

McLaurin, Melton. "Rituals of Initiation and Rebellion: Adolescent Responses to Segregation in Southern Autobiography." *Southern Cultures* 3 (Summer 1997): 5–24.

McRae, Elizabeth Gillespie. "To Save a Home: Nell Battle Lewis and the Rise of Southern Conservatism, 1941–1956." *North Carolina Historical Review* 81 (July 2004): 261–87.

Meigs, Cornelia. *What Makes a College? A History of Bryn Mawr.* New York: Macmillan Company, 1956.

Moffett, Edna V. "Wellesley North and South." Typescript, 1948, Anne Elizabeth Lee Papers, Alumnae Biographical Files, Wellesley College Archives, Margaret Clapp Library, Wellesley College, Wellesley, Massachusetts.

Montgomery, Rebecca S. *The Politics of Education in the New South: Women and Reform in Georgia, 1890–1930.* Baton Rouge: Louisiana State University, 2006.

―――――. "Southern Gender Reform and the Role of Women's Education: Celeste Parrish and the Critique of 'Hedonistic Ethics.' " Paper presented at the History of Education Society, 1998.

Nielsen, Kim. "The Southern Ties of Helen Keller." Unpublished paper in author's possession, 2004.

Oates, Mary J., and Susan Williamson. "Women's Colleges and Women Achievers." *Signs* 3 (1978): 795–806.

Palmieri, Patricia Ann. *In Adamless Eden: The Community of Women Faculty at Wellesley.* New Haven, Conn.: Yale University Press, 1995.

―――――. "Patterns of Achievement of Single Academic Women at Wellesley College, 1880–1920." *Frontiers* 5 (1980): 63–67.

Peacock, Jane Bonner, ed. *Margaret Mitchell, a Dynamo Going to Waste: Letters to Allen Edee, 1919–1921.* Atlanta: Peachtree Publishers, 1985.

Perkins, Linda M. "The African American Female Elite: The Early History of African American Women in the Seven Sister Colleges, 1880–1960." *Harvard Educational Review* 67 (Winter 1997): 718–56.

Perun, Pamela J., and Janet Z. Giele. "Life after College: Historical Links between Women's Education and Women's Work." In *The Undergraduate Woman: Issues in Educational Equity*, ed. Pamela J. Perun, 375–98. Lexington, Mass.: Lexington Books, 1982.

Pokempner, Elizabeth. " 'Unusual Qualifications': Teachers at the Bryn Mawr School, 1885–1901." *Maryland Historical Magazine* 93 (Spring 1998): 77–87.

Pressly, Paul M. "Educating the Daughters of Savannah's Elite: The Pape School, the Girl Scouts, and the Progressive Movement." *Georgia Historical Quarterly* 80 (Summer 1996): 246–75.

Pruitt, Paul M., Jr. "The Education of Julia Tutwiler: Background to a Life of Reform." *Alabama Review* 46 (July 1993): 199–226.

Pyron, Darden. "Nell Battle Lewis (1893–1956) and 'The New Southern Woman.'" *Perspectives on the American South* 3 (1982): 63–85.

———. *Southern Daughter: The Life of Margaret Mitchell.* New York: Oxford University Press, 1991.

Radway, Janice. *Reading the Romance: Women, Patriarchy, and Popular Literature.* Chapel Hill: University of North Carolina Press, 1984.

Randolph, Ruth Elizabeth. "Another Day Will Find Me Brave: Clarissa Scott Delaney, 1901–1927." *Sage: A Scholarly Journal on Black Women, Student Supplement* (1988): 14–17.

Reiman, Richard A. "Helen Keller." In *American National Biography,* 12:472–74.

Roberts, Giselle. "Sarah Morgan Dawson: A New Southern Woman in Postwar Charleston." In *South Carolina Women: Their Lives and Times,* ed. Marjorie Spruill, Valinda Littlefield, and Joan Johnson. Athens: University of Georgia Press, forthcoming.

Rogers, Agnes. *Vassar Women: An Informal Study.* Poughkeepsie, N.Y.: Vassar College, 1940.

Rosenzweig, Linda W. *The Anchor of My Life: Middle Class American Mothers and Daughters, 1880–1920.* New York: New York University Press, 1993.

Rota, Tiziana. "Between 'True Women' and 'New Women': Mount Holyoke Students, 1837–1908." PhD diss., University of Massachusetts, 1983.

Rountree, Moses. *Strangers in the Land: The Story of Jacob Weil's Tribe.* Philadelphia: Dorrance and Company, 1969.

Rousmaniere, John P. "Cultural Hybrid in the Slums: The College Woman and the Settlement House, 1889–1894." *American Quarterly* 22 (Spring 1970): 45–66.

Rubin, Anne Sarah. *A Shattered Nation: The Rise and Fall of the Confederacy, 1861–1868.* Chapel Hill: University of North Carolina Press, 2005.

Rubin, Louis. Introduction to *The Yemassee Lands: Poems of Beatrice Ravenel,* ed. Louis Rubin, 3–28. Chapel Hill: University of North Carolina Press, 1969.

Rupp, Leila J. "Imagine My Surprise: Women's Relationships in Mid-Twentieth-Century America." In *Hidden from History: Reclaiming the Gay and Lesbian Past,* ed. Martin Duberman, Martha Vicinus, and George Chauncey, Jr., 395–410. New York: New American Library, 1989.

Sahli, Nancy. "Smashing: Women's Relationships before the Fall." *Chrysalis* 8 (Summer 1979): 17–27.

Schafer, Elizabeth. "Julia Strudwick Tutwiler." In *American National Biography,* 22:45–46.

Scott, Anne Firor. "The Ever Widening Circle: The Diffusion of Feminist Values from the Troy Female Seminary, 1822–1872." *History of Education Quarterly* 19 (Spring 1979): 3–25.

———. *Natural Allies: Women's Associations in American History.* Urbana: University of Illinois Press, 1991.

———. "The 'New Woman' of the New South." In *Making the Invisible Woman Visible,* 212–21. Urbana: University of Illinois Press, 1984.

————. "On Seeing and Not Seeing." *Journal of American History* 71 (June 1984): 7–21.

————. *The Southern Lady: From Pedestal to Politics.* Chicago: University of Chicago Press, 1970.

Shadron, Virginia, Eleanor Hinton Hoylt, Margaret Parsons, Barbara B. Reitt, Beverly Guy Sheftall, Jacqueline Zalumas, and Darlene R. Roth. "The Historical Perspective: A Bibliographical Essay." In *Stepping off the Pedestal: Academic Women in the South,* ed. Patricia Stringer and Irene Thompson, 145–68. New York: Modern Language Association, 1982.

Shaw, Stephanie J. *What a Woman Ought to Be and to Do: Black Professional Women Workers during the Jim Crow Era.* Chicago: University of Chicago Press, 1996.

Shea, Charlotte King. "Mount Holyoke College, 1975–1910: The Passing of the Old Order." PhD diss., Cornell University, 1983.

Sicherman, Barbara. "Colleges and Careers: Historical Perspectives on the Lives and Work Patterns of Women College Graduates." In *Women and Higher Education in American History,* ed. John Mack Faragher, 130–64. New York: W. W. Norton, 1988.

————. "Reading and Ambition: M. Carey Thomas and Female Heroism." *American Quarterly* 45 (March 1993): 73–103.

Silber, Nina. *Romance of Reunion: Northerners and the South, 1865–1900.* Chapel Hill: University of North Carolina Press, 1993.

Sim, Jillian A. "My Secret History." *American Heritage Magazine* (1999). Reprinted in *Utne Reader,* May–June 1999, 70–76.

Sims, Anastasia. *The Power of Femininity in the New South: Women's Organizations and Politics in North Carolina, 1880–1930.* Columbia: University of South Carolina Press, 1997.

Smith, D. Anthony, and Arthur H. Keeney. "Linda Neville (1873–1961): Kentucky Pioneer against Blindness." *Filson Club History Quarterly* 64 (July 1990): 360–76.

Smith, Daniel Scott. "Family Limitation, Sexual Control, and Domestic Feminism in Victorian America." In *Clio's Consciousness Raised: New Perspectives on the History of Women,* ed. Mary Hartman and Lois W. Banner, 119–36. New York: Harper and Row, 1974.

Smith, Margaret Supplee, and Emily Herring Wilson. *North Carolina Women: Making History.* Chapel Hill: University of North Carolina Press, 1999.

Smith-Rosenberg, Carroll. "The Female World of Love and Ritual: Relations between Women in Nineteenth Century America." In *A Heritage of Her Own: Toward a New Social History of American Women,* ed. Nancy Cott and Elizabeth Pleck, 311–42. New York: Simon and Schuster, 1979.

Solomon, Barbara Miller. *In the Company of Educated Women: A History of Women and Higher Education in America.* New Haven, Conn.: Yale University Press, 1985.

Solomon, Barbara Miller, with Patricia M. Nolan. "Education, Work, Family, and Public Commitment in the Lives of Radcliffe Alumnae, 1883–1928." In *Changing Education: Women as Radicals and Conservators,* ed. Joyce Antler and Dari Knopp Biklen, 139–55. Albany: State University of New York Press, 1990.

"Sophonisba Preston Breckinridge." *Wellesley Magazine,* October 1948, 35.

Stewart, Ruth Ann. *Portia: The Life of Portia Washington Pittman, the Daughter of Booker T. Washington.* New York: Doubleday, 1977.

Stoddart, Jess. *The Quare Women's Journals: Summers in the Kentucky Mountains and the Founding of the Hindman Settlement School.* Ashland, Ky.: Jess Stuart Foundation, 1997.

Stohlman, Martha Lou. "Connie M. Guion: Physician Extraordinary." *Sweet Briar Alumnae News*, March 1958, 16–18.

Stowe, Steven M. "The Thing Not Its Vision: A Woman's Courtship and Her Sphere in the Southern Planter Class." *Feminist Studies* 9 (Spring 1983): 113–30.

Strauch, Ileana. *Ashley Hall.* Charleston: Arcadia Publishing, 2003.

Sutherland, Daniel. *The Confederate Carpetbaggers.* Baton Rouge: Louisiana State University Press, 1988.

———. "Southern Fraternal Organizations in the North." *Journal of Southern History* 53 (November 1987): 587–612.

Taylor, A. Elizabeth. *The Woman Suffrage Movement in Tennessee.* New York: Bookman Association, 1957.

Thompson, Eleanor. *Education for Ladies, 1830–1860.* New York: King's Crown Press, 1947.

Tidball, M. Elizabeth. "Women's Colleges and Women Achievers Revisited." *Signs* 5 (1980): 504–17.

Turnbull, Pauline. *May Lansfield Keller: Life and Letters, 1877–1964.* Verona, Va.: McClure Press, 1975.

Turner, Elizabeth Hayes. *Women, Culture, and Community: Religion and Reform in Galveston, 1880–1920.* New York: Oxford University Press, 1997.

Wedell, Marsha. *Elite Women and the Reform Impulse in Memphis, 1875–1915.* Knoxville: University of Tennessee Press, 1991.

Wethey, Harold. "An American Pioneer in Hispanic Studies: Georgiana Goddard King." *Parnassus* 11 (November 1939): 33–35.

Wharton, Vernon L. "Reconstruction." In *Writing Southern History: Essays in Historiography in Honor of Fletcher M. Green*, ed. Arthur S. Link and Remember W. Patrick, 295–315. Baton Rouge: Louisiana State University Press, 1965.

Wilkerson-Freeman, Sarah. "The Emerging Political Consciousness of Gertrude Weil: Education and Women's Clubs, 1879–1914." Master's thesis, University of North Carolina, 1985.

———. "Women and the Transformation of American Politics: North Carolina, 1898–1940." PhD diss., University of North Carolina, 1995.

Zschoche, Sue. "Dr. Clarke Revisited: Science, True Womanhood, and Female Collegiate Education." *History of Education Quarterly* 29 (Winter 1989): 545–69.

INDEX

Abbott, Edith, 117, 152

Adair, Barbara (McClung), 55, 89

Addams, Jane, 4, 93, 127–28, 133, 146, 151–52, 157

African Americans, 7, 95–108

Agnes Scott College, 11, 17, 19–21, 124, 144

Alliance for Guidance of Rural Youth (Southern Woman's Educational Alliance), 124, 136

American Association of University Women (AAUW), 45–46, 53, 173

Ashley Hall School, 47, 139

Association of Colleges and Secondary Schools of the Southern States, 51

Association of Collegiate Alumnae (ACA), 23, 53, 55, 112, 173

Atlanta Girls High School, 42

Atlanta Vassar Club, 171

Atlantic Magazine, 87

Atwood, Charlotte, 101

Belknap, Eleanor, 35, 127

Birney, Alice McLellan, 156

Blanding, Sarah Gibson, 51

Booth, Margaret, 47

Borden, Sallie, 138

Breckinridge, Curry, 157

Breckinridge, Issa, 24, 31, 64, 88, 103, 117, 128, 167

Breckinridge, Sophonisba, 23–24, 31–32, 34–35, 68, 74, 109, 145; and African Americans, 103–5; homesickness of, 64; nonmarriage of, 117–18; preparation of, for college, 50–51, 54; reform work of, 148, 151–52, 157; and southern identity, 83, 84–86, 88, 89, 92–93; and wage work, 128–31; woman suffrage work of, 161, 164

Breckinridge, William, 54, 74, 167; attitude of, toward African Americans,

104; influence of, on Sophonisba's career, 109, 128, 130; support of, for Sophonisba's education, 31, 64; view of, on women, 31, 84–85

Briney, Melville, 158

Brown, Varina Davis, 72, 89, 93

Browne, Ethel, 138

Browne, Jennie N., 138

Browne, Jennie Nicholson, 138

Browne, Mary, 138

Bruce, Sarah, 123

Bryn Mawr College: African American students at, 99; and alumnae employment, 134; extracurricular activities at, 146; history of, 16, 60; lack of preparatory department at, 43; liberal arts curriculum at, 26–27; number of southern students at, 8, 123; preparation for, 43–44, 48, 50; reputation of, 18–19, 56–57

Bryn Mawr School, 8, 43–44, 47–48, 54

Burdick, Dorothy, 116

Burney, Minnie Melton, 172

Caldwell, Agnes, 88

Capen School, 43

Career. *See* Wage work

Carson, Katherine, 172–73

Cecil, Martha, 35, 94, 138, 153

Century Magazine, 87

Chase, Mary, 133

Cheek, Mary Ashby, 137, 156

Choate, Augusta, 154

Christensen, Abby Holmes, 157–58

Christensen, Abby Winch, 157–58

Clara Conway Institute, 49–50, 133

Clarke, Edward H., 23, 113; *Sex in Education*, 23

Cleghorn, Sarah Norcliffe, 162

College Settlement Association, 150
Colton, Elizabeth Avery, 41
Columbia University, New York, 54
Comer, Mary, 33, 38, 56, 63, 68, 76, 147, 151
Commission on Interracial Cooperation,
    103, 142
Consumer's League, 150–51
Converse, D. E., 64
Converse, Florence, 94, 122
Converse College, 20, 40, 64
Conway, Clara, 49–50, 114, 163–64
Cook, May Estelle, 93, 109, 129
Cornell University, 9–10
Crane, Edith Campbell, 18–19
Crawford, Eleanor, 83
Cromwell, Otelia, 100

Dagan, Jessie, 67, 89
Dana Hall School, 43, 168
Daviess, Maria, 32, 48–49, 96, 162
Dawson, Sarah Morgan, 120
Delaney, Clarissa Scott, 96
DeSaussure, Nancy Bostick, 87, 94
Dimmick, Annie May, 170
Dixon, Brandt Van Blarcom, 18, 20–21
Domestic science, 25–29, 34–35
Durant, Henry, 16, 59, 78–79, 138, 150
Durant, Pauline, 16, 59, 78–79, 83, 138
Durr, Virginia Foster, 6, 29, 50, 68, 145, 151;
    and African American students, 105–6,
    108; on marriage, 114; on wage work,
    125

Edwards, Ann, 88
Eginton, Louise, 88
Eliot, Charles, 21
Ellett School, 44, 50–51
Entrance examinations, 47–48, 51–53

Fearn, Anne, 125
Felter, William, 22
Ferger, Nellie, 138
Finnigan, Annette, 161

Fitzgerald, Marguerite, 152
Florida Female College, 20–21
Freeman, Alice (Palmer), 21, 104, 117–18
Fuller, Mary, 29

Galbraith, Mary, 47, 134
General Federation of Women's Clubs,
    53–54
Georgia Female College (Georgia State
    Woman's College), 15, 27
Gilman, Arthur, 60
Girls' Preparatory School, Chattanooga,
    44, 49, 51
Goucher, John Franklin, 17–18
Goucher College, 11, 17–18, 21, 53
Grant, Emma, 55
Gude, Mary, 84, 102
Guion, Connie, 40, 46, 83, 91, 116, 122, 138,
    152–53
Guion, Laura, 40
Guion, Mrs., 40

Hall, B. Frank, 74, 85
Hall, Jessie, 53, 74, 85, 88, 138, 166
Hall, Maggie, 53, 166
Hall, Susan (Sue), 35, 43–44, 67, 133,
    148–50, 166; and African Americans,
    96–97, 103; on entrance examinations,
    52–53; southern identity of, 83, 86,
    88–91
Hamilton, Katherine, 96
Hammond, Julia, 56, 159; devotion of,
    to family, 121, 134; difficulties of, at
    Radcliffe, 24, 65–66, 67, 76; southern
    identity of, 79, 83, 86
Hammond, Katherine, 85
Hardy, Cora Armistead, 149
Harrison, Annie Poe, 78–79
Harrison, Florence, 38
Hartridge, Emelyn, 45, 52, 83
Hartridge, Kathryn, 45
Harvard Annex. See Radcliffe College
Haskell, Alex, 40

Haskell, Mary, 45, 55–56, 86
Hatcher, Frances Bell, 41
Hatcher, Oranie Snead, 167
Hatcher, Orie Latham, 5, 27, 32, 84, 107, 167; preparation of, for college, 40–42; on women and work, 124, 126, 135–36
Hatcher, William, 32
Heiskell, Augusta Lamar, 172
Hemmings, Anita Florence, 100
Hero, Ann, 162
Higher education for women: curriculum of, 15–16, 25–26; debate over purpose of, 22–29; and health, 23–25; history of, 15–17; independence gained through, 74–77; liberal arts in, 25–29, 34–35; and marriage, 109–23; preparation for, 40–62; study of literature in, 36–38; and wage work, 109–11, 123–42
Hobbs, Mary Mendenhall, 46
Holley, Margaret Josephine, 45
Home economics, 25–29, 34–35
Horace Mann School, Columbia Teachers' College, New York, 50
Houk, Elizabeth Messick, 10
Howard, Ellen, 123
Howard, Mary, 123

Irvine, Julia, 89

Jackson, May, 93
Jenkins, Helen, 46–47
Jewell, Frances. *See* McVey, Frances Jewell
Johnson, Elizabeth, 6, 144, 169
Johnson, Lilian Wyckoff, 17, 27, 29, 90, 107; influence of mother on, 169; on marriage and career, 114, 133–34, 137
Johnston, Phillip, 1, 118
Jones, Louisa, 162
Jones, Mattie, 172

Kearny, Belle, 33, 125, 144
Keller, Helen, 34, 38, 83, 93, 148
Keller, May Lansfield, 53

Kelley, Florence, 4, 150–52
King, Georgiana Goddard, 115, 137

Lancaster, Mary, 173
Lantz, Augusta, 54
League of Women Voters, 1, 153, 162, 170, 172
Lee, Annie Elizabeth, 63, 78, 82, 83, 95–96
Lee, Carrie, 100
Lewis, Nell Battle, 20, 139–40, 147, 149, 163
Liberal arts education, 13–15, 25–29, 34–35
Limestone College, 20
Literature, students' love of, 36–38
Livy, Caroline, 44
Lost Cause, 7, 20, 79, 82–83
Louisville Girls High School, 43, 49
Lyon, Mary, 15, 57–58

Marks, Sophie, 173
Marriage rates of college women, 6, 109–23
Martin, Juliet, 48
Mary Baldwin College, 17, 21
Mary Sharp College, 15
McBee, Mary Vardrine, 47, 122, 139, 147
McBryde, John M., 18
McClung, Barbara Adair, 55, 89
McCrackin, Elizabeth, 93
McGhilvary, Cornelia, 138
McVey, Frances Jewell, 51, 94, 118, 137
Mendenhall, Gertrude, 46
Meriwether, Lide, 6, 45, 144
Merrick, Caroline, 6, 144
Miss Burnham School, 43
Misses Holley School for Girls, 45
Misses Neville School, 49
Misses Shipleys' School, 43
Misses Waldo School, Houston, 46
Miss Florence Baldwin's School, 43
Miss Kate Shipp's School, 40
Miss Mary E. Stevens' School, 43
Miss Patty Blackburn Semple's Collegiate School, 43, 49

Mitchell, Margaret, 13, 33, 49, 53, 63, 69, 74–76, 120; and African American students, 105; southern identity of, 83; and wage work, 131–33; and woman suffrage, 169–70

Mitchell, Maria, 123, 153–54, 159

Mitchell, May Belle Stephens, 13, 54, 131, 169–70

Mitchell, Stephen, 33

Mitchell, S. Weir, 26

Morris, Emma Garrett Boyd, 42, 55, 83, 91–92, 148, 154, 170–71

Mount Holyoke College: African American students at, 99; and alumnae employment, 134; alumnae marriage rates of, 111, 113; courses at, 156; fathers' occupations for students of, 10; history of, 16–17, 57–58; liberal arts curriculum at, 26; number of southern students at, 8, 58, 123; preparatory department at, 42; reputation of, 57

Nelson, Carolyn Peyton, 79

Nelson, Carrie, 83

Nelson, Jenny, 46, 78–79, 83

Neville, John, 32, 126

Neville, Mary, 32, 49, 54, 70, 122, 158

Neville, Zelinda (Linda), 84, 116, 158, 162; father's influence on, 32, 126; influence of, on Margaret Preston, 54, 70; as teacher, 49, 122

New Southern Woman ideal, 4, 6, 12, 145

Nisbet, Virginia, 162

Norfolk College for Young Ladies, 44, 47

North Carolina Normal and Industrial College, 20, 46, 56, 112

Northfield Seminary, 40

Offut, Jane Bolin, 96

Page, Walter Hines, 76, 78, 90–91

Palmer, Alice Freeman, 21, 104, 117–18

Pape, Nina, 45

Pape School, 44, 51

Parrish, Celeste, 27, 115

Pendleton, Miss, 40

Penniman, Lucy, 35

Pettit, Katherine, 157–58

Petty, Mary, 46

Phelps, Almira Lincoln, 44

Phelps, Aphra, 119

Pierpont, Julia, 44

Pinckney, Josephine, 138–39

Poppenheim, Christie (Kitty), 52, 90

Poppenheim, Christopher, 52

Poppenheim, Ida, 26, 52, 90, 126

Poppenheim, Louisa (Lulu), 30, 70, 72–74, 148, 155–56; and entrance examinations, 52, 55; and marriage, 116–17, 119–21; mother's support of, 168–69; southern identity of, 83, 89; southern woman ideal of, 164–66; on wage work, 125–26

Poppenheim, Mary (May), 29, 30, 32, 53, 70–74, 147–49, 155–56, 173; and entrance examinations, 52, 55; homesickness of, 65; independence gained by, 62; love of, for literature, 36–38; and marriage, 117, 119–22; mother's support of, 168–69; southern identity of, 76, 83, 87–89, 90, 92; southern woman ideal of, 164–65; on wage work, 125–26

Poppenheim, Mary Elinor (Mrs.), 29, 30, 72–74, 119, 147–48, 155; and entrance examinations, 52, 97; misses daughters, 65; southern identity of, 86–87; support for daughters by, 168–69; on wage work, 125–26

Powers, Mamie, 55

Poynter, Wiley Taul, 48

Preston, Margaret, 1–2, 32, 34, 134; dislike of, for Bryn Mawr social life, 70, 71; and health, 22–24; homesickness of, 64, 66–67; on marriage, 118–19; preparation of, for college, 54; relationship of, with mother, 160, 168; social activism of, 158–59; southern identity of, 11, 81–83

Preston, Sarah, 1, 22–24, 54, 66, 168
Prichard, Lucy, 55, 92
Pullen, Nettie Garrett, 48

Radcliffe College: and alumnae survey, 14;
    history of, 60; liberal arts curriculum
    at, 26; reputation of, 56
Randolph-Macon College, 17–18, 21, 112,
    124
Raoul, Agnes, 33, 49, 67–68, 74, 76,
    83, 114; and entrance examinations,
    52; homesickness of, 63; southern
    identity of, 89–90; on woman suffrage
    movement, 161–62
Ravenel, Beatrice Witte, 138–39
Rhyne, Loula, 135, 162
Rice, Harriett Alleyne, 99
Richmond, Grace, 33, 35, 94–95, 114, 123
Richmond, Harriett, 33, 94, 148–49
Richmond, Theodore, 94
Richmond Female Institute, 42, 135
Robbins, Mary Lafayette, 172

Salmon, Lucy, 38, 91–92, 153–55, 159, 163
Sawitzky, Susan Clay, 33
Science Hill Academy, 32, 44, 48, 51, 54
Scudder, Vida, 94, 122, 150–51
Seelye, L. Clark, 28
Seifert, Aida, 63
Semple, Ellen, 49, 131, 162
Semple, Patty, 49
Semple Collegiate School, 43, 49
Sex in Education (Clarke), 23
Sherrill, Elizabeth, 44
Simpson, Edith, 152
Simpson, Georgiana, 104–5
Simrall, Charles, 35
Simrall, Isabella, 23, 29, 30
Simrall, Josephine (Josie), 22, 23, 29, 30,
    35, 83, 114, 150; career of, 133, 137; on
    domestic servants, 97–98
Simrall, Mary Barton (Bart), 30
Smith, Ella, 104

Smith, Grace Carlisle, 172
Smith, Sophia, 16, 28–29
Smith College: African American
    students at, 100; alumnae marriage
    rates of, 111, 113; courses at, 143, 151;
    extracurricular activities at, 146, 149;
    fathers' occupations for students of,
    10; founding of, 28–29; history of, 16,
    59; lack of preparatory department at,
    43; liberal arts curriculum at, 26–29;
    number of southern students at, 8–9;
    preparation for, 43, 45, 52; recruitment
    of southern students to, 53; reputation
    of, 13, 55–57; social regulations at, 74–75;
    southern club at, 53, 92–93
Sophie Newcomb College, 10, 17–18, 21,
    112, 159–60
South Carolina Female Collegiate
    Institute (Barhamville, S.C.), 15, 44
Southern Association of College Women
    (SACW), 3, 55, 90; and promotion of
    college education, 11, 53; and social
    reform, 170–71; and southern school
    improvements, 42, 173; and woman
    suffrage, 159
Southern Club of Smith College, 53, 92
Southern Clubs, 88, 90–92
Southern identity, 7, 79–95
Southern lady ideal, 2, 18–21, 72–77, 145
Southern Woman's Educational Alliance
    (Alliance for Guidance of Rural Youth),
    124, 136
Southern women at northern colleges:
    academic struggles of, 66–68;
    graduation rates of, 63; history of
    attendance of, 7–8; homesickness of,
    63–66; independence gained by, 2, 6,
    62–63, 75–77; and marriage, 109–23;
    preparation for, 40–62; and race issues,
    95–108; social activism of, 143–74; and
    social life, 69–75; and southern identity,
    79–95; support for, by fathers, 31–32;
    support for, by mothers, 30–31; and

Southern women at northern colleges (*continued*)
    wage work, 109–11, 123–42; and woman suffrage, 159–66
Southern women's colleges, 3; compared to northern colleges, 15–21; and marriage rates, 112; social activism at, 144–45; on wage work, 124
Sparks, Alice, 88, 135
Stanley, Eva, 24, 135, 160, 167, 173
Stanley, Irene, 160, 167
Statesboro Female College, 42
Stewart, Daisy, 89
Stone, May, 103–4, 157
Stress, 1–2, 22–25
St. Timothy's School, 43
Suffrage. *See* Woman suffrage movement
Summerall, Hope, 30
Sweet Briar College, 46

Talbot, Marion, 10, 26, 109, 117
Taylor, Joseph Wright, 60
Temple, Mary Boyd, 172
Terry, Adolphine Fletcher, 107–8
Thomas, M. Carey, 37, 120; and Bryn Mawr College, 21, 26, 60, 113; and Bryn Mawr School, 47–48; racist views of, 99, 145
Thompson, C. Mildred, 27, 53, 94, 107–8, 137, 162–64
Thorsby Institute, 46–47
Thwing, Charles, 21, 27
Toof, Ruth, 153
Troy Female Seminary, 4, 15, 44–45
Tunnell, Barbara, 64, 93–94
Tutwiler, Ida, 36
Tutwiler, Julia, 36, 136–37
Tyler, W. S., 28

United Daughters of the Confederacy (UDC), 53, 80, 82, 87–88, 91, 155, 173
University of Chicago, 10, 53, 109, 129–30

Vassar College: African American students at, 7, 98–100; and alumnae employment, 123–24; alumnae marriage rates of, 111, 113; and alumnae survey, 31; benefits of education at, 35; class fight at, 71; domestic science at, 26–27, 113; and entrance examinations, 52; extracurricular activities at, 146, 149, 154; history of, 16, 58–59; liberal arts curriculum at, 26–27; number of Southern students at, 8–9; preparation for, 52; preparatory department at, 42; reputation of, 56–57, 64; social regulations at, 74; southern club at, 92–93; and woman suffrage, 159–60
Veach, Frances, 135
Virginia Association of Colleges and Schools for Girls, 42, 135

Wage work, 6, 109–11, 123–42
Waldo, Lula, 46
Waldo, Virginia, 46
Walker, Lucy, 70
Walnut Hill School, 43–44, 88
Warner, Katherine Burch, 162
Washington, Booker T., 96, 100–101
Washington, Portia, 96, 100–102
Washington Seminary (Atlanta), 44, 47, 49, 51
Watkins, Alice, 94–95
Weil, Gertrude, 26, 149, 151, 171–72; independence of, 75; preparation of, for college, 50; on race, 98, 103, 108; relationship of, with mother, 31, 167–68; southern identity of, 83, 92; support of, for woman suffrage, 143, 145, 153, 160–61, 164; on wage work, 140–42
Weil, Mina, 31, 75, 140–41, 167–68
Weil, Sarah, 31, 168
Wellesley College: African American students at, 7, 99–105; and alumnae employment, 134; alumnae marriage rates of, 113; alumnae records of,

9; benefits of education at, 35, 47, 51; courses at, 151; and entrance examinations, 53; extracurricular activities at, 150–52; faculty of, 113–14, 125, 160; history of, 16, 59–60, 78–79; liberal arts curriculum at, 26, 109; number of southern students at, 8–9, 123–24; preparation for, 40–41, 43–46, 48, 52; preparatory department at, 42; recruitment of southern students to, 40; reputation of, 56–57; southern club at, 91–92

Western College for Women, 134

Westhampton College, 21, 53

Wetzel, Anne Audubon, 93

Wey, Frances Liggett, 171

Wheeler, Anna, 94

Whitaker, Eloise, 56

Willard, Emma, 4, 6, 15, 44–45, 144, 169

Willard, Frances, 169

Winthrop Normal and Industrial School (Rock Hill, S.C.), 20, 124

Woman's College of Baltimore. *See* Goucher College

Woman suffrage movement, 1, 145, 153, 159–66

Women's clubs, 46, 49, 118, 133–34, 138, 158; activism of, 143–44, 159, 163, 165, 168, 170–71, 172–73; involvement of mothers in, 166–70; Nell Lewis's involvement in, 139–40, 163; Louisa Poppenheim's involvement in, 155, 165, 169, 172; Margaret Preston's involvement in, 1, 159, 168; Gertrude Weil's involvement in, 141–42, 143, 153, 167–68, 171–72

Worthington, Daisy, 22, 120